First World War

and Army of Occupation

War Diary

France, Belgium and Germany

15 DIVISION
Divisional Troops
Machine Gun Corps
15 Battalion Machine Gun Corps
17 March 1918 - 31 March 1919

WO95/1930/2

The Naval & Military Press Ltd
www.nmarchive.com
Published in association with The National Archives

Published by

The Naval & Military Press Ltd

Unit 10 Ridgewood Industrial Park,
Uckfield, East Sussex,
TN22 5QE England
Tel: +44 (0) 1825 749494

www.naval-military-press.com
www.nmarchive.com

This diary has been reprinted in facsimile from the original. Any imperfections are inevitably reproduced and the quality may fall short of modern type and cartographic standards.

Contents

Document type	Place/Title	Date From	Date To
Miscellaneous	WO95/1930/2		
Heading	15th Division. 15th Bn Machine Gun 1918 Mar-Mar 1919		
Heading	15th Divisional Troops Formed 17th March 1918 from the 4 companies of the 15th Division. 15th Battalion Machine Gun Company March 1918		
Heading	War Diary of 15th Battalion Machine Gun Corps form 17th March 1918 to 31st March 1918 Volume 1		
War Diary	Arras	17/03/1918	26/03/1918
War Diary	Duisans	27/03/1918	31/03/1918
Miscellaneous	15th. Battn. Machine Gun Corps. Operations Order No. 2.	29/03/1918	29/03/1918
Miscellaneous	15th. Battn. Machine Gun Corps. Operation Order No. 3	31/03/1918	31/03/1918
Miscellaneous	15th. Battn. Machine Gun Corps.	24/04/1918	24/04/1918
Miscellaneous	15th-Bn Machine Gun Corps	31/03/1918	31/03/1918
Heading	15th Division War Diary. 15th Divisional Machine Gun Battalion April 1918		
Heading	War Diary of 15th Battalion Machine Gun Corps from 1st to 30th April 1918 Volume 2		
War Diary	Warlus	01/04/1918	30/04/1918
Operation(al) Order(s)	15th. Bn. Machine Gun Corps. Operation Order No. 4.	01/04/1918	01/04/1918
Operation(al) Order(s)	15th. Battn. Machine Gun Corps. Operation Order No. 5	02/04/1918	02/04/1918
Operation(al) Order(s)	15th. Battn. Machine Gun Corps. Operation Order No. 6	03/04/1918	03/04/1918
Operation(al) Order(s)	15th. Battn. Machine Gun Corps. Operation Order No. 7.	03/04/1918	03/04/1918
Operation(al) Order(s)	15th. Battn. Machine Gun Corps. Operation Order No. 8.	06/04/1918	06/04/1918
Operation(al) Order(s)	15th. Battn. Machine Gun Corps. Operation Order No. 8	06/04/1918	06/04/1918
Operation(al) Order(s)	15th. Battn. Machine Gun Corps. Operation Order No. 9	13/04/1918	13/04/1918
Operation(al) Order(s)	15th. Bn. Machine Gun Corps. Operation Order No. 10	16/04/1918	16/04/1918
Miscellaneous	15th. Bn. Machine Gun Corps No. M.G./T.20.	18/04/1918	18/04/1918
Operation(al) Order(s)	15th. Battn. Machine Gun Corps. Operation Order No. 11.	23/04/1918	23/04/1918
Miscellaneous	15th. Bn. Machine Gun Corps No. M.G./T.30	23/04/1918	23/04/1918
Operation(al) Order(s)	15th. Battn. Machine Gun Corps. Operation Order No. 12	23/04/1918	23/04/1918
Operation(al) Order(s)	15th. Bn. Machine Gun Corps. Operation Order No. 13	24/04/1918	24/04/1918
Heading	War Diary of 15th Battalion Machine Gun Corps from 1st to 31st May 1918 Volume 3		
War Diary	Hurionville	01/05/1918	31/05/1918
Operation(al) Order(s)	15th. Battn. Machine Gun Corps. Operation Order No. 15	03/05/1918	03/05/1918
Operation(al) Order(s)	15th. Battn. Machine Gun Corps. Operation Order No. 16	04/05/1918	04/05/1918
Operation(al) Order(s)	15th. Bn. Machine Gun Corps. Operation Order No. 17	06/05/1918	06/05/1918

Operation(al) Order(s)	15th. Battn. Machine Gun Corps. Operation Order No. 18	08/05/1918	08/05/1918
Operation(al) Order(s)	15th. Battn. Machine Gun Corps. Operation Order No. 19	15/05/1918	15/05/1918
Operation(al) Order(s)	15th. Battn. Machine Gun Corps. Operation Order No. 20	15/05/1918	15/05/1918
Operation(al) Order(s)	15th. Bn. Machine Gun Corps. No. M.G./T.136. Reference 15th. Bn. M.G.C. Operation Order No. 20	15/05/1918	15/05/1918
Operation(al) Order(s)	15th. Bn. Machine Gun Corps. No. M.G./T.156. Amendment to 15th. Bn. M.G.C. Operation Order No. 20	18/05/1918	18/05/1918
Operation(al) Order(s)	15th Battn. Machine Gun Corps. Operation Order No. 21	23/05/1918	23/05/1918
Operation(al) Order(s)	15th Battn. Machine Gun Corps. Operation Order No. 22	29/05/1918	29/05/1918
Operation(al) Order(s)	15th Bn. Machine Gun Corps. M.G./T.275. Amendment No. 1 to 16th Bn. Machine Gun Corps Operation Order No. 28. dated 29.5.18	30/05/1918	30/05/1918
Operation(al) Order(s)	15th Bn. Machine Gun Corps. M.G./T.276. Addendum To Operation Order No. 22	30/05/1918	30/05/1918
Miscellaneous	15th Bn. Machine Gun Corps. M.G./T.279.	30/05/1918	30/05/1918
Operation(al) Order(s)	15th Bn. Machine Gun Corps. M.G./T.282. Addendum No. 2 to 15th Bn. M.G.C. Operation Order No. 22 dated 29.5.18	31/05/1918	31/05/1918
Operation(al) Order(s)	15th Bn. Machine Gun Corps. M.G./T.287. Addendum No. 3 to 15th Bn. M.G.C. Operation Order No. 22 Dated 29.5.18	31/05/1918	31/05/1918
Operation(al) Order(s)	15th Bn. Machine Gun Corps. Operation Order No. 23	31/05/1918	31/05/1918
Heading	War Diary Vol. IV 15th Battn. Machine Gun Corps. 1st to 30th. June 1918		
War Diary		01/06/1918	30/06/1918
Operation(al) Order(s)	15th. Bn. Machine Gun Corps. Operation Order No. 24	07/06/1918	07/06/1918
Operation(al) Order(s)	15th. Bn. Machine Gun Corps. Operation Order No. 25	07/06/1918	07/06/1918
Operation(al) Order(s)	15th Bn. Machine Gun Corps. M.G./T.372. Addendum 1. to Operation Order No. 25.	08/06/1918	08/06/1918
Operation(al) Order(s)	15th Bn. Machine Gun Corps. M.G./T.411. Reference 15th Bn. Machine Gun Corps Operation Order No. 26. Dated 13th June 1918.	16/06/1918	16/06/1918
Operation(al) Order(s)	15th. Battn. Machine Gun Corps Operation Order No. 26.	13/06/1918	13/06/1918
Operation(al) Order(s)	15th. Bn. Machine Gun Corps No. M.G./T.395. Amendment No. 1 to 15th. Bn. M.G.C. Operation Order No. 26. d/13/6/18.	13/06/1918	13/06/1918
Operation(al) Order(s)	15th Bn. Machine Gun Corps. Operation Order No. 27	16/06/1918	16/06/1918
Operation(al) Order(s)	15th Bn. Machine Gun Corps. Operation Order No. 28	17/06/1918	17/06/1918
Operation(al) Order(s)	15th Bn. Machine Gun Corps. M.G./T.448. Ref. 15th Bn. M.G.C. Operation Order No. 29. d/19.6.18 and M.G./T.438. d/19.6.18	20/06/1918	20/06/1918
Operation(al) Order(s)	15th Bn. Machine Gun Corps. M.G./T.438.	19/06/1918	19/06/1918
Operation(al) Order(s)	15th Bn. Machine Gun Corps. M.G./T.439. Amendment No. 1 to 15th Bn. M.G.C. Operation Order No. 28. d/17.6.18	19/06/1918	19/06/1918
Operation(al) Order(s)	15th Bn. Machine Gun Corps. Operation Order No. 29	18/06/1918	18/06/1918
Operation(al) Order(s)	15th Bn. Machine Gun Corps. Operation Order No. 30	22/06/1918	22/06/1918

Operation(al) Order(s)	15th Bn. Machine Gun Corps. M.G./T.47 1. Amendment No. 1 to 15th Bn. M.G.C. Operation Order No. 30 d/22.6.18	23/06/1918	23/06/1918
Operation(al) Order(s)	15th Bn. Machine Gun Corps. Operation Order No. 31.	28/06/1918	28/06/1918
Operation(al) Order(s)	15th Bn. Machine Gun Corps. M.G./T.530. Amendment No. 1 To Operation Order No. 32 of 15th Bn. M.G.C. d/29.6.18	30/06/1918	30/06/1918
Operation(al) Order(s)	15th Bn. Machine Gun Corps. Operation Order No. 32	29/06/1918	29/06/1918
Heading	Volume V From 1st July 1918 To 31st July 1918		
War Diary		01/07/1918	31/07/1918
Operation(al) Order(s)	15th Bn. Machine Gun Corps. Operation Order No. 33.	05/07/1918	05/07/1918
Operation(al) Order(s)	15th Bn. Machine Gun Corps. Operation Order No. 34	09/07/1918	09/07/1918
Operation(al) Order(s)	15th Bn. Machine Gun Corps. M.G/T.597. Ref. Operation Order No. 34. d/9.7.18	10/07/1918	10/07/1918
Operation(al) Order(s)	15th Bn. Machine Gun Corps. Operation Order No. 35	11/07/1918	11/07/1918
Operation(al) Order(s)	15th Bn. Machine Gun Corps. Operation Order No. 36	13/07/1918	13/07/1918
Operation(al) Order(s)	15th Bn. Machine Gun Corps. Operation Order No. 37	15/07/1918	15/07/1918
Operation(al) Order(s)	15th Bn. Machine Gun Corps. Operation Order No. 38	18/07/1918	18/07/1918
Operation(al) Order(s)	15th Bn. Machine Gun Corps. Operation Order No. 39	25/07/1918	25/07/1918
Operation(al) Order(s)	15th Bn. Machine Gun Corps. Operation Order No. 40	27/07/1918	27/07/1918
Operation(al) Order(s)	15th Bn. Machine Gun Corps. Operation Order No. 41	29/07/1918	29/07/1918
Operation(al) Order(s)	15th Bn. Machine Gun Corps. Operation Order No. 42	31/07/1918	31/07/1918
Heading	War Diary of 15th Battn. Machine Gun Corps 1st to 31st August 1918 Volume VI		
War Diary		01/08/1918	31/08/1918
Operation(al) Order(s)	15th Bn. Machine Gun Corps. Operation Order No. 43	03/08/1918	03/08/1918
Operation(al) Order(s)	15th Bn. Machine Gun Corps. Operation Order No. 44	05/08/1918	05/08/1918
Miscellaneous	15th Div. No. G.S.	08/05/1918	08/05/1918
Operation(al) Order(s)	15th Bn. Machine Gun Corps. Operation Order No. 45	15/08/1918	15/08/1918
Operation(al) Order(s)	15th Bn. Machine Gun Corps. Operation Order No. 46	18/08/1918	18/08/1918
Miscellaneous	15th Bn. Machine Gun Corps. M.G. 158	22/08/1918	22/08/1918
Operation(al) Order(s)	15th Bn. Machine Gun Corps. Operation Order No. 47	20/08/1918	20/08/1918
Operation(al) Order(s)	15th Bn. Machine Gun Corps. Operation Order No. 48	22/08/1918	22/08/1918
Operation(al) Order(s)	15th Bn. Machine Gun Corps. Operation Order No. 49	27/08/1918	27/08/1918
Heading	War Diary of 15th Battn. Machine Gun Corps From. 1st to 30th September 1918 Volume VII		
War Diary		01/09/1918	30/09/1918
Operation(al) Order(s)	15th Bn. Machine Gun Corps. Operation Order No. 50	01/09/1918	01/09/1918
Operation(al) Order(s)	15th Bn. Machine Gun Corps. Operation Order No. 51	02/09/1918	02/09/1918
Operation(al) Order(s)	15th Bn. Machine Gun Corps. Operation Order No. 52	04/09/1918	04/09/1918
Operation(al) Order(s)	15th Bn. Machine Gun Corps. M.G. 281. Ref. Operation Order No. 54. d/6.9.18	07/09/1918	07/09/1918
Operation(al) Order(s)	15th Bn. Machine Gun Corps. Operation Order No. 54	06/09/1918	06/09/1918
Operation(al) Order(s)	15th Bn. Machine Gun Corps. M.G. 375. Reference 15th Bn. M.G.C. Operation Order No. 56 d/16th September 1918	16/09/1918	16/09/1918
Operation(al) Order(s)	15th Bn. Machine Gun Corps. Operation Order No. 56	16/09/1918	16/09/1918
Operation(al) Order(s)	15th Bn. Machine Gun Corps. Operation Order No. 57	15/09/1918	15/09/1918
Operation(al) Order(s)	15th Bn. Machine Gun Corps. Operation Order No. 58	17/09/1918	17/09/1918
Operation(al) Order(s)	15th Bn. Machine Gun Corps. Operation Order No 59	22/09/1918	22/09/1918
Operation(al) Order(s)	15th Bn. Machine Gun Corps. Operation Order No. 60	28/09/1918	28/09/1918
Operation(al) Order(s)	15th Bn. Machine Gun Corps M.G. 501. Amendment No. 1 to Operation Order No. 60 d/28.9.18	29/09/1918	29/09/1918
Heading	War Diary of 15th Bn. Machine Gun Corps. From 1st to 31st October 1918 Vol VIII		
War Diary		01/10/1918	31/10/1918

Operation(al) Order(s)	15th Bn. Machine Gun Corps. Operation Order No. 62	04/10/1918	04/10/1918
Operation(al) Order(s)	15th Bn. Machine Gun Corps. Operation Order No. 63	07/10/1918	07/10/1918
Operation(al) Order(s)	15th Bn. Machine Gun Corps. Operation Order No. 64	08/10/1918	08/10/1918
Operation(al) Order(s)	Appendix I to 15th Bn. Machine Gun Corps Operation Order No. 64	08/10/1918	08/10/1918
Operation(al) Order(s)	15th Bn. Machine Gun Corps. M.G.598. Ref. 15th Bn. M.G.C. Operation Order No. 64. d/8.10.18	08/10/1918	08/10/1918
Operation(al) Order(s)	15th Bn. Machine Gun Corps. M.G. 606. Ref. Appendix I to 15th Bn. Machine Gun Corps. Operation Order No. 64	10/10/1918	10/10/1918
Operation(al) Order(s)	15th Bn. Machine Gun Corps. Operation Order No. 65	10/10/1918	10/10/1918
Operation(al) Order(s)	15th Bn. Machine Gun Corps. M.G. 623. Operation Instructions No. 1		
Operation(al) Order(s)	15th Bn. Machine Gun Corps. M.G.630. Addendum I to Operation Instructions No. I. d/11.10.18	12/10/1918	12/10/1918
Miscellaneous	15th Bn. Machine Gun Corps. M.G. 634. Addendum 2 to Operation Instructions No. 1. d/11.10.18	12/10/1918	12/10/1918
Miscellaneous	15th Bn. Machine Gun Corps. M.G.646. Addendum 3 to Operation Instructions No. 1. d/11.10.18	13/10/1918	13/10/1918
Operation(al) Order(s)	15th Bn. Machine Gun Corps. Operation Order No. 67.	23/10/1918	23/10/1918
Operation(al) Order(s)	15th Bn. Machine Gun Corps. Operation Order No. 68.	24/10/1918	24/10/1918
Operation(al) Order(s)	15th Bn. Machine Gun Corps. Operation Order No. 69.	31/10/1918	31/10/1918
Miscellaneous	15th Bn. Machine Gun Corps. No. M.G.699.	30/10/1918	30/10/1918
Heading	War Diary of 15th Batt. Machine Gun Corps From. 1st November 1918 To 30th November 1918		
War Diary		01/11/1918	30/11/1918
Operation(al) Order(s)	15th Bn. Machine Gun Corps. Order No. 71	21/11/1918	21/11/1918
Operation(al) Order(s)	March Table issued in conjunction with 15th Bn. Machine Gun Corps. Order No. 71. d.21.11.18		
Heading	War Diary of 15th Battn Machine Gun Corps From 1st December 1918 to 31st December 1918 Volume X		
War Diary	In The Fields	01/12/1918	06/12/1918
War Diary	Field	07/12/1918	13/12/1918
War Diary	In The Field	14/12/1918	24/12/1918
War Diary	Field	25/12/1918	29/12/1918
War Diary	In The Field	30/12/1918	31/12/1918
Operation(al) Order(s)	15th. Bn. Machine Gun Corps. Order No. 73	14/12/1918	14/12/1918
Operation(al) Order(s)	15th Bn. Machine Gun Corps. Order No. 72	03/12/1918	03/12/1918
Heading	War Diary of 15th Battn. Machine Gun Corps From 1st January 1919 to 31st January 1919 Volume XI		
War Diary	Field	01/01/1919	31/01/1919
Heading	War Diary of 15th Battn. Machine Gun Corps From 1st February 1919 To 28th February 1919 Volume XII		
War Diary	Lillois-Witterzee	01/02/1919	28/02/1919
Miscellaneous	D.A.G. 3rd Echelon G.H.Q. France	09/04/1919	09/04/1919
Heading	War Diary of 15th Battn Machine Gun Corps From 1st March 1919 To 31st March 1919 Volume XIII		
War Diary	Lillois-Witterzee	01/03/1919	06/03/1919
War Diary	Wauthier-Braine	06/03/1919	22/03/1919
War Diary	Lembecq	23/03/1919	24/03/1919
War Diary	Dunkirk	25/03/1919	31/03/1919
Operation(al) Order(s)	15th Bn. Machine Gun Corps. Order No. 74	04/03/1919	04/03/1919

15TH DIVISION

15TH BN MACHINE GUN ~~CORPS~~ Battalion

1918 MAR ~~JLY 1917~~-MAR 1919

15th Divisional Troops

Formed 17th March 1918 from the 4 companies of the 15th Division.

)))

15th BATTALION

MACHINE GUN COMPANY

MARCH 1918

Instructions regarding War Diaries and Intelligence Summaries are contained in F. S. Regs., Part II. and the Staff Manual respectively. Title pages will be prepared in manuscript.

WAR DIARY
or
INTELLIGENCE SUMMARY.
(*Erase heading not required.*)

Army Form C. 2118.

Vol I

Place	Date	Hour	Summary of Events and Information	Remarks and references to Appendices
			CONFIDENTIAL WAR DIARY OF 15th Battalion MACHINE GUN CORPS From:- 17th March 1918. To:- 31st March 1918 VOLUME I R. Nasmith Lieut. Col. Commdg 15th Bn Machine Gun Corps	

D. D. & L., London, E.C.
(A8004) Wt. W1771/M2-31 750,000 5/17 Sch. 52 Forms/C2118/14

Instructions regarding War Diaries and Intelligence Summaries are contained in F. S. Regs., Part II. and the Staff Manual respectively. Title pages will be prepared in manuscript.

WAR DIARY

or

~~INTELLIGENCE~~ SUMMARY.

(Erase heading not required.)

Army Form C. 2118.

Place	Date	Hour	Summary of Events and Information	Remarks and references to Appendices
ARRAS	17/3/18		From instructions received from HQrs 15th Div, Lieut-Col Naismith M.C. assumed tactical command of the 44th, 45th, 46th and 228th Machine Gun Coys., these Coys in future to be known as A, B, C and D Coy respectively. HQrs of the Battalion were opened at 15 Rue de Four St Adrien. The Headquarter Staff at this time consisting of Lieut-Col Naismith M.C. Commanding Officer, Lieut H. M. Burns (45th MG Coy) Adjutant and Capt Scott R.A.M.C. Medical Officer. Lieut & Qm. Donaldson (9th Manchester Regt) and Lieut J. R. Stage (45th MG Coy.) The four Companies at this time were commanded by A Coy. Lieut Smeltzer, B Coy Capt. Newton, C Coy Capt. Hamilton M.C. D Coy Capt. Forrester.	
	18/3/18		Major F. Davies joined the Battalion and assumed duties of Second in Command. Formation of the Battalion proceeded with.	
	19/3/18		Commanding Officer visited Coys accompanied by Major Davies. The Medical Officer also made a tour of inspection. Except for the usual harassing fire by our Artillery and Machine Guns the day and night were quiet.	
	20/3/18		Work continued for the formation of the Battalion, and preparations made for expected enemy Offensive.	
	21/3/18		Great enemy Offensive launched against third and fifth Armies, intense shelling on our front about 5 am when enemy attack developed. Raids were made by enemy on the Division on our right, otherwise the rest of our Divisional front was	

D. D. & L., London, E.C. (A8004) Wt. W1771/M2·31 750,000 5/17 Sch. 52 Forms/C2118/14

Instructions regarding War Diaries and Intelligence Summaries are contained in F. S. Regs., Part II. and the Staff Manual respectively. Title pages will be prepared in manuscript.

WAR DIARY
or
INTELLIGENCE SUMMARY.
(Erase heading not required.)

Army Form C. 2118.

Place	Date	Hour	Summary of Events and Information	Remarks and references to Appendices
ARRAS	21/3/18 (Cont.)		Quiet except for intermittent Artillery activity on both sides. Active harassing fire was carried out by our guns during the night in conjunction with our Artillery.	
	22/3/18		Enemy attack to the South still proceeding with great violence	
		9pm.	Owing to events in the South, orders were received to withdraw to front line of third system at 1am. 23/3/18. Operation orders prepared and sent out by Priority Wire to Coys.	
	23/3/18	5am.	Withdrawal to third System complete. Bn. HQrs. closed at Rue Louis St Adrien at 10.30am. and reopened at the Citadel Arras at 12noon close by Divisional HQrs. During the withdrawal to third System all Coys. left two guns at the disposal of each Brigade. 'B' Coy. reported that owing to the morning haze masses of enemy advanced right on to their ~~two~~ guns before they could be observed and after inflicting many casualties on the enemy only succeeded in withdrawing one gun. The enemy followed up our withdrawal very quickly and by 10.30am was reported in CONGO TR and in les Fosses Farm and in front of Monchy le Preux. Our transport moved from ARRAS to DAINVILLE after suffering slight casualties in animals	

D. D. & L., London, E.C. (A8004) Wt. W1771/M2031 750,000 5/17 Sch. 52 Forms/C2118/14

Instructions regarding War Diaries and Intelligence Summaries are contained in F. S. Regs., Part II. and the Staff Manual respectively. Title pages will be prepared in manuscript.

WAR DIARY
or
INTELLIGENCE SUMMARY.
(*Erase heading not required.*)

Army Form C. 2118.

Place	Date	Hour	Summary of Events and Information	Remarks and references to Appendices
ARRAS	23/3/18 (contd.)		from effects of enemy long range shell fire.	
	24/3/18		Reports from all Coys received and preparations made for withdrawal to the ARMY LINE in the case of emergency. Intermittent Artillery activity on our front otherwise everything Normal	HMS
	25/3/18		Preparations completed for ARMY LINE withdrawal and warning orders issued to all Coys.	HMS
	26/3/18		Divl Hqrs moved from Citadel ARRAS to DUISANS, Bn. Hqrs. moved accordingly reopening at ~~[illegible]~~ DUISANS 4pm.	HMS
DUISANS	27/3/18		Owing to Corps Headquarters returning to DUISANS, Divl. Hqrs moved to WARLUS. Bn. Hqrs. opening in WARLUS at 4.30pm.	HMS
	28/3/18		About dawn the enemy launched an attack along the whole Corps front, and after severe fighting we occupied the ARMY LINE. The third division on our right at 12 noon was reported to be still in third system with exception of centre Brigade which was back in Army line. The fourth division on our left also appears to have checked the enemy whose objective according	HMS

D. D. & L., London, E.C.
(A8004) Wt. W1771/M2131 750,000 5/17 Sch. 52 Forms/C2118/14

Army Form C. 2118.

Instructions regarding War Diaries and Intelligence Summaries are contained in F. S. Regs., Part II. and the Staff Manual respectively. Title pages will be prepared in manuscript.

WAR DIARY
or
INTELLIGENCE SUMMARY.
(Erase heading not required.)

Place	Date	Hour	Summary of Events and Information	Remarks and references to Appendices
	28/3/18 cont.		to prisoners statement was ARRAS. No reports received until very late from Coys who appear to have suffered heavy casualties but have fought well and inflicted very heavy losses on the enemy. Reports received by runner from A and B Coys at 11pm showing heavy casualties in guns and personnel. Reports received from Brigades with reference to remaining Coys bring our estimated casualties to the following total.	Report on Operations attached
			Offrs. (Killed Wounded and missing) 9	HWS
			O.R. (Killed Wounded and missing) 285	Detailed list attd
	29/3/18	9.30 am	C.O. left HQrs. to visit all Coy HQrs in the line.	HWS
			Several reports from Coys received during the morning saying several missing men had reported. Three men arrived from 4th Bn and reported at HQrs having lost touch with their Coys and got mixed with units of the 4th Divn during the heavy fighting	HWS
	30/3/18	9.45 am	C.O. visited Coys in the line. Intermittent shelling of ARRAS otherwise everything quiet on our front	HWS
	31/3/18	9.30 am	C.O. left for the line. 38 Guns and various accessories received from DADOS	

D. D. & L., London, E.C. (A8004) Wt. W1771/M2231 750,000 5/17 Sch. 52 Forms/C2118/14

Army Form C. 2118.

Instructions regarding War Diaries and Intelligence Summaries are contained in F. S. Regs., Part II. and the Staff Manual respectively. Title pages will be prepared in manuscript.

WAR DIARY
or
INTELLIGENCE SUMMARY.
(Erase heading not required.)

Place	Date	Hour	Summary of Events and Information	Remarks and references to Appendices
	31/7/18 Cont		to replace losses. Enemy shelling ARRAS and RONVILLE heavily during the day.	[illegible initials]

R. Rasmith LIEUT.-COL.
COMMANDING 15TH BATT. MACHINE GUN CORPS.

D. D. & L., London, E.C.
(A3004) Wt. W1771/M2031 750,000 5/17 Sch. 52 Forms/C2118/14

SECRET. COPY No. 8

15th. Battn. MACHINE GUN CORPS.

OPERATION ORDER No. 2. 29th. March 1918

1. 2 Batteries (16 Guns) 1st. Canadian M. G. Battalion will relieve the guns of 15th. Bn. M.G.Corps and 6 Guns of 7th. Squadron in the following area to-night.

Southern Corps Boundary to a Line Cross Roads H.1.c.70.40. – Cross Roads H.8.c.22.80. – Cross Roads H.4.c.05.75.

2. The following guns will be relieved:-

5 Guns of "B" Coy. at H.13.d.70.90.
1 " " "A" " at H.1.d.
1 " " "A" " at H.7.b.

2 Guns of 7th. Squadron at H.13.b.1.3
2 " " " " at H.6.d.3.4
2 " " " " at H.13.b.1.9

3. Guides from Coys. and Squadron to be at Railway Bridge at G.30.b.90.60 at 8.0 p.m.

4. On complitition of Relief

4 Guns 7th. Squadron will take up Position at H.8.a.30.25

2 Guns 7th. Squadron will take up Position at H.8.d.30.60

5 Guns of "B" Coy. and 2 Guns of "A" Coy. will move to LONDON CAVES, G.29.d.90.90. in reserve.

"A" Coy. Hd.Qrs. will also move to LONDON CAVES.

5 ACKNOWLEDGE.

[signature]

Lieut. & Adjt.

15th. Bn. Machine Gun Corps.

Copy No.1. "A" Coy.
" " 2. "B" "
" " 3. 44th. Infantry Brigade.
" " 4. 45th. Infantry Brigade.
" " 5. 15th. Division "G"
" " 6. 1st. Canadian M.G. Bn.
" " 7. File.
" " 8. War Diary.
9. 7th MG Squadron

SECRET. COPY NO. 10

15th. BATTN. MACHINE GUN CORPS.

OPERATION ORDER NO. 3.

The following moves and reliefs will take place to-morrow (1st. prox-) and night 1/2nd. April.

"A" 6 guns of "D" Coy. at present under tactical command of "A" Coy. to rejoin "D" Coy. at LEICESTER CAVES.

4 Guns of "B" Coy. at present under command of "D" Coy. to rejoin "B" Coy., but to be accomodated at LEICESTER CAVES.

"B" 2 Guns of "B" Coy. to relieve 2 guns of "C" Coy. at N.1.a.5.9.

The 2 Guns of "C" Coy. on relief to be withdrawn as Coy. reserve. at Coy. Hd. Qrs.

1 Gun of "C" Coy. to relieve 1 Gun of "D" Coy. at H.25.c.15.10

The gun of "D" Coy. on relief to be withdrawn as reserve at Coy. Hd. Qrs.

Moves in "A" will be completed as soon as possible after receipt of orders, in daylight.

Reliefs in "B" not to take place by daylight.

All necessary arrangements to be made by Coy. Commanders concerned.

Completion of "A" to be reported by code word " LOCK "

Completion of "B" to be reported by code word "SPRING "

ACKNOWLEDGE.

[signature]

Capt. & Adjt.

31.3.18. 15th. Bn. Machine Gun Corps.

Copy NO. 1 "A" Coy.
2. "B" "
3. "C" "
4. "D" "
5. 15th. Division "G"
6. 44th. Infantry Brigade.
7. 45th. Infantry Brigade.
8. 46th. Infantry Brigade.

9. FILE.
10. War Diary.

15th. Battn. MACHINE GUN CORPS.

I have the honour to attach herewith my report on the action of the 15th. Bn. M.G.C. during the operations of 21st. and 28th. March 1918.

At about 9.0.p.m. on ~~that date~~ 21st March an order was received that the Division was to withdraw to the Front Line 3rd. System, & that Machine Guns were to conform with the move, two guns in each Brigade Front being left as a rearguard. The necessary orders were issued to all Companies, and the withdrawal was successfully carried out with the exception of two guns which were slightly South and in front of MONCHY VILLAGE at O.1.d.15.90. who held on too long and were both captured in spite of the gallant fight made by Serjt. EDWARDS the N.C.O. in charge.

This sudden change of plans left the guns in the following positions:-

2 Guns at	N.10.d.70.00.	2 Guns at	N.4.a.70.15.
2 " "	N.11.c.00.30.	2 " "	N.4.a.65.77.
2 " "	N.11.a.50.15.	4 " "	N.8.d.00.60.
2 " "	N.11.a.50.60.	4 " "	N.9.b.45.37.
2 " "	N.5.c.60.35.	4 " "	N.2.b.61.05.
2 " "	H.35.a.50.25.	4 " "	N.9.b.15.80.
1 " "	N.16.b.10.90.	4 " "	H.35.c.90.80.
1 " "	N.10.b.10.45.	4 " "	H.35.b.10.05.
2 " "	N.4.d.50.00.	4 " "	H.33.b.10.25.
1 " "	N.5.a.00.40.	1 " "	N.5.a.10.70.

Coy. H.Q. :-	"A" Coy.	N.8.a.70.80.	- 3 Guns.
" "	"B" "	H.33.a.10.00.	- 4 Guns.
" "	"C" "	H.32.b.60.25.	- 4 Guns.
" "	"D" "	H.31.b.50.00.	

Of these, 12 were in M.G. Nests connected with tunnelled dug-outs and were in the Front Line, from which position, though some were destroyed in the preliminary bombardment the remainder were able to bring continuous and effective fire on the attacking enemy until the Brigade on the Right of the Line withdrew; when these Posts were attacked in the rear and overwhelmed only one fighting his way out owing to the skill and initiative of its Section Officer :- 2nd. LT. PETERKIN.

The remaining guns were with the exception of 2 guns in the old Power Station, in four gun batteries, placed in old bits of trenches and Artillery Positions away from the General Trench Line.

"A" Coy. on the right of the line had two of these batteries, one at N.8.d.00.50. under 2nd. LT. POOLE and one at N.9.b.50.40. under 2nd. LT. LITTLEJOHN. Both these batteries fired on their S.O.S. lines until they were joined by our Infantry when they engaged direct targets with great success. 2nd.LT. POOLE continued in Action though much worried by enemy snipers until the enemy were within 25 to 50 yards of him , when having finished all his belts and fired 15000 rounds from his battery, he succeeded in successfully withdrawing his guns to the ARMY LINE. 2nd. LT. LITTLEJOHN also successfully withdrew his battery; but came under heavy Artillery & Machine Gun Fire & suffered severe casualties, himself being wounded which necessitated all these 4 guns being abandoned, one certainly being destroyed by a direct hit. The reserve guns of this Company came into action close to their Headquarters; one was soon destroyed by a shell, the other two remained in action, fired personally by LT.SMELTZER, and LT.ROGERS for two hours or more in spite of both these Officers suffering from the effects of gas, and when the Infantry withdrew they successfully withdrew those two guns, alternately covering each other to fresh positions in rear.

"B" Coy. who were covering the Centre Brigade had all their forward guns except one destroyed by shell fire early in the action. Some of them however succeeded in coming into action for short periods. The one that escaped was situated in INVERGORDON TRENCH and had many and good direct targets until the Infantry retired when it withdrew to the Coy. H.Q.

The remaining guns were a 4 gun battery at N.2.b.70.30. South of the CAMBRAI ROAD, and a 4 gun Battery at H.32.d.70.85. at Coy. H.Q. These batteries as soon as the situation became clear opened direct fire on the enemy crossing the ridge running through N.5. N.4. and N.10.

The Southern Battery was forced to retire first, owing to their right flank being turned, and took up position in the ARMY LINE, one gun covering their retreat.
At about 12.45 p.m. Capt. NAWTON with 4 guns at Coy. H.Q. was informed that there was no infantry in front of him, and therefore he sent back 3 guns keeping one himself to cover their withdrawal. This was successfully done and this gun having finished its remaining belts was also withdrawn to conform with the line of Infantry, these two batteries finally occupying positions on TELEGRAPH HILL and N.1.a.60.10. supporting the Line held by the Infantry.

North of the CAMBRAI ROAD the left Brigade of the Division was covered by "C" Coy. This Coy. had no guns in front at all and had all its guns arranged in 4 gun batteries distributed in schelons to its rear. This Coy. opened on its Barrage lines at an early hour and when at 8.30.a.m. the enemy launched their first attack opened rapid on its S.O.S. Lines. As a result of this and the fire brought to bear from the Front Line guns in Nests enemy attacks did not succeed but about 9.0.a.m. the enemy having penetrated to the South parties of the Infantry commenced to retire and small bodies of the enemy commenced to appearon the Crest Line of ORANGE HILL and were moving down its Western slopes towards the CAMBRAI ROAD. These troops were engaged and heavy casualties caused. About mid-day masses of the enemy were seen on the crest of ORANGE HILL and were dispersed by the fire of these guns, as was a similar target on the ridge South of the CAMBRAI ROAD.
Shortly after 1.0 p.m. the whole of the Infantry having passed through them these batteries successfully effected their retirement to cover the ARMY LINE, leaving 2 guns on the forward slope of OBSERVATION RIDGE AND ONE battery at Coy. H.Q. These guns had several excellent targets and much assisted by the good fire observation obtained on the dusty ground, completely dispersed several waves of attacks. The Battery finally withdrew to the ARMY LINE about 3.0.p.m. The guns of this Coy. were in Action from 7.30.a.m. to 3.0.p.m. practically continuously, inflicted heavy losses on the enemy, covered our own Infantry effectively, and finally successfully covered their own withdrawal when it became necessary.

As regards the action of "D" Coy. it is very difficult to say what happened. 12 Guns were in the Front Line in Nests and 1 four gun battery rather close up at AIRY CORNER. Of these 12 Front Line guns 8 were South of the CAMBRAI ROAD in the Front Line, and 4 were North of it. These guns were heard firing at an early hour and as not a single man escaped from the Front Line guns except from the extreme left pair of guns which though surrounded fought their way out, it is believed that these guns fought to a finish and were finally surrounded and overwhelmed.

The one gun that escaped under 2nd. LT. PETERKIN obtained magnificent targets and inflicted tremendous casualties on the enemy and continually broke up attempts to approach his position from the Front, firing about 15000 rounds especially engaging attempts of the enemy to establish his Machine Guns among his forward Infantry. This Officer on finding himself surrounded turned his guns on the enemy who were behind him and then brought off his remaining gun and two teams and joined 7/8 K.O.S.B. and protected their flank until they established themselves in the ARMY LINE. This force which was a considerable way behind the rest of the Infantry suffered heavy casualties from the accurate fire of our heavy artillery who apparently mistook them for an enemy attack.

As a result of the Action the Battalion had 27 guns left out of 62 and a loss in personnel of 11 Officers and 142 Other Ranks, Killed, Wounded, and Missing.

LESSONS LEARNT FROM THE ACTION.

The chief of these was the great fire power and handiness of the 4 gun battery. These batteries were self-contained, easy to control, had great moral and material effects on the enemy were very successful in covering our Infantry and when it was necessary in mutually covering their own withdrawal without undue loss.

Pairs of guns in Nests succeeded in inflicting loss on the enemy; but were finally overwhelmed by flank and rear attacks only one gun succeeding in escaping. These guns being near trench lines suffered from the preliminary bombardment and were definite objects of the enemy's attack, in comparision to the 4 gun Batteries which were placed in positions away from the trench lines, in a large manner escape the bombardment and their fire when delivered came as a complete surprise to the enemy.

The necessity of protection of these batteries by snipers to meet enemy snipers who were their chief damger, was clearly brought out.

The preliminary M.G. Barrage at the commencement of the attack was unable to be developed to its utmost owing to the shortage of belts and the necessity of retaining a good proportion for direct targets. This would have been overcome had ammunition been packed in Papier-Maché belts.

The necessity of siting all Barrage batteries primarily for direct fire over their sights, as indirect will not stop determined attacks by large forces. Fortunately this was done in every case and was fully justified by results.

Signalling communication either between Batteries or Headquarters was non-existant except when buried cable was available and in any case the establishment allowed renders any proper signalling communication impossible. Pigeons at Coy. H.Q. would have been of great value in enabling Coys. to keep Battn. H.Q. informed of their progress rendering possible the accurate direction of reserves and reinforcements where most required.

One Company (A) who received an issue of anti-gas capsules before the action, were unanimous as to the good effects obtained from their use during the periods of gas shelling they were subjected to.

R. Rasmith

Lieut. Colonel.

12. 4. 18. Commanding 15th. Battn. Machine Gun Corps.

15th Bn Machine Gun Corps

List of Officer Casualties in Operations 28/3/18

RANK	NAME	CASUALTY	DATE
2nd LIEUT:	FINIGAN W.J.	Killed	28-3-18
— " —	PARROTT S.A.	Wounded	— " —
— " —	LITTLEJOHN A.R.	— " —	— " —
— " —	SMITH E.A.	— " —	— " —
— " —	STAGG H.W.	Missing	— " —
— " —	ASHBURNER J.C.	— " —	— " —
— " —	KIRK J.T.	— " —	— " —
— " —	TAYLOR W.J.	— " —	— " —
LIEUT:	WINN L.S.	— " —	— " —
— " —	ROGERS E	Wounded Gas	— " —
2nd LIEUT.	POOLE A.F.	Wounded Gas	— " —

15TH BATTALION.
MACHINE GUN
CORPS.
No. W.D.1
Date 31/3/18.

ROUTE NATIONALE.

(d) When artillery barrage is moving, rate of fire will be 1 belt per 3 minutes.

When artillery barrage is standing, rate of fire will be 1 belt per 6 minutes.

at least 3,000 rounds per gun will be retained for dealing with enemy counter attacks.

3\. (a) O.C., B.Coy. will detail one section to assist in consolidation of first objective with 46th Inf. Bde. and will arrange for approximate positions for guns to take up with G.O.C. 46th Inf. Bde.

(b) O.C., C.Coy. will detail two sections to assist in consolidation of final objective with 44th Inf. Bde. and will arrange for approx. positions for these guns to take up with G.O.C., 44th Inf. Bde.

These two sections will move forward from VIERZY with pack animals, and O.C., C.Coy. will arrange with G.O.C. 44th Inf. Bde. to be notified when final objective has been taken, and times at which guns will move forward.

Twelve pack animals will report at C.Coy. Hqrs. at 4 a.m. tomorrow August 1st.

4\. O.Cs. B. and D. Coys. will show G.O.Cs. 46th and 45th Inf. Bdes. respectively, and O.C., C. Coy. will show G.O.C. 44th Inf. Bde. details of barrages to be fired.

5\. Zero hour will be notified later.

6\. ACKNOWLEDGE.

Capt. & Adjt.
15th Bn. Machine Gun Corps.

Distribution :- Copies 1-4. Coys.
5. 44th Inf. Bde.
6. 45th Inf. Bde.
7. 46th Inf. Bde.
8. 15th Div. "G".
9. 15th Bn. M.G.C. (Rear Hqrs.)
10. War Diary.
11. File.

15th Division

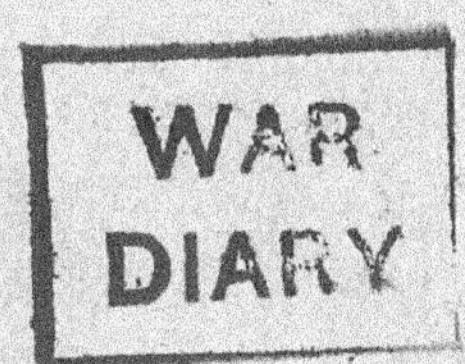

15th DIVISIONAL

MACHINE GUN BATTALION

APRIL 1 9 1 8

Operation Orders attached.

Army Form C. 2118.

Instructions regarding War Diaries and Intelligence Summaries are contained in F. S. Regs., Part II. and the Staff Manual respectively. Title pages will be prepared in manuscript.

WAR DIARY
or
INTELLIGENCE SUMMARY.
(Erase heading not required.)

Vol 2

Place	Date	Hour	Summary of Events and Information	Remarks and references to Appendices

CONFIDENTIAL.

WAR DIARY

OF

15th Battalion MACHINE GUN CORPS

From 1st to 30th April 1918

VOLUME 2.

R. Nasmith Lieut; Col.
Commdg 15th Bn Machine Gun Corps

30th April 1918

D. D. & L., London, E.C. (A8004) Wt. W1771/M2 31 750,000 5/17 Sch. 52 Forms/C2118/14

Army Form C. 2118.

Instructions regarding War Diaries and Intelligence Summaries are contained in F. S. Regs., Part II. and the Staff Manual respectively. Title pages will be prepared in manuscript.

WAR DIARY
or
INTELLIGENCE SUMMARY.
(Erase heading not required.)

Place	Date	Hour	Summary of Events and Information	Remarks and references to Appendices
WARLUS	1/4/18	6pm	Draft of 8 Offrs and 250 O.R arrived from Base Depot. These were immediately posted to Coys to replace casualties. HWS	
			B Coy relieved four guns of 7th MG Squadron	O.O. attached
	2/4/18	9.30 am	Officers and men posted to Coys left HQrs to join Coys in the line	
			Owing to adjustments in Divisional boundaries, B Coy placed four extra guns in the line HWS	O.O. attached
	3/4/18		A Coy withdrew into Reserve to cellars in GRANDE PLACE ARRAS	O.O. attached
			At night, various inter Coy reliefs took place to adjust guns of Coys. HWS	O.O. attached
	4/4/18		Normal activity on both sides during the day, our Artillery active at night HWS	
	5/4/18		Intermittent Artillery activity by enemy, chiefly gas shells. HWS	
	6/4/18		Enemy Artillery active, counter battery work chiefly with gas shells	
		9pm	Lieut Buchanan, 2/Lieuts Crawder and Baxter reported from Base Depot HWS	
	7/4/18		On night 7/8th A Coy relieved B Coy in the line. Relief reported complete by wire at 12.30am 8-4-18 HWS	O.O. attached
		10am	Adjutant visited Coy HQrs in the line also Battery positions of B Coy	
	8/4/18		Battalion defence scheme completed, and issued at 8pm by D.R.L.S. HWS	

D. D. & L., London, E.C.
(A8004) Wt. W1771/M2-31 750,000 5/17 Sch. 52 Forms/C2118/14

Instructions regarding War Diaries and Intelligence Summaries are contained in F. S. Regs., Part II. and the Staff Manual respectively. Title pages will be prepared in manuscript.

WAR DIARY
or
INTELLIGENCE SUMMARY.
(Erase heading not required.)

Army Form C. 2118.

Place	Date	Hour	Summary of Events and Information	Remarks and references to Appendices
	9/4/18	7.30 am	Major Devine and Transport Officer proceeded to GOUY-en-ARTOIS to draw 6 riders for HQrs from Remounts	HWS
	10/4/18	9.30 am	C.O. left HQrs to visit Coys in the line	HWS
	11/4/18	10am	C.O. and Major Devine reconnoitred positions in ARRAS for close defence in case of withdrawal. Activity on both sides normal throughout the day.	HWS
	12/4/18		Quiet day. Enemy shelled front and support lines intermittently during the afternoon.	HWS
	13/4/18		D Coy relieved 4 guns of B Coy at K Battery. (O.O. attached.)	HWS
	14/4/18		Very quiet day. Active harassing fire was carried out by our Artillery throughout the night.	HWS
	15/4/18		Normal day. Stores sent to ARRAS by transport for gun positions for close defence. These were received by Lieut Rosher C Coy and distributed by him.	HWS
	16/4/18	9am 3pm	C.O. left HQrs and visited all Coys in the trenches. Conference of Coy Commanders at HQrs C Coy, attended by all Coy Commanders and C.O. and Adjutant.	HWS

D. D. & L., London, E.C.
(A8004) Wt. W1771/M2031 750,000 5/17 Sch. 52 Forms/C2118/14

Army Form C. 2118.

Instructions regarding War Diaries and Intelligence Summaries are contained in F. S. Regs., Part II. and the Staff Manual respectively. Title pages will be prepared in manuscript.

WAR DIARY
or
INTELLIGENCE SUMMARY.
(*Erase heading not required.*)

Place	Date	Hour	Summary of Events and Information	Remarks and references to Appendices
	17/4/18		Very quiet day. Our Artillery carried out active harassing fire during the night, and engaged several parties of the enemy during the morning. HWS	
	18/4/18		Relief orders for relief of C Coy by B Coy issued by D.R. at 8 pm. Normal Day. HWS	
	19/4/18		CO visited C Coy to arrange co-operation by this Coy in raid to be carried out by 11th A. & Suth. Highrs. Relief between B and C Coys postponed 24 hrs. HWS	
	20/4/18	6.30 am	Argyll & Suth. Highrs. carried out a successful minor operation, capturing 32 prisoners and three M.G.s of 10th Coy. 25th R.I.R. 185th Divn. C Coy guns "stood by" for counter attack. Enemy Artillery active during the morning. Relief of B and C Coys postponed a further 24 hrs. HWS	
	21/4/18		B Coy relieved C Coy. Relief reported complete 12.30 am. (22nd.) C Coy withdrew to cellars in Grande Place. HWS	
	22/4/18		Warning order received that Division was being relieved by 56th Divn. All preparations for relief made, and Coys warned. HWS	
	23/4/18		Operation orders for relief issued by runner at 7.30 am. C and D Coys reached 8 Huts DUISANS by 5.30 pm. HQrs. closed at WARLUS and opened	O.O. attached

D. D. & L., London, E.C. (A8004) Wt. W1771/M2631 750,000 5/17 Sch. 52 Forms/C2118/14

Instructions regarding War Diaries and Intelligence Summaries are contained in F. S. Regs., Part II. and the Staff Manual respectively. Title pages will be prepared in manuscript.

WAR DIARY
or
INTELLIGENCE SUMMARY.
(Erase heading not required.)

Army Form C. 2118.

Place	Date	Hour	Summary of Events and Information	Remarks and references to Appendices
	23/4/18 cont.		at 8 Huts DUISANS at 6pm.	
			Operation Orders prepared for move to XIII Corps area 24th inst, and issued at 2pm (24th.)	O.O. attd. HMS
	24/4/18		Battalion entrained at 9am. Transport moving by Road	O.O. attd
		2pm	Battalion arrived at RAIMBERT. Transport arriving at 5pm.	HMS
	25/4/18	10am	Warning order received that Battalion was to move to HURIONVILLE. Battn. moved by march route, starting time 2pm. Arriving at HURIONVILLE 3.30pm.	HMS
	26/4/18		Reconnaissance of the line carried out by C.O. and all Coy Commanders. Remainder of Battalion spent the day cleaning up and re-organising	HMS
	27/4/18	8.30 – 12.30	Coys carried out training as per programme.	HMS
	28/4/18	11.30 am	C of E. Church parade under Senior C of E. Chaplain.	
		11am.	Presb. Church Parade.	HMS
		10.30.	R.C. parade at BURBURE Church.	
	29/4/18	8.30 am	C.O. inspected A Coy.	
			B and C Coys paraded for Baths at AUCHEL. D Coy carried on parades as per	

D. D. & L., London, E.C. (A8004) Wt. W1771/M2 31 750,000 5/17 Sch. 52 Forms/C2118/14

Army Form C. 2118.

WAR DIARY
or
INTELLIGENCE SUMMARY.
(Erase heading not required.)

Instructions regarding War Diaries and Intelligence Summaries are contained in F. S. Regs., Part II. and the Staff Manual respectively. Title pages will be prepared in manuscript.

Place	Date	Hour	Summary of Events and Information	Remarks and references to Appendices
	29/4/18		Programme of training	
	30/4/18	8.30 am	C.O. inspected B Coy. Remainder of Battn. carried on with Bn. Training Programme.	HW3

30th April 1918

R. Rasmith
Lieut. Col.
Commdg 15th Bn Machine Gun Corps

D. D. & L., London, E.C.
(A8004) Wt. W1771/M2931 750,000 5/17 Sch. 52 Forms/C2118/14

SECRET. **COPY NO. 8**

15th. BN. MACHINE GUN CORPS.

OPERATION ORDER NO. 4. **1st. April 1918.**

1. "B" Coy. will relieve 4 Guns of 7th. M.G. Squadron at M.6.a.00.20. and 2 Guns of 7th. M.G. Squadron at M.6.d.40.60. as soon as possible to-night April 1/2nd.

2. All necessary arrangements to be made between O.C. "B" Coy. and O.C. 7th. M.G. Squadron.

3. On completion of relief the 6 guns of 7th. M.G. Squadron will proceed to WAGONLIEU.

4. Completion of relief to be wired to Bn. Hqrs. by code word "THROUGH".

5. ACKNOWLEDGE.

[signature] Capt. & Adjt.
15th. Battn. Machine Gun Corps.

Copy NO. 1. "B" Coy.
2. 7th. M.G. Squadron.
3. 44th. Infantry Brigade.
4. 45th. Infantry Brigade.
5. 46th. Infantry Brigade.
6. 15th. Division "G".
7. FILE.
8. War Diary.

SECRET.

COPY NO. 11

15th. Battn. MACHINE GUN CORPS.

OPERATION ORDER NO. 5.

2nd. April 1918.

1. On night 3/4th. April the Divisional & Inter Brigade Boundaries will be readjusted as follows:-

(a) SOUTHERN DIVISIONAL BOUNDARY :- GRID LINE running between M. & H.

(b) INTER BRIGADE BOUNDARY :- G.35.a.00.70. - G-36.a.00.70. - H.31.a.00.70 - H.32.a.00.70. - H.33.a.00-60.

(c) NORTHERN DIVISIONAL BOUNDARY :- G.29.a.00.40. - G.30.a.00.40. - H.25.a.00.40. - H.26.a.50.40. - H.27.a.90.20. - BROKEN MILL exclusive.

2. Reference above the following reliefs and moves will take place on night 3/4th. April.

1st. Canadian M.G. Bn. will relieve "B" Coy. as follows:-

3 Guns at N.1.a.50.15.
2 Guns at H.6.d.45.82.

3. Details of relief to be arranged between Coy. Commanders concerned. Canadians Officers will visit "B" Coy. Hdqrs. in LONDON CAVES on morning 3rd. April.

4. "B" Coy. will place 4 Guns in position at about G.36.c.30.50.
"B" Coy. will on completion of moves have 6 guns in reserve at Coy. Hdqrs.
"B" Coy. will select a position for 3 of their reserve guns at about G.30.a.50.00. for use in case of attack.

5. Completion of relief will be reported by wire by the code word "GOOD NIGHT".

6. ACKNOWLEDGE.

Capt. & Adjt.

15th. Battn. Machine Gun Corps.

Copy NO. 1. "A" Coy.
2. "B" "
3. "C" "
4. "D" "
5. 1st. Canadian M.G. Bn.
6. 15th. Division "G".
7. 44th. Infantry Brigade.
8. 45th. Infantry Brigade.
9. 46th. Infantry Brigade.
10. FILE.
11. War Diary.

SECRET. COPY NO. 10

15th. Battn. MACHINE GUN CORPS.

OPERATION ORDER NO. 6. 3rd. April 1918.

The following moves and reliefs will take place to-night 3/4th. inst.

1. "C" Coy. will withdraw the 2 Guns at H.31.b.9.9.

2. "B" Coy. will relieve 4 Guns of "C" Coy. at G.36.d.10.~~85~~.75

3. "C" Coy. will place 4 Guns in position at G.30.b.75.45.

Completion of above instructions to be wired to Battn. Hdqrs. by Coys. concerned by Code Word" RUM"

H M Barons, Capt. & Adjt.

15th. Bn. Machine Gun Corps.

Copy. NO.
1. "A" Coy.
2. "B" "
3. "C" "
4. "D" "
5. 15th. Division "G".
6. 44th. Infantry Brigade.
7. 45th. Infantry Brigade.
8. 46th. Infantry Brigade.
9. FILE.
10. War Diary.

SECRET. **COPY NO. 10**

15th. Battn. MACHINE GUN CORPS.

OPERATION ORDER NO. 7. **3rd. April 1918.**

1. "A" Coy. will move to cellars in GRANDE PLACE to-day.

2. On completion of move "A" Coy. will reconnoitre a position for 4 Guns at about G.30.a.00.50. This position will be prepared as soon as selected and occupied by 4 Guns of "A" Coy. as soon as possible.

3. Completion of move to be reported by wire to Bn. Hdqrs. by code word "HAPPY".

H M Bares Capt. & Adjt.
15th. Bn. Machine Gun Corps.

Copy. NO. 1. "A" Coy.
2. "B" "
3. "C" "
4. "D" "
5. 15th. Division "G".
6. 44th. Infantry Brigade.
7. 45th. Infantry Brigade.
8. 46th. Infantry Brigade.
9. FILE.
10. War Diary.

SECRET. **COPY NO.** ______

18th. BATTN. MACHINE GUN CORPS.

OPERATION ORDER NO. 8. **6th. April 1918.**

1. On night 7/8th. inst. "A" Coy. will relieve "B" Coy. in the Line.

2. All necessary arrangements will be made by O.C. Coys. concerned. On completion of relief "B" Coy. will withdraw into reserve to cellars in the GRANDE PLACE, ARRAS., leaving 2 guns under tactical control of O.C. "A" Coy. and 2 guns under tactical control of O.C. "C" Coy. These guns to be left at Hdqrs. of above mentioned Coys in reserve.

3. "B" Coy. will also place 4 guns at G.30.a.00.80. (approx:)

4. Completion of relief to be wired to Bn. Hdqrs. by code word "WINDY".

ACKNOWLEDGE.

5.

H. M. Barr[illegible]
Capt. & Adjt.
18th. Bn. Machine Gun Corps.

Copy NO. 1. "A" Coy.
2. "B" "
3. "C" "
4. "D" "
5. 18th. Division "G".
6. 1st. Canadian M.G. Bn.
7. 44th. Infantry Brigade.
8. 45th. Infantry Brigade.
9. 46th. Infantry Brigade.
10. FILE.
11. War Diary.

SECRET. **COPY NO. 11**

15th. BATTN. MACHINE GUN CORPS.

OPERATION ORDER NO. 8. **6th. April 1918.**

1. On night 7/8th. inst. "A" Coy. will relieve "B" Coy. in the Line.

2. All necessary arrangements will be made by O.C. Coys. concerned. On completion of relief "B" Coy. will withdraw into reserve to cellars in the GRANDE PLACE, ARRAS. leaving 2 guns under tactical control of O.C. "A" Coy. and 2 Guns under tactical control of "C" Coy. These guns to be left at Hdqrs. of above mentioned Coys. in reserve.

3. "B" Coy. will also place 4 guns at G.30.c.00.80.(approx.)

4. Completion of relief to be wired to Bn. Hdqrs. by code word "WINDY".

5. ACKNOWLEDGE.

H M Barnes.
Capt. & Adjt.
15th. Bn. Machine Gun Corps.

Copy. NO. 1. "A" Coy.
2. "B" "
3. "C" "
4. "D" "
5. 15th. Division "G".
6. 1st. Canadian M.G. Bn.
7. 44th. Infantry Brigade.
8. 45th. Infantry Brigade.
9. 46th. Infantry Brigade.
10. FILE.
11. War Diary.

SECRET. COPY No. 10

15th. Battn. MACHINE GUN CORPS.

OPERATION ORDER NO. 9. 15th. April 1918.

1. As soon as possible after receipt of these orders "D" Coy. will relieve 4 guns of "B" Coy. at "K" Battery (G.30. a.00.50.) with the 2 guns from R.1. Position (G.35.d.05.62.) and 2 guns from "H" Battery (G.35.b.00.90.)

2. On completion of relief "B" Coy. will withdraw their guns from "K" Battery to Coy. Hdqrs. at GRANDE PLACE, ARRAS.

3. Completion of relief to be notified by "B" Coy. to Bn. Hdqrs. by code word "BREEZE ".

4. ACKNOWLEDGE.

Capt. & Adjt.
15th. Bn. Machine Gun Corps.

Copy No. 1. "A" Coy.
2. "B" "
3. "C" "
4. "D" "
5. 15th. Division "G".
6. 44th. Infantry Brigade.
7. 45th. Infantry Brigade.
8. 46th. Infantry Brigade.
9. FILE.
10. War Diary.

SECRET.

COPY No. 10

15th. Bn. Machine Gun Corps.

OPERATION ORDER No. 10. 16th. April 1918.

1. On night 19/20th. "B" Coy. will relieve "C" Coy. in the Line.

2. Details to be arranged by Coy. Commanders concerned.

3. On completion of relief "C" Coy. will withdraw to reserve to cellars in GRANDE PLACE, ARRAS.

4. Completion of relief to be wired by by "B" Coy. to Bn. Hdqrs. by code word "PETROL".

H M Bowers Capt. & Adjt.

15th. Bn. Machine Gun Corps.

Copy No. 1. "A" Coy.
2. "B" "
3. "C" "
4. "D" "
5. 15th. Division.
6. 44th. Infantry Brigade.
7. 45th. Infantry Brigade.
8. 46th. Infantry Brigade.
9. FILE.
10. War Diary.

SECRET.

15th. Bn. Machine Gun Corps No. M.G./T.20.

O.C. "A" Coy.
O.C. "B" "
O.C. "D" "
O.C. "C" "
15th. Division "G".
44th. Inf. Bde.
45th. Inf. Bde.
46th. Inf. Bde.

File

Ack B.74/192

Reference 15th. Bn. M.G.C. Operation Order No. 10. dated 16th. April 1918.

The above Operation Order is postponed for 24 hours.

Please acknowledge.

Capt. & Adjt.
15th. Bn. Machine Gun Corps.

18. 4. 18.

SECRET. 15th. Battn. MACHINE GUN CORPS. COPY NO. 11

OPERATION ORDER NO. 11. 23rd. April 1918.

Ref. Sheet 51.c N.E.

1. Section The 15th. Division less Artillery will hand over Left XV11 Corps to 56th. Division.

2. Machine Gun Reliefs will be carried out as follows:-

(a). "C" Coy. will withdraw to "Y" Hutments at L.2.c.00.60. Route :- G.21.a.3.7. - ST. POL Road.
Time of leaving GRANDE PLACE 1.30. p.m. 23rd. inst.
Transport Officer will arrange for 5 limbers to report at "C" Coy. Hd.Qrs. at 1.0 p.m. 23rd. inst.

(b). "D" Coy. will withdraw all guns and belt boxes in position to Coy. H.Q. by 12.30. p.m. and will march to "Y" Huts L.2.c.00.60. leaving Coy. Hd.Qrs. at 2.0 p.m. Route:- G.21.a.3.7. - ST. POL Road.
Transport Officer will arrange for 5 limbers to remove guns etc. from Coy. Hd.Qrs. Only 1 limber to move E. of Railway Bridge at G.28.b.9.6. at a time. First limber to arrive outside Coy. Hd.Qrs. at 1.15 p.m.

(c). "A" Coy. will withdraw the following guns to Coy. Hd.Qrs. as soon as possible after dark on night 23rd. inst:-

1 Gun BOIS des BOEUFS POSITION.
1 " CAMBRAI ROAD "
2 " TILLOY "
4 " "B" Battery.

56th. Bn. M.G.C. will relieve "A" & "C" Batteries on night 23/24th. inst. Details re guides, transport etc. will be notified later. On completion of relief "A" Coy. will move to "Y" Huts. Route as for "D" Coy.

(d). "B" Coy. will withdraw the following guns to Coy. Hd.Qrs. as soon as possible after dark on night 23/24th. inst:-

"E" Battery.

56th. Bn. M.G.C. will relieve the following guns on night 23/24th. inst:-

2 Guns at Battery Valley Position.
4 " of "D" Battery.
4 " of "F" "

Details re guides, transport etc. will be notified later.
On completion of relief "B" Coy. will move to "Y" Huts. Route as for "D" Coy.

3. "A" Coy. will bring out belt boxes from the BOIS des BOEUFS, CAMBRAI ROAD, and TILLOY POSITIONS; but will hand over belt boxes at "A" & "C" Batteries. Half the belt boxes at "B" Battery will be taken to each "A" & "C" Batteries and will be handed over there.
"B" Coy. will hand over all belt boxes belonging to guns in position. Half of those at "E" Battery to be taken to each of "D" & "F" Batteries and handed over there.
In all cases belt boxes at Coy. Hd.Qrs. will be brought out and all improvised boxes either at Positions or Coy. Hd.Qrs. will be brought out.

4. Arrangements are being made for billeting of Coys. at "Y" Huts.

5. Transport Officer will arrange for the removal to "Y" Huts with "C" Coy. of the Field Kitchen & Maltese Cart at "C" Coy. Hd.Qrs. GRANDE PLACE, and also for horses for Coy. Commanders and Medical Officer.

The Medical Officer will move with "C" Coy.

6. Completion of relief of "A" & "B" Coys. will be reported by wire to Battn. Hd.Qrs. by code word "OIL".

7. Duplicate receipts of trench stores etc. handed over will be sent to Bn. Hd.Qrs. as soon as possible after reaching "Y" Huts.

8. Battn. Hd.Qrs. will close at WARLUS and open at "Y" Huts at a time to be notified later.

9. ACKNOWLEDGE.

Issued by Runner
at 7.0,a.m.

[signature] Capt. & Adjt.
15th. Bn. Machine Gun Corps.

Distribution:-

Copy No. 1. "A" Coy.
2. "B" "
3. "C" "
4. "D" "
5. Medical Officer.
6. Transport Officer.
7. 56th. Bn. Machine Gun Corps.
8. 15th. Division "G".
9. 15th. Division "Q".
10. Quartermaster.
11. FILE.
12. War Diary.

SECRET.   15th. Bn. Machine Gun Corps No. M.G./T.30.

"A" Coy.
"B" "
"C" "
"D" "
15th. Division "G".
15th. Division "Q".
56th. Bn. Machine Gun Corps.
Transport Officer.
Quartermaster.

Reference 15th. Bn. M.G.C. Operation Order No. 11.

1. "C" Coy. 56th. Bn. M.G.C. will relieve those guns of "A" and "B" Coys. which are being relieved.

2. Ref. Para 2. (d).
"D", "E" & "F" Batteries will be relieved as follows and not as therein stated.

2 Guns of 56th. Bn. M.G.C. will relieve "D" Battery.
4 " " " " " " " "E" Battery.
2 " " " " " " " "F" Battery.

Belt boxes of guns of batteries which are not being relieved will be distributed among those that are being relieved.

Details re guides etc. will be arranged between Coy. Commanders concerned. Transport Officer will arrange for 5 limbers to be outside "B" Coy. Hd.Qrs. at 10.0 p.m. to-night.

3. Ref. Para 2. (c). "A" Coy.
All details of relief will be arranged between Coy. Commanders concerned.
Transport Officer will arrange for 5 limbers to be outside "A" Coy. Hd.Qrs. at 9.30. p.m. to-night.

4. All maps (except sheet LENS 11.) Defence Schemes etc. of this area will be handed over.

5. Please acknowledge. by wire

[signature] Capt. & Adjt.

23. 4. 18.   15th. Bn. Machine Gun Corps.

SECRET. 15th. Battn. MACHINE GUN CORPS. COPY NO.

OPERATION ORDER NO. 12. 23rd. April 1918.

1. The 15th. Division (less @rtillery) will move by bus to ~~XXXX~~ X111 Corps Area.

2. The Battalion will embuss at "Y" Huts on the 24th. inst. at a time to be notified later. Destination:- BRUAY Area. (to billets vacated by 46th. Division).
Route for busses:- ACQ - ESTREE CAUCHIE - HOUDAIN.

All personnel embussing will carry full marching order and 1 blanket per man.

All Guns, Tripods, Spare Parts and 10 belt boxes per gun will be taken by bus.
The 323 belt boxes taken over from 56th. Bn. M.G.C. will be carried by the transport.
All improvised boxes will also be carried by the transport.
The Quartermaster will arrange to load his G.S. Wagon and send same to Transport Lines. This wagon will move with the transport; but the Quartermaster and his staff will move with the Battalion.

3. The Transport will move unders orders to be issued by Brig. Genrl. Cmdg. 46th. Inf. Bde. Destination:- BRUAY Area.
Route for Transport:- ACQ - ESTREE CAUCHIE - HOUDAIN - DIVION - CAMBLAIN CHATELAIN - CALONNE RICOUART.

BRUAY is not to be entered.

Distances of 500 yards will be maintained between Transport of Units during the move.
The Transport will carry all Officers valises which will be stacked at a time and place to be notified later.

4. The unexpended portion of rations for 24th. inst. will be carried on the man. Dixies will also be taken.

Water Bottles will be filled before embussing.

Attention of O.C. Coys. is directed to 15th. Div. No. ~~Q/XX/X~~ Q/64/205 dated 22. 4. 18.- Instructions for Embussing - issued to Coys. 22. 4. 18.

5. ACKNOWLEDGE.

Capt. & Adjt.

15th. Bn. Machine Gun Corps.

Distribution:-

Copy No. 1. "A" Coy.
2. "B" "
3. "C" "
4. "D" "
5. Transport Officer.
6. Quartermaster.
7. Medical Officer.
8. 56th. Bn. Machine Gun Corps.
9. 15th. Division "G".
10. 15th. Division "Q".
11. FILE.
12. War Diary.

SECRET

15th. Bn. MACHINE GUN CORPS

Copy No..........

Ref. LENS 11
1/100,00 A
HAZEBROUCK 5.A.
1/100,000

OPERATION ORDER No. 12.

24.4.18.

1. The Battalion will move to billets in RAIMBERT, BURBURE today, 24th. inst. by bus.
   Transport will move by march route.

2. Battalion will parade in column of route on road outside Camp facing S.W. at 8.30 a.m.
   Order of March H.Q. "A" "B" "C" "D" Coys.
   Head of column to be opposite Flying Corps hangars.
   Battalion will march thence to K.6.d.8.4. and thence embus.

3. 1 lorry per Company has been provided to carry all guns, tripods, beltboxes etc. These lorries will be outside Camp at 8.40 a.m. by which time Coys. will have all guns, tripods, etc., ready for loading. 1 N.C.O. and 6 men per Coy. will be detailed to load lorries and will proceed with these lorries to debussing point.
   "D" Coy's loading party will report to Adjutant at 8 a.m. to act as guides to bring lorries to Camp.
   1 N.C.O. per Company and 1 N.C.O. for H.Q. will report to Lieut. BARLOW at Battalion Hd. Qrs. at 6 a.m. for billeting in the new area. This party will proceed to cross road K.6.c.2.8. and report by 6.30 a.m. to Captain POWER, 10th. Scottish Rifles.

4. Lieut. [illegible] will act as Embussing Officer for the Battalion and will report to Captain POWER at cross roads at K.6.c.2.8. at 6.15 a.m. This Officer will also act as Debussing Officer and will travel on first bus occupied by the Battalion.
   Embussing will be carried out in accordance with 15th. Division No. G/64/206 dated 22.4.18.

5. The Transport will move by road under orders of the 46th. Inf. Bde. Transport Officer.
   Starting Point Cross Roads ½ mile North of AGNEZ-les-DUISANS. Time 6.10 a.m.
   ROUTE - AGNEZ-les-DUISANS - HAUTE AVESNES - ACQ ESTREE CAUCHIE - HOUDAIN - DIVION - CAMBLAIN - CHATELAIN - RAIMBERT.
   Approx time of leaving Camp 7.40 a.m.

6. Transport Officer will detail a reliable N.C.O. to report to Captain POWER at cross road K.6.c.2.8. at 6.15 a.m. to go ahead to arrange for billeting for Transport.
   This N.C.O. will travel in the first bus used by the Battalion.

7. ACKNOWLEDGE.

Captain & Adjt.

15th. Bn. MACHINE GUN CORPS.

Distribution -

Copy No. 1 "A" Company
2. "B" "
3. "C" "
4. "D" "
5. Transport Officer
6. Quartermaster
7. File.
8. War Diary.

Instructions regarding War Diaries and Intelligence Summaries are contained in F. S. Regs., Part II. and the Staff Manual respectively. Title pages will be prepared in manuscript.

WAR DIARY
or
~~INTELLIGENCE SUMMARY.~~
(Erase heading not required.)

Army Form C. 2118.

Vol 3

Place	Date	Hour	Summary of Events and Information	Remarks and references to Appendices
			CONFIDENTIAL WAR DIARY OF 15th Battalion MACHINE GUN CORPS From 1st to 31st May 1918 VOLUME 3	

31st May 1918

R. Rasmith Lieut: Col
Commanding 15th Battn. Machine Gun Corps

D. D. & L., London, E.C. (A8004) Wt. W1771/M2 31 750,000 5/17 Sch. 52 Forms/C2118/14

Instructions regarding War Diaries and Intelligence Summaries are contained in F. S. Regs., Part II. and the Staff Manual respectively. Title pages will be prepared in manuscript.

WAR DIARY
or
INTELLIGENCE SUMMARY.
(Erase heading not required.)

Army Form C. 2118.

Place	Date	Hour	Summary of Events and Information	Remarks and references to Appendices
HURIONVILLE	1/5/18	8.30/am	A.B.D. Coys continued training as per programme of work	
		12.30/pm	C Coy were inspected by Commanding Officer at 8.30 am	
"	2/5/18	7.45	D Coy A Coy and HQrs paraded for baths at AUCHEL.	
			B.C. Coys continued training as per programme	
		8pm	Warning orders received that Division was moving next day to XVII Corps area.	
"	3/5/18	2am	Operation Orders for move issued by runner. A B Coys and HQrs moved to XVII Corps area. Dispositions on night 3/4th — HQrs DUISANS A and B Coys ARRAS (in billets) C and D Coys HURIONVILLE	O.O. 15 attd
	4/5/18	1pm	C and D Coys arrived at MAROEUIL by train and moved to No. 3 Camp Duisans. A and B Coys moved into the line, relieving Batteries of 1st Canadian MG Bn. Completion of relief reported by wire at 2am 5th May.	O.O. 16 attd
	5/5/18	9am	HQrs opened at ECURIE C and D Coy relieved Batteries of 1st Canadian MG Bn. Completion of relief reported about 1am 6th May	O.O. 16 attd
	6/5/18		Adjustments made in dispositions, and operation orders issued for various reliefs	O.O. 17 attd
	7/5/18		Reliefs carried out successfully as per O.O. 17, completion duly reported to Bn HQrs Bn HQrs moved from ECURIE to ETRUN, re-opening at 4pm	
	8/5/18		Last series of reliefs as per O.O. 17 completed.	

D. D. & L., London, E.C. (A8004) Wt. W1771/M2631 750,000 5/17 Sch. 52 Forms/C2118/14

Army Form C. 2118.

WAR DIARY
or
INTELLIGENCE SUMMARY.
(*Erase heading not required.*)

Instructions regarding War Diaries and Intelligence Summaries are contained in F. S. Regs., Part II. and the Staff Manual respectively. Title pages will be prepared in manuscript.

Place	Date	Hour	Summary of Events and Information	Remarks and references to Appendices
	9/5/18		51st Div. took over portion of Northern Div front. A Coy were relieved on night 8/9th by a Coy of 51st Bn. M.G.C.	O.O. 18 attd.
	10/5/18		Normal quiet day, 11,000 rounds were fired in harassing fire by guns of B and D Coys.	
	11/5/18		Usual harassing fire carried out, quiet day	
	12/5/18		Normal Day. Harassing fire continued.	
	13/5/18		Night firing continued, 11,000 rounds being expended	
	14/5/18		Normal Day. Harassing fire continued.	
	15/5/18	1.30 pm	Operation Order issued for B Coy to co-operate in raid by 45th Inf Bde.	O.O. 19 attd.
	16/5/18	3.45 am	Raid by 13th Royal Scots carried out. Very successful results. Three prisoners captured, one M.G. destroyed and several casualties inflicted on the enemy. Own casualties light.	
	17/5/18		During the night A Coy relieved B Coy in the left front. Relief reported complete about 12.30 am 18/5/18	O.O. 20 attd.
	18/5/18		C Coy relieved D during the night. Dispositions after relief were as follows A Coy left front, C Coy Right Front, D Coy Support Position. B Coy reserve.	
	19/5/18		Normal Day. Our night firing guns fired 9,000 rounds during the night.	

D. D. & L., London, E.C.
(A8004) Wt. W1771/M2 31 750,000 5/17 Sch. 52 Forms/C2118/14

Army Form C. 2118.

Instructions regarding War Diaries and Intelligence Summaries are contained in F. S. Regs., Part II. and the Staff Manual respectively. Title pages will be prepared in manuscript.

WAR DIARY
or
INTELLIGENCE SUMMARY.

(Erase heading not required.)

Place	Date	Hour	Summary of Events and Information	Remarks and references to Appendices
	20/5/18		Normal Day Harassing fire carried out as usual Lieut Sassoon MC joined from Base Depot	[illegible]
	21/5/18		2/Lieut Wilson 2/Lieut Wentle Lieut Draper and Lieut Bryson joined the Battalion from 52 MG Bn. Normal Day.	[illegible]
	22/5/18		Normal Day Harassing fire carried out as usual at night	[illegible]
	23/5/18		OO 21 issued No harassing fire carried out by special request of Brigade Commander	OO 21 att [illegible]
	24/5/18		Normal Day. Harassing fire was again stopped by special request	
	25/5/18		D Coy relieved A Coy in the left front. A Coy on relief took over support position 3,000 rounds were expended in harassing fire	[illegible]
	26/5/18		B Coy relieved C Coy in the right front. C Coy on relief withdrew to Reserve Billets in St. Nicholas 7,000 rounds were expended in harassing fire at night	[illegible]
	27/5/18		Our harassing fire above normal, 8,000 rounds being expended	[illegible]
	28/5/18		Normal Day Our guns again active at night firing 9,000 rounds	[illegible]
	29/5/18		OO 22 issued for D Coy to co-operate in raid to be carried out by 4/5th BLACK WATCH (116th Inf. Bde) Harassing fire guns fired 7,000 rounds	[illegible] OO 22 att
	30/5/18		Instructions received that raid by Black Watch is postponed. Notification sent by wire to all concerned	[illegible]

D. D. & L., London, E.C.
(A8004) Wt. W1771/M2 31 750,000 5/17 Sch. 52 Forms/C2118/14

Instructions regarding War Diaries and Intelligence Summaries are contained in F. S. Regs., Part II. and the Staff Manual respectively. Title pages will be prepared in manuscript.

WAR DIARY
or
INTELLIGENCE SUMMARY.

(*Erase heading not required.*)

Army Form C. 2118.

Place	Date	Hour	Summary of Events and Information	Remarks and references to Appendices
	31/5/18		Notification received that raid will take place on early morning of June 1st Zero hour to be 12.35am Addendum to 00.22 sent to all concerned	

R. Nasmith Lieut Colonel
Commanding 15th Battn Machine Gun Corps

31st May 1918

D. D. & L., London, E.C.
(A8004) Wt. W1771/M2 31 750,000 5/17 Sch. 52 Forms/C2118/14

~~SECRET~~. 15th. Battn. MACHINE GUN CORPS. Copy No. 12

OPERATION ORDER NO. 15. 3rd. May 1918.

1. The 15th. Division (less Artillery) is being transferred to XVll Corps. Dismounted personnel will move by rail, transport by road.

2. The Battalion will move as follows:-
"B" Coy. with 45th. Inf. Bde. to-day.
"~~B~~"
"A" Coy. with 46th. Inf. Bde. to-day.
"C" & "D" Coys. will move on 4th. inst. under instructions to be issued later.
Destination for "A" & "B" Coys. :- ARRAS.

3. "B" Coy. will move off head of column to pass Ed.rs Mess at 8.45 a.m. Route :- BURBURE -RAIMBERT- Cross Roads ½ mile N.of Y. in CAUCHY -A-LA-TOUR -RICOURT Station. where this Coy. will entrain. 1 Officer and 2 N.C.O.s will be at I.5.c.2.2. at 7.45 a.m. where they will meet a lorry conveying billeting parties of 45th. Inf. Bde. This party will take over billets and act as guides, meeting Coy. at BAUDIMONT GATE, ARRAS.
Detraining station :- ACQ. Probable time of arrival :- 2.40 p.m.
An Officer from "B" Coy. will report to R.T.O. at CALINNE RICOURT Station at 11.10 a.m. and will hand him a Parade State.
1 N.C.O. and 8 men are to be left behind as brakesmen to limbers.

"A" Coy. will march off at 4.15 p.m. and pass Cross Roads ½ mile N. of Y in CAUCHY-A- LA TOUR at 5.30 p.m.
Route:- BURBURE - RAIMBERT - FLORINGHEM - PERNES Station.
An Officer of "A" Coy. will report to Capt. POWER M.C. 10th. Scottish Rifles at PERNES Station at 5.30 p.m. at R.T.O.s Office with Parade State.
"A" Coy. will have a party of 1 N.C.O. and 8 men as brakesmen to their limbers.
"A" Coy. will send a billeting party of 1 Officer and 2 N.C.O.s to be at BURBURE Church at 7.40 a.m. when they will proceed with Staff Captain of 46th. Inf. Bde. and act as billeting party. This party will send 1 man as a guide to meet Coy. at detraining station and guide Coy. to billets.
Detraining Station :- MAROEUIL. Probable time of arrival:- 10.0 p.m.
Blankets of "A" & "B" Coys. to be rolled in bundles of 10 and dumped at Quartermaster Stores by 7.45 a.m.
1 guide for rations from eavh Coys. billeting party to report to Quartermaster at DUISANS after Billets have been arranged in ARRAS.
Location of Quartermaster Stores to be obtained from Area Commandant DUISANS.

4. TRANSPORT of "A" & "B" Coys. under 2nd.LT. CUMMINGS will move to old standings at DUISANS by road, moving off at 12.20 p.m. to pass Starting point :- Cross Roads ½ mile N. of Y. in CAUCHY-A-LA TOUR at at 1.25 p.m.
Route:- CAUCHY-A-LA TOUR -HOUDAIN - ESTREE CAUCHEE- CAMBLIGNEUL-AUBIGNY - HAUTE AVESNES - DUISANS.
Strict March discipline will be maintained. There will be a halt of 1 hour for watering and feeding besides normal hourly halts of 10 minutes. This transport will move with 46th. Inf.Bde. Transport and will move under orders of 46th. Inf.Bde. T.O. during the march.

Capt. & Adjt.
15th. Bn. Machine Gun Corps.

Issued by Runner
and D.R.L.S. at 2.0 a.m.

Distribution over leaf.

Distribution :-.

Copy No. 1 "A" Coy.
2 "B" "
3 "C" "
4 "D" "
5 Transport Officer.
6 Quartermaster.
7 15th. Division "G"
8 44th. Inf. Bde.
9 45th. Inf. Bde.
10 46th. Inf. Bde.
11 FILE.
12 WAR DIARY.

SECRET. 15th. Battn. MACHINE GUN CORPS. Copy No. 10

Ack. BM435

OPERATION ORDER NO. 16. 4th. May 1918.

Ref. 51 B. N.W.1/20000

1. The 15th. Division will relieve the 1st. Canadian Division in the Line on nights 4/5th. and 5/6th. inst. Relief to be completed by 6.0 a.m. 6th. inst.

2. Machine Gun Reliefs will be carried out as follows:-

(a) On night 4/5th.inst.

(i) "A" Coy. 15th. Bn. M.G.C. will relieve "H" Battery, 1st. Canadian M.G. Bn.
(ii) "B" Coy. 15th. Bn. M.G.C. will relieve "F" Battery, 1st. Canadian M.G. Bn.

Until completion of relief "A" & "B" Coys. will come under tactical control of O.C. 1st. Canadian M.G. Bn.

(b) Night 5/6th. inst.

(i) "C" Coy. 15th. Bn. M.G.C. will relieve "B" Battery, 1st. Canadian M.G. Bn.
(ii). "D" Coy. 15th. Bn. M.G.C. will relieve "G" Battery, 1st. Canadain M.G. Bn.

3. On completion of relief each Coy. will have 1 Section in reserve. Sections of "A" & "B" Coys. will remain in billets in ARRAS till night of 5/6th. inst. when all reserve sections of Coys. will take over billets vacated by "E" Battery, 1st. Canadian M.G. Bn. at ST. NICHOLAS.

An Officer of "B" Coy. is reconnoitring positions occupied by reserve sections in case of emergency and will be responsible that all Sections know the route to billets in ST. NICHOLAS.

4. Details of all reliefs to be arranged between Coy. Commanders concerned. Signalling Officer will arrange for Signal Relief.

Transport Officer will arrange for 3 limbers containing guns of Coys. to be at "A" & "B" Coy. Hdqrs. by 7.30 p.m. on night 4th. inst.

Rations for "A" & "B" Coys. will be delivered to billets in ARRAS by 7.30 p.m. 4th. inst.

All Coys. going into the Line will wear "Battle Order". Packs of "A" & "B" Coys. will be left in billets in ARRAS under charge of Reserve Sections. Disposal of these will be arranged by Bn. Hdqrs.

5. Belt Boxes and Trench Stores will be taken over and receipts given. Copies of receipts for trench stores taken over will be sent to Bn. Hdqrs. by 10.0 a.m. day after relief.

6. Completion of relief to be wired to Bn. Hdqrs. by code word :"ASS".

Battalion Hdqrs. will open at ECURIE on completion of relief.

7. ACKNOWLEDGE.

[signature] Capt. & Adjt.
15th. Bn. Machine Gun Corps.

Distribution over leaf.

Distribution :-

Copy No. 1. "A" Coy.
2. "B" "
3 "C" "
4 "D" "
5. Transport Officer.
6. Quartermaster.
7. 15th. Division "G".
8. 44th. Inf. Bde.
9. 45th. Inf. Bde.
10 46th. Inf. Bde.
11 1st. Canadian M.C. Bn.
12. FILE.
13 War Diary.

SECRET. **15th. Bn. MACHINE GUN CORPS.** **COPY No. 13**

6th. May 1918.

OPERATION ORDER NO. 17.

1. The following reliefs will take place on nights 7/8th. and 8/9thinst.

(a) Night 7/8th. "A" Coy. will relieve Guns Nos. 33,34,35,36, from "B" Coy.
"B" Coy. will relieve Guns Nos. 19 and 20 from "D" Coy.

(b) Night 8/9th. "D" Coy. will relieve Guns Nos. 11,12,13,14,15, & 16, from "C" Coy.
"B" Coy. will relieve Guns Nos. 23,24,25,26,29,30. from "C" Coy.

2. On completion of relief "C" Coy. will withdraw into reserve to billets at ST. NICHOLAS.

3. All details of relief to be arranged between Coy. Commanders concerned.

4. O.C. Coys. will inform Battn. Hdqrs. of details of transport required to move the reserve Sections.

5. Completion of relief in Para 1 (a) to be wired to Battn. Hdqrs. by code word "HORSE"
Completion of relief in Para 1 (b) to be wired to Battn. Hdqrs. by code word "MARE"

6. ACKNOWLEDGE.

H M Sa[illegible] Capt. & Adjt.

15th. Bn. Machine Gun Corps.

Distribution:-

Copy No. 1. "A" Coy.
2. "B" "
3. "C" "
4. "D" "
5. 15th. Division "G"
6. 15th. Division "Q".
7. 44th. Inf. Bde.
8. 45th. Inf. Bde.
9. 46th. Inf. Bde.
10. 51st. Bn. M.G.C.
11. 56. Bn. M.G.C.
12. FILE.
13. War Diary.

SECRET. 15th. Battn. MACHINE GUN CORPS. COPY NO. 15

OPERATION ORDER NO. 18. 8th. May 1918.

Ref. 51B. N.W. 1/20,000.

1. The Northern Divisional Boundary will be altered to-night 8/9th. inst.) as follows:-

H.5.a.(07 75.55. - H.9.a.99.70. - H.9.a.3.7. - H.1.d.35.00. - G.6.d.9.2. - G.5.d.1.3. - H.3.c.3.4.

2. In consequence of above alteration the following M.G. reliefs will take place on night 9/10th. inst.

"A" Coy. 15th. Bn. M.G.C. will be relieved by a Coy. of 51st. (H) Bn. M.G.C.

3. All necessary arrangements will be made between Coy. Commanders concerned. Requirements for transport to be notified to Bn. Hdqrs. as soon as possible.

4. Belt Boxes and Trench Stores will be handed over and receipts taken. Copy of list of Trench Stores handed over will be sent to Bn. Hdqrs. by 1st. D.R.L.S. on day following relief.

5. On completion of relief "A" Coy. will withdraw to billets at present occupied by "C" Coy. "C" Coy. will move forward into Support Positions. Details of this move will be notified later.

6. Completion of relief to be notified to Bn. Hdqrs. by code word "CAMEL"

7. ACKNOWLEDGE.

H M [signature] Capt. & Adjt.
15th. Bn. Machine Gun Corps.

Distribution :-

Copy No. 1. "A" Coy.
2. "B" "
3. "C" "
4. "D" "
5. Signalling Officer.
6. Transport Officer.
7. Quartermaster.
8. 44th. Inf. Bde.
9. 45th. Inf. Bde.
10. 46th. Inf. Bde.
11. 15th. Div. "G".
12. 15th. Div. "Q".
13. 51st. (H) Bn. M.G.C.
14. 56th. Bn. M.G.C.
15. War Diary.
16. File.

SECRET. 15th. Battn. MACHINE GUN CORPS. COPY NO. 8

OPERATION ORDER NO. 19. 15th. May 1918.

Ref. Map 51B. N.W. 1/20,000.

1. (a). The 13th. The Royal Scots. (45th. Inf. Bde.) are raiding the enemy's Trenches in the area H.5.d.80.20. - H.6.c.00.15. - H.6.c.08.40. on the night of the 15/16th. inst.

(b). The object of the raid is to capture prisoners.

2. Guns of the 15th. Bn. M.G.C. and 51st. Bn. M.G.C. will co-operate as follows:-

(a). 15th. Bn. M.G.C. ("B" Coy.)

2 Guns at approx. H.10.c.40.85.
Targets :- H.5.b.80.35. to H.6.a.22.70. Traverse 2 degrees Right.

2 Guns at approx. H.10.c.40.85.
Targets :- H.5.b.90.23. to H.6.a.33.60. Traverse 2 degrees Left.

1 Gun at approx. H.10.c.45.15.
Targets H.6.a.55.20. to H.6.a.80.35. Traverse 4 degrees Right.

1 Gun at approx. H.10.c.45.15.
Targets H.6.a.78.00. to H.6.a.96.15. Traverse 4 degrees Left.

(b). 51st. Bn. M.G.C.

2 Guns, Targets :- H.6.d.00.55. to H.6.d.58. 59.

2 Guns, Targets :- H.6.a.61.59. to H.6.a.60.38.

(c). RATES OF FIRE.

Z + 2 minutes	to Z + 15 minutes,		4 Belts.
Z + 15 "	to Z + 17	"	1 Belt.
Z + 17 "	to Z + 22	"	3 Belts.
Z + 22 "	to Z + 30	"	2 Belts.

2. An Officer from "B" Coy. 15th. Bn. M.G.C. and from 51st. Bn. M.G.C. will synchronise watches at Hdqrs. 13th. The Royal Scots (H.4.c.45.40.) at 10.30 p.m. to-night (15th. inst.)

3. (a). Zero hour will be notified later.
(b). The actual moment of Zero will be when the Artillery opens Fire.

4. Acknowledge.

Capt. & Adjt.

15th. Bn. Machine Gun Corps.

Distribution overleaf.

Distribution :-.

Copy No. 1. "B" Coy.
2. 51st. BN. M.G.C.
3. "C" Coy. 15th. Bn. M.G.C.
4. "D" Coy. "
5. 45th. Inf. Bde.
6. 15th. Division "G".
7. File.
8. War Diary.
9. File

SECRET. **15th. Battn. MACHINE GUN CORPS.** COPY NO. 16

OPERATION ORDER NO. 20. 15th. May 1918.

Ref. Map. 51.B. N.W. 1/20,000.

1. The following reliefs will take place on nights 17/18th. and 18/19th. inst.

2. Night 17/18th. inst.

"A" Coy. will relieve "B" Coy. in the Left Front.
All necessary arrangements to be made between Coy. Commanders concerned.
Belt Boxes and tripods will be handed over.
On completion of relief "B" Coy. will withdraw into reserve to billets in ST. NICHOLAS.
Transport requirements will be notified direct to Transport Officer.
Completion of relief to be wired to Bn. Hdqrs. by code word "WASP".

3. Night 18/19th. inst.

"C" Coy. will relieve "D" Coy. in the Right Front.
All necessary arrangements to be made by Coy. Commanders concerned.
Belt Boxes and tripods will be handed over.
On completion of relief "D" Coy. will withdraw to Support Positions occupied at present by "C" Coy.
Tran sport Requirements to be wired to Bn. Hdqrs. by code word "BEE".

4. ACKNOWLEDGE.

H M Saunders Capt.& Adjt.
15th. Bn. Machine Gun Corps.

Distribution :-

Copy No. 1. C.O.
2. "A" Coy.
3. "B" "
4. "C" "
5. "D" "
6. Transport Officer.
7. Quartermaster.
8. 44th. Inf. Bde.
9. 45th. Inf. Bde.
10. 46th. Inf. Bde.
11. 15th. Division "G".
12. 15th. Division "Q".
13. 51st. Bn. M.G.C.
14. 56th. Bn, M.G.C.
15. File.
16. War Diary.

SECRET. 15th. Bn. Machine Gun Corps No. M.G./T.136.

Reference 15th. Bn. M.G.C. Operation Order No. 20.

Ref. Para 3. Line 8.

Delete " Transport requirements to be wired to Battn. Hdqrs. by code word "BEE" " and substitute the following. :-

"Transport requirements will be notified to Transport Officer direct."

Completion of relief to be wired to Bn. Hdqrs. by code word "BEE".

Capt. & Adjt.

15. 5. 18. 15th. Bn. Machine Gun Corps.

Addressed to all recipients of Operation Order No. 20.

SECRET. 15th. Bn. Machine Gun Corps No. M.G./T.156.

Amendment to 15th. Bn. M.G.C. Operation Order No. 20.

Reference Para 3.

1. "C" Coy. will not relieve Guns Nos. 1,2,3, & 4. of "D" Coy. ; but will relieve Guns Nos. 19, and 20. of "A" Coy. with 4 guns.

2. The 2 Guns of "A" Coy. relieved will be in Coy. Reserve and accomodated in dug-outs in H.13.a.

3. On completion of relief "D" Coy. will be occupying Positions as follows :- Nos. 1,2,3,4. S.5, S.6, S.7, S.8, S.9, S.10. S.11, S.12, S.13, S.14. and 2 guns in reserve at Coy. Hdqrs. (In case of attack these two guns will occupy Positions R.3. and R.4.)

4. ACKNOWLEDGE.

[signature] Capt. & Adjt.

18. 5. 18. 15th. Bn. Machine Gun Corps.

Copies to all recipients of O.O. No. 20.

SECRET. 15th Battn. MACHINE GUN CORPS. COPY NO. 13

OPERATION ORDER NO. 21. 23.5.18.

1. The following reliefs will take place on nights 25/26th and 26/27th inst.

2. Night 25/26th inst.

(a) "D" Coy. will relieve "A" Coy. in the left front.
(b) All necessary arrangements to be made between Coy. Commanders concerned.
(c) Completion of relief to be wired to Bn. Hqrs. by code word "P.E.N".
(d) On completion of relief "A" Coy. will withdraw to support positions at present occupied by "D" Coy.

3. Night 26/27th inst.

(a) "B" Coy. will relieve "C" Coy. in the right front.
(b) All necessary arrangements to be made between Coy. Commanders concerned.
(c) Completion of relief to be notified to Bn. Hqrs. by code word "N I B".
(d) On completion of relief "C" Coy. will withdraw into reserve to Billets in St. Nicholas.
(e) Transport Officer will arrange to replace "B" Coy. transport by "C" Coy. transport on night 27/28th.

4. All Transport requirements to be notified direct to Transport Officer.

5. ACKNOWLEDGE.

Issued at by D.R.L.S.

[signature]
Capt. & Adjt.
15th Bn. Machine Gun Corps.

Distribution:-
Copy No.1. C.O.
2. "A" Coy.
3. "B" "
4. "C" "
5. "D" "
6. Transp. Officer.
7. Quartermaster.
8. Signalling Officer.
9. 15th Division "G".
10. 44th Inf. Bde.
11. 45th Inf. Bde.
12. 46th Inf. Bde.
13. War Diary. ✓ 1st File

SECRET. COPY NO. 13

15th BATTN. MACHINE GUN CORPS.

OPERATION ORDER NO. 22.

29th May, 1918.

1. (a) The 4/5th Black Watch (46th Inf. Bde.) will carry out a raid on the enemy's Trenches in H.11.d and the Sunken Road immediately WEST of it on the night 30/31st May 1918.

(b) 1st Objective - Trench from H.11.d.55.00 (CAMEL AVENUE inclusive) to H.11.d.65.29.
2nd Objective - SUNKEN ROAD from H.17.b.60.99 to H.11.d. 70.30.

2. "D" Coy. 15th Bn. M.G.C. will co-operate as follows:-
(a) 2 guns at H.17.a.62.80.
Target H.17.b.60.55 to H.17.b.60.80.
Rate of fire, Zero to Z plus 10, 5 belts per gun.

(b) 3 guns at about H.16.a.00.80.
Target H.17.b.60.30. to H.17.b.60.55.
Rate of fire, Zero plus 1 to Z plus 8, 3 belts per gun.
Z " 8 to Z " 16 2 " " "
Z " 16 to Z " 20 2 " " "
Z " 20 to Z " 40 4 " " "

(c) 3 guns at about H.10.c.40.82.
Target H.11.d.80.60. to H.11.d.80.90.
Rate of fire, Zero plus 1 to Z plus 8, 3 belts per gun.
Z " 8 to Z " 16 2 " " "
Z " 16 to Z " 20 2 " " "
Z " 20 to Z " 40 4 " " "

3. The Infantry Garrison of the front line in H.17.b. will be withdrawn during the Raid.

4. The Artillery Barrage will open at Zero. Machine Guns will not open fire until Artillery Barrage opens.

5. An officer of "D" Coy. will synchronise watches at 10:30 p.m. 30th inst. at H.Q. 4/5 Black Watch. (H.14.a.00.90.)

6. Zero hour will be notified later.

7. Acknowledge.

[signature]
Capt. & Adjt.
15th Bn. Machine Gun Corps.

Copies to:-
No.1. C.O.
2. "D" Coy.
3. 46th Inf. Bde.
4. 44th Inf. Bde.
5. 45th Inf. Bde.
6. 15th Div. "G".
7. C.M.G.O. XVII Corps.
8. "A" Coy.
9. "B" Coy.
10. "C" Coy.
11. 56th Bn. M.G.C.
12. 51st Bn. M.G.C.
13. War Diary.
14. File.

15th Bn. Machine Gun Corps. M.G./T.275.

S E C R E T.

AMENDMENT NO.1. to 15th Bn. MACHINE GUN CORPS OPERATION ORDER NO.32. dated 29.5.18.

30th May, 1918.

PARA.5 :- For 10:30 p.m. read 8:30 p.m.

ACKNOWLEDGE.

[illegible] 2Lt for
Capt. & Adjt.
15th Bn. Machine Gun Corps.

Copies to all recipients of Operation Order No.32.

SECRET. 15th Bn. Machine Gun Corps. M.G./T.276.

ADDENDUM TO OPERATION ORDER NO.22.

1. Reference PARA. 6. Zero hour will be 12:15 a.m. 31st May.

2. Please ACKNOWLEDGE.

[signature]
Capt. & Adjt.
15th Bn. Machine Gun Corps.

30.5.18.

S E C R E T. 15th Bn. Machine Gun Corps. M.G./T.279.

Reference Operation Order No.22. This operation is postponed.

Capt. & Adjt.
15th Bn. Machine Gun Corps.

30.5.18.

To all recipients of O.O.No.22.

S E C R E T.   15th Bn. Machine Gun Corps. M.G./T.282.

ADDENDUM NO. 2 to 15th Bn. M.G.C. Operation Order No.22
dated 29.5.18.

31st May, 1918.

1. The operation will be carried out on the night 31st May/1st June 1918.

2. Zero hour will be notified later.

3. An Officer of "D" Coy. will synchronise watches at 8:30 p.m. at H.Q. 4/5 Black Watch.

4. Acknowledge.

Capt. & Adjt.
15th Bn. Machine Gun Corps.

Copies to all recipients of O.O.22.

SECRET.   15TH Bn. Machine Gun Corps. M.G./T. 287.

ADDENDUM NO.3 to 15th Bn. M.G.C. Operation Order No.22. dated 29.5.18.

31st May, 1918.

1. Reference ADDENDUM No. 2 to O.O. No.22. Para 2.

ZERO hour will be 12:35 a.m. 1st June 1918.

2. ACKNOWLEDGE. by Wire

H McLennan
Capt. & Adjt.
15th Bn. Machine Gun Corps.

Copies to all recipients of O.O.22.

SECRET. COPY NO 13

15th Bn. MACHINE GUN CORPS.

OPERATION ORDER NO.23.

Hqrs.
15th Bn. M.G.C.

31st May 1918.

1. The following reliefs will take place on nights 2nd/3rd June, 3rd/4th June.

2. (a) Night 2/3rd June.

"A" Coy. will relieve "B" Coy. in the Right Front.
All details of relief to be arranged between Coy. Commanders concerned.
On completion of relief "B" Coy. will withdraw to support positions at present occupied by "A" Coy.
Transport requirements to be notified direct to Transport Officer.
Completion of relief to be wired to Bn. Hqrs. by code word "PETER".

(b) Night 3/4th June.

"C" Coy. will relieve "D" Coy. in the Left Front.
All necessary arrangements to be made between Coy. Commanders concerned.
On completion of relief "D" Coy. will withdraw into reserve to Billets at ST. NICHOLAS.
Transport requirements to be notified direct to Transport Officer.
Completion of relief will be wired to Bn. Hqrs. by code word "PAN".

3. All Harassing fire Maps, Trench Stores and Programmes of Work in hand will be handed over on relief and receipts taken. Copies of receipts for trench stores handed over will be forwarded to Bn. Hqrs. by 12 noon on day following relief.

4. Acknowledge.

H M Sams
Capt. & Adjt.
15th Bn. Machine Gun Corps.

Issued through Signals
at 1:38 p.m.

Distribution:-
No.1. C.O.
2. "A" Coy.
3. "B" "
4. "C" "
5. "D" "
6. 15th Div. "G".
7. 44th Inf. Bde.
8. 45th Inf. Bde.
9. 46th Inf. Bde.
10. 51st Bn. M.G.C.
11. 56th Bn. M.G.C.
12. C.M.G.O. XVII Corps.
13. War Diary.
14. File.

Instructions regarding War Diaries and Intelligence Summaries are contained in F. S. Regs., Part II. and the Staff Manual respectively. Title pages will be prepared in manuscript.

WAR DIARY
or
INTELLIGENCE SUMMARY.
(Erase heading not required.)

Army Form C. 2118.

Vol 4

Place	Date	Hour	Summary of Events and Information	Remarks and references to Appendices
			CONFIDENTIAL.	
			WAR. DIARY	
			VOL. IV	
			15th BATTN. MACHINE GUN CORPS. 1st to 30th JUNE. 1918.	
			7th July 1918	
			R. Nasmith Lieut. Col.	
			O.C. 15th Battn. Machine Gun Corps	

A5834 Wt. W4973/M687 750,000 8/16 D. D. & L. Ltd. Forms/C.2118/13.

Instructions regarding War Diaries and Intelligence Summaries are contained in F. S. Regs., Part II. and the Staff Manual respectively. Title pages will be prepared in manuscript.

WAR DIARY
or
INTELLIGENCE SUMMARY.
(Erase heading not required.)

Army Form C. 2118.

Place	Date	Hour	Summary of Events and Information	Remarks and references to Appendices
	1/6/18		During the night our night firing guns fired 2000 rounds on enemy tracks and approaches. Work continued on emplacements for firing on enemy's field batteries in "BATTERY VALLEY." The day was quite normal. J.K.	
	2/6/18		C & D Coys issue their own orders re. Relief on the night 3/4. The day was quiet & normal. A & B Coy commence relief. J.K.	
	3/6/18		A & B Coy complete relief. The ~~day~~ was quite normal. C & D Coy commence relief. J.K.	
	4/6/18		D Coy after relief occupy Reserve Position. Enemy art was more active than ordinary. Our night firing guns fired 1,750 rounds at usual targets. Work on dugouts & emplacements continued. J.K.	
	5/6/18		Usual harassing fire 12,750 rds were fired. The day was quiet. Enemy aircraft active. A map was received showing good results of our harassing fire programme. Several tracks are obviously no longer in use. J.K.	
	6/6/18		During the night 10,000 rds ~~were~~ fired. Some new targets on the left were engaged. The day was normal. J.K.	
	7/6/18		Usual harassing fire was carried out	
		1.30pm	Operation Order for inter-relief of Coys on the nights 10/11 and 11/12 [illegible] was issued.	OO 24 [illegible]
		5pm	Operation Order for the co-operation of B & C Coys in a raid by the 6th Cameron Hrs was issued.	OO [illegible]
			Defence Scheme was issued.	
			J.K.	

D. D. & L., London, E.C.
(A8004) Wt. W1771/M2 31 750,000 5/17 Sch. 52 Forms/C2118/14

Instructions regarding War Diaries and Intelligence Summaries are contained in F. S. Regs., Part II. and the Staff Manual respectively. Title pages will be prepared in manuscript.

WAR DIARY
or
~~INTELLIGENCE SUMMARY.~~
(*Erase heading not required.*)

Army Form C. 2118.

Place	Date	Hour	Summary of Events and Information	Remarks and references to Appendices
	8/6/18		The day was extremely quiet. We carried out our usual fire on the night of 7th 8th but owing to preparations for raid in ~~OO~~ 25 no definite scheme was arranged for night of 8th 9th. Work on emplacements & dugouts most satisfactory.	Add. I to OO25 att.
		7pm.	Addendum I to ~~OO~~ 25 issued at 7pm J.K.	
	9/6/18	2am 2.40am	Our guns fired 22,000 rounds in support of the raid by the Camerons. Enemy opened a heavy barrage on our trenches and followed it by a raid. The guns fired on their S.O.S. lines. The remainder of the day was quiet. Four [illegible] of 'B' Coy were wounded. J.K.	
	10/6/18		While engaged in harassing enemy field batteries 2nd Lt DAVIES was wounded. At the same time one man was wounded. 'B' Coy took over from 'C' Coy in the [illegible] front [illegible]. 'C' moved back to "support". ~~While~~ returning to his Coy by cycle an 'A' Coy runner was killed. J.K.	
	11/6/18		The day was very quiet. We carried out our usual harassing fire. 'D' Coy relieved 'A' Coy in the left front sector. 'A' Coy occupied reserve position. J.K.	
	12/6/18		During the night the usual harassing fire was carried out. The period was very quiet. J.K.	
	13/6/18		Our guns fired 12,000 rounds. The period was very quiet. O.O. No 26 and Amendment No 1 to same issued. J.K.	O.O. No 26 Amendment No 1 to O.O. 26

D. D. & L., London, E.C.
(A8004) Wt. W1771/M2 31 750,000 5/17 Sch. 52 Forms/C2118/14

Instructions regarding War Diaries and Intelligence Summaries are contained in F. S. Regs., Part II. and the Staff Manual respectively. Title pages will be prepared in manuscript.

WAR DIARY
or
~~INTELLIGENCE SUMMARY.~~
(*Erase heading not required.*)

Army Form C. 2118.

Place	Date	Hour	Summary of Events and Information	Remarks and references to Appendices
	14 6/18		Normal day. Our guns fired usual harassing fire. [illegible]	
	15 6/18		Normal day. Our guns fired 6,000 rounds [illegible]	
	16 6/18	4am	Operation Order No 27 Issued. Normal day. [illegible]	OO No 27
	17 6/18	2am	Our guns fired 18000 in support of two raids carried out simultaneously by Seaforths & B. Watch. OO. 28 issued respecting relief. [illegible]	OO No 28
	18 6/18		Normal day. Our guns fired 10000 rounds. OO No 29 issued at 5 pm [illegible]	OO No 29
	19 6/18	3pm	Amendment No 1 to OO. No 28 postponing relief until 21/22 & 22/23. Harassing fire carried out as usual. 6000 rounds fired [illegible]	Amdt No 1 to OO. No 28
	20 6/18.		Normal day. Harassing fire carried out as usual. [illegible]	
	21 6/18.	1.30am	70000 rounds fired in support of raid by 13 Bn. R. Scots. Day very quiet. Usual harassing fire carried out at night. C Coy relieved D Coy in left front. D Coy moving support position [illegible]	
	22 6/18	5pm	OO No 30 issued. Quiet day. Harassing fire carried out as usual. A Coy relieved B Coy in left front. B Coy moving into Reserve Billets at [illegible] [illegible]	OO No 30 Att.
	23 6/18	10.30pm	~~[illegible]~~ Amdt No 1 to OO No 30 issued postponing [illegible]. Quiet day. No harassing fire carried out. [illegible]	
	24 6/18	11.30pm	Our guns fired 15000 rds in support of raid by K.O.S.Bs. Quiet day. [illegible]	
	25 6/18		Normal day. Our guns fired usual harassing fire. [illegible]	
	26 6/18		Normal Day. 8 shells fell in vicinity of reserve Billets. One man of B Coy killed. [illegible]	
	27 6/18		Normal Day. Our guns fired 6000 rounds Harassing fire. [illegible]	

D. D. & L., London, E.C.
(A8004) Wt. W1771/M2 31 750,000 5/17 Sch. 52 Forms/C2118/14

Army Form C. 2118.

WAR DIARY
or
INTELLIGENCE SUMMARY.
(Erase heading not required.)

Instructions regarding War Diaries and Intelligence Summaries are contained in F. S. Regs., Part II. and the Staff Manual respectively. Title pages will be prepared in manuscript.

Place	Date	Hour	Summary of Events and Information	Remarks and references to Appendices
	26/6/18		Normal day. Owing to epidemic coy strength so depleted that no harassing was carried out. GG 31 issued JK.	GG 31 att.
	29/6/18		Normal day. No harassing fire. GG 32 issued JK	GG 32 att.
	30/6/18		Normal day. Amendt to GG no 32 issued JK.	Amendt to GG 32 att.

R. Nasmith LIEUT-COL
COMMANDING 15TH BATT. MACHINE GUN CORPS.

D. D. & L., London, E.C.
(A8004) Wt. W1771/M2 31 750,000 5/17 Sch. 52 Forms/C2118/14

SECRET.   COPY NO 15

15th Bn. MACHINE GUN CORPS.

OPERATION ORDER NO.24.

Hqrs.
15th Bn. M.G.C.
June 7th 1918.

1. The following reliefs will take place on nights 10/11th inst. and 11/12th inst.

2.(a) Night 10/11th inst.

"B" Coy. will relieve "C" Coy. in the Left Front.
Details of relief to be arranged between Coy. Commanders concerned.
On completion of relief "C" Coy. will occupy support positions vacated by "B" Coy.
Transport requirements to be notified direct to Transport Officer.
Completion of relief to be reported by wire by phrase "Rations received at___"

(b) Night 11/12th inst.

"D" Coy. will relieve "A" Coy. in the Right Front.
Details of relief to be arranged between Coy. Commanders concerned.
On completion of relief "A" Coy. will withdraw into reserve to billets at ST.NICHOLAS.
Transport requirements to be notified direct to Transport Officer.
Completion of relief to be reported by wire by phrase "Message received at___".

3.(a) Harassing fire maps, Trench Stores (including water bottles of anti-gas solution), Programmes of work in hand, will be handed over.

(b) Transport Officer will arrange to relieve "D" Coy. transport (at present at ST.NICHOLAS) by "C" Coy. transport on night 12/13th inst.

4. ACKNOWLEDGE.

H W Barra.
Capt. & Adjt.
15th Bn. Machine Gun Corps.

Issued through Signals
at 1:30 p.m.

Distribution:- No.1. C.O.
2. "A" Coy.
3. "B" Coy.
4. "C" Coy.
5. "D" Coy.
6. Qmrmaster.
7. Transp. Offr.
8. Signal Officer.
9. 15th Div. "G".
10. 44th Inf. Bde.
11. 45th Inf. Bde.
12. 46th Inf. Bde.
13. 51st Bn. M.G.C.
14. 56th Bn. M.G.C.
15. War Diary.
16. File.

War Diary

SECRET.

COPY NO 11

15th Bn. MACHINE GUN CORPS.

OPERATION ORDER NO.25.

Hqrs.
15th Bn. M.G.C.
June 7th 1918.

Ref. 1/10000 Feuchy Trench Map.

1. The 6th Cameron Highrs. will raid enemy post at H.22.c.71.12. on night 8/9th June 1918.

2. 15th Bn. M.G.C. will cooperate as follows:-

(a) "C" Coy.

2 guns at ab out H.16.a.47.75.
Target H.22.d.12.12. to H.28.b.19.72.
2 guns at about H.16.a.47.75.
Target H.22.d.17.13. to H.28.b.24.74.
2 guns at about H.16.c.33.99.
Target H.22.d.22.14. to H.28.b.29.76.
Rate of fire:-
Z. to Z plus 5 3 belts.
Z plus 5 to Z plus 12 2 belts.
Z " 12 to Z " 20 4 belts.

(b) "A" Coy.

4 guns at about H.15.d.15.27.
Target H.22.d.53.31. to H.23.c.21.70.
Rate of fire:-
Z. to Z plus 5 3 belts.
Z plus 5 to Z plus 12 2 belts.
Z " 12 to Z " 20 4 belts.

3. Zero hour will be notified later, also time for synchronization of watches.

4. Machine Guns will wait for the Artillery Barrage to commence before opening fire.

5. Acknowledge.

H. Barnes
Capt. & Adjt.
15th Bn. Machine Gun Corps.

Issued through Signals at 8 p.m.

Distribution:-

Copy No.1. "A" Coy.
2. "B" "
3. "C" "
4. "D" "
5. 15th Divn. "G".
6. 44th Inf. Bde.
7. 45th Inf. Bde.
8. C.M.G.O. XVII Corps.
9. 51st Bn. M.G.C.
10. 56th Bn. M.G.C.
11. War Diary.
12. File.

SECRET. 15th Dn. Machine Gun Corps.M.G./T.372.

ADDENDUM 1. to OPERATION ORDER NO. 33.

Ref. Operation Order No. 33. PARA. 3.

Watches will be synchronised at Headqrs. 6th Cameron Highrs. (H.19.b.40.40.) at 10 p.m. to-night

ZERO hour will be 2 A.M. 9th inst.

ACKNOWLEDGE.

Capt. & Adjt.
15th Dn. Machine Gun Corps.

8.8.18.

Copies to all recipients of O.O.33.

Secret. 15th Bn. Machine Gun Corps. M.G./T.411.

Reference 15th Bn. Machine Gun Corps Operation Order No.26.
Dated 13th June 1918.

This Operation Order is hereby cancelled.

Please acknowledge.

J Kutcher[?] 2/Lieut. & A/Adjt.
16.6.18. 15th Bn. Machine Gun Corps.

Copies to all recipients of O.O.26.

SECRET. 15th. Battn. MACHINE GUN CORPS COPY NO. 14

OPERATION ORDER NO. 26. 13th. June 1918.

Ref. Special 1/10,000 FEUCHY Trench Map attchd.

1. At a date to be notified later the 168th. Inf. Bde. (56th. Div.) will carry out a raid on the enemy's positions in Squares H.28., H.22.d.& H.23.c., and H.29.a.

2. The raid will be carried out by three Battalions, two in Front and 1 in Support.

3. The boundaries of the area to be raided will be :-
On the North.:- The marshy valley of the River SCARPE as far as LANCER LANE H.23.b.20.45.
On the East.:- LANCER LANE to its junction with PELVES LANE at H.29.d.15.80.
On the South.:- PELVES LANE from H.29.d.15.80. to our Front Line in H.32.a.

4. First Objective. :- ICELAND-IONIAN Trench System.

Second Objective :- MORAY TRENCH.

Third Objective :- The INDIAN-ITALIAN Trench Systems in H.29.a. and H.23.c.

Left Flank Objective.:- The defensive works and dug-outs in the Railway Cutting and in the Bank to the North of the Railway Cutting in H.28.a., H.22.d., and H.23.c.
The Support Battalion is forming a defensive flank to the South during the raid.

5. The general plan of the artillery action is as follows:- At Zero a hurricane bombardment by Field Artillery of the enemy's Outpost Positions in H.27.d., and bombardment by Field & Heavy Artillery of the ICELAND - IONIAN TRENCH SYSTEM and the wire protecting it. As the leading battalions advance to the ICELAND-IONIAN Trench System the barrage will roll forward in advance of the Infantry to INDIAN-ITALIAN Trench System, the heavy artillery barrage jumping first to MORAY TRENCH then to the INDIAN-ITALIAN Trench System. As the leading battalions advance against this system the barrage will roll forward and will stand on the Line LANCER LANE, forming a protective barrage.

6. The 15th. Battalion Machine Gun Corps will co-operate as follows:-
(a). "C" Company.
"A" Battery 4 guns at about H.16.a.15.50.
(guns to be used, S.5., S.6., S.7., S.8.)
"B" Battery 4 guns at about H.10.c.50.50.
(guns to be used, S.9., S.10., S.11., S.12.)

Barrage.	Battery.	Target.	Time.
"A"	("A"	H.28.a.75.91. to H.28.a.85.11.)	Z to Z + 13
	("B"	H.28.a.85.93. to H.28.a.95.13.)	
"B"	("A"	H.22.d.31.11. to H.28.b.42.35.)	Z + 13 to
	("B"	H.22.d.41.17. to H.28.b.53.37.)	Z + 21.

Barrage.	Battery.	Target.	Time.
"C"	("A" ("B"	H.22.d.87.38. to H.29.a.05.60. H.22.d. 98.41 to H.29.a.17.62.	) Z + 21 to) Z + 26
"D"	("A" ("B"	H.23.c.77.81. to H.23.d.02.05. H.23.c.86.87. to H.23.d.11.12.	) Z + 26 to) Z + 33
"E"	("A" ("B"	H.23.b.22.10. tp H.23.d.52.34. H.23.b.27.12. to H.23.d.55.39.	) Z + 33 tp) Z + 38
"F"	("A" ("B"	H.23.b.56.25. to H.23.d.88.49. H.23.b.65.30. to H.23.d.98.55.	) Z + 38 to Z +) 40. Z + 60 to) stop.

Rate of fire :- Z to Z + 40 , 16 belts per gun at a rate of 1 belt per 2½ minutes.
After Z + 40 M.G. Barrage will cease.
Until Z + 60 when it will re-open at a rate of 1 belt per 4 minutes until the artillery standing barrage stops.

In the event of the enemy counter-attacking or the Artillery Barrage becoming intense the M.G. Barrage will quicken to 1 belt per 2½ minutes for 15 minutes when it will again drop to 1 belt per 4 minutes.

(b) "D" Company.

"C" Battery of 4 guns at about H.15.d.15.25.
(guns to be used, 11, 11a, 12 and the 1 Gun in Coy. Reserve.)

Barrage.	Battery.	Target.	Time.
"G"	"C"	H.22.c.81.18. to H.28.a.62.80.	Z to Z + 13.
"H"	"C"	H.22.d.35.25. to H.28.b.33.86.	Z+ 13 to Z + 21
"L"	"C"	H.23.c.02.67. to H.22.d.90.27.	Z + 21 to Z + 26
"M"	"C"	H.23.b.00.24. to H.23.c.97.90.	Z + 26 to Z + 33
"P"	"C"	H.23.b.72.58. to H.23.b.60.21.	(Z + 33 to Z + 40 (Z + 60 to stop.

Rate of Fire :-Z to Z + 40, 16 belts at a rate of 1 belt per 2½ minutes.
After Z + 40 the M.G. Barrage will cease until Z + 60 when it will re-open at a rate of 1 belt per 4 minutes until the Artillery Standing Barrage stops.

In the event of the Artillery Barrage again becoming intense the Machine Gun Barrage will quicken to 1 belt per 2½ minutes for 15 minutes when it will drop to 1 belt per 4 minutes.

(c) Water jackets will be refilled after every 4 belts to keep down steam. This is most important.
Extra Petrol Tins, 8 to "C" Coy. and 4 to "D" Coy. are being sent up to be used as condensers.
Each gun will have in addition its own two petrol tins of water. These to be refilled immediately after raid.

(d). "C" Coy. will arrange for an Officer to observe from the Artillery Observation Post in CAM AVENUE about H.16.c.45.80.
The Signalling Officer will arrange for telephonic communication from this O.P. to "A" Battery.

(e). The Quartermaster will arrange to send up 1 gallon of gun oil to "C" Coy. and ½ gallon to "D" Coy. with a supply of 4 x 2" to-night.

(f). Coys. will arrange to fit up 1 good belt filling machine in a dug-out near each of their battery positions and will report on their use.

"C" Coy. will use the "Machine positioning cartridges in belt" which is being sent up to them and report on its value.

(g). All guns will be brought back to battle positions as soon as possible after raid is over.

(h). Arrangements are being made to send up loaded belts for this raid and belts at present with Coys. will not be used.

7. Arrangements for synchronization of watches & Zero Hour will be notified later. Zero hour will probably be between 7.0 p.m. and 7.45 p.m.

8. ACKNOWLEDGE.

[signature] Capt. & Adjt.

15th. Bn. Machine Gun Corps.

Distribution :-

Copy No. 1. "C" Coy.
2. "D" "
3. "A" "
4. "B" "
5. Signalling Officer.
6. Quartermaster.
7. 15th. Division "G".
8. 44th. Inf. Bde.
9. 46th. Inf. Bde.
10)
11). 56th. Bn. M.G.C.
12. C.M.G.O. XVII Corps.
13. 51st.(H)Bn. M.G.C.
14. War Diary.
15. File.

SECRET. 15th. Bn. Machine Gun Corps No. M.G./T.395.

AMENDMENT NO.1 to 15th. Bn. M.G.C. Operation Order No. 26. d/13/6/18.

13th. June 1918.

Para 6. (a). "C" Company.

For" "A" Battery 4 guns at about H.16.a.15.50. " read
" "A" Battery 4 Guns in EEEIE H.16.a.66.45."

For" "B" Battery 4 guns at about H.10.c.50.50. " read
" "B" Battery 4 guns in GUN PITS H.10.c.52.35. "

Acknowledge.

Capt. & Adjt.

13. 6. 18. 15th. Bn. Machine Gun Corps.

Copies to all recipients of O.O. 26.

SECRET.

Copy No.____

15th Bn. Machine Gun Corps.

OPERATION ORDER No.27.

16th June 1918.

Ref. Point du Jour &
Fouchy Maps. 1/10,000

1. The following raids will be carried out tonight 16/17th inst.

   (a) The 4/5th Black Watch will raid enemy front line from H.5.d.70.62. to H.5.d.70.80.

   (b) The 8th Seaforths will raid enemy front line from H.17.b.60.80. to H.11.d.56.03.

   Both raids will be carried out simultaneously.

2. The 15th Bn. Machine Gun Corps will cooperate as follows:-

   (a) "B" Coy. 2 guns at H.10.c.50.35. Target H.6.c.10.49. to H.6.c.00.34.
   3 guns at about H.10.c.50.35.
   Target H.6.c.58.08. to H.6.c.42.47.

   (b) 51st Bn. M.G.C.
   2 guns. Target H.6.a.05.43. to H.5.b.88.19.
   2 guns. Target H.6.a.46.46. to H.6.a.44.20.

   (c) "C" Coy.
   2 guns H.16.a.15.55. Target H.11.d.69.49. to H.11.d.80.08.
   2 guns H.16.a.15.55. Target H.12.c.00.49. to H.12.c.08.67.

3. Rate of Fire:- Z. to Z plus 6 3 belts.
   Z plus 6 to Z plus 14 2 belts.
   Z plus14 to Z plus 20 3 belts.
   Guns to be used "B" Coy. B1.B1a.B2. B2a. B3.
   "C" Coy. C9. C10. C11. C12.
   Guns will be returned to their battle positions immediately after firing ~~period~~. Barrage
   The filled belts sent up on the night of the 15th, and now in the possession of "B" Coy. will be used by both "B" and "C" Coys.
   Zero hour will be notified later, but will be about 1 a.m.
   "B" and "C" Coys. and 51st Bn.M.G.C. will send a representative to synchronise watches at 44th Inf. Bde. HQ.(G.12.b.85.35.) at 6 p.m. tonight.

4. Acknowledge.

2/Lieut. & A/Adjt.
15th Bn. Machine Gun Corps.

Distribution:
"B" Coy. "C" Coy.
51st Bn.M.G.C.
44th Inf. Bde.
15th Div. "G".

SECRET.

COPY NO 15

15th Bn. MACHINE GUN CORPS.

OPERATION ORDER NO.28.

Hqrs.
15th Bn. M.G.C.
June 17th 1918.

1. The following reliefs will take place on the nights 20/21st inst. and 21/22nd inst.

2. (a) Night 20/21st inst.

"C" Coy. will relieve "D" Coy. in the Right Front.
Details of relief to be arranged between Coy. Commanders concerned.
On completion of relief "D" Coy. will occupy support positions vacated by "C" Coy.
Transport requirements to be notified direct to Transport Officer.
Completion of relief to be reported by wire by code word "Pickwick"

(b) Night 21/22nd inst.

"A" Coy. will relieve "B" Coy. in the Left Front.
Details of relief to be arranged between Coy. Commanders concerned.
On completion of relief "B" Coy. will withdraw into reserve billets at ST. NICHOLAS.
Transport requirements to be notified direct to Transport Officer.
Completion of relief to be reported by wire by code word "Papers".

3. (a) Harassing fire map s, Trench Stores (including water bottles of anti-gas solution), Programmes of work in hand, will be handed over.

(b) Transport Officer will arrange to relieve "A" Coy transport (at present at ST.NICHOLAS) by "B" Coy. transport on night 22/23rd inst.

4. ACKNOWLEDGE.

G Kitchin 2/Lieut. & A/Adjt,
15th Bn. Machine Gun Corps.

Issued through Signals
at 1:30 p.m.

Distribution:- No.1. C.O.
2. "A" Coy.
3. "B" Coy.
4. "C" Coy.
5. "D" Coy.
6. Quartermaster.
7. Transport Officer.
8. Signal Officer.
9. 15th Div. "G".
10. 44th Inf. Bde.
11. 45th Inf. Bde.
12. 46th Inf. Bde.
13. 51st Bn. M.G.C.
14. 56th Bn. M.G.C.
15. War Diary.
16. File.

SECRET. 18th Bn. Machine Gun Corps. M.G./S.468.

Ref. 18th Bn. M.G.C. OPERATION ORDER NO.20. d/18.6.18 and M.G./S.430. d/19.6.18.

1. Zero day will be 21st June 1918.

2. Zero hour will be 3 a.m.

3. Acknowledge by wire.

2/Lieut. & A/Adjt.
20.6.18. 18th Bn. Machine Gun Corps.

Distribution:- "B" Coy.
"C" "
51st Bn. M.G.C.

SECRET. 15th Bn. Machine Gun Corps. M.G./T.438.

Reference Operation Order 29. dated 18th June. The raid by the 13th Royal Scots will take place on the night 20/21st inst.

Acknowledge.

J Ketchin 2/Lieut. & A/ADjt.
19.6.18. 15th Bn. Machine Gun Corps.

Copies to all recipients of O.O.29.

SECRET. 15th Bn. Machine Gun Corps. M.G./T.459.

AMENDMENT NO.1. to 15th Bn. M.G.C. OPERATION ORDER NO.28.d/17.6.18.

Para. 1. Instead of nights 20/21st inst. and 21/22nd inst.
Read nights 21/22nd inst. and 22/23rd inst.

Para. 2. (a) Instead of Night 20/21st inst.
Read Night 21/22nd inst.
(b) Instead of Night 21/22nd inst.
Read Night 22/23rd inst.

Para. 3. (b) Instead of night 22/23rd inst.
Read night 23/24th inst.

Acknowledge.

[signature] 2/Lieut. & A/Adjt.
15th Bn. Machine Gun Corps.

19.6.18.

Copies to all recipients of O.O.28.

SECRET. COPY NO. 6.

15th Bn. Machine Gun Corps.

OPERATION ORDER NO. 29.

18th June 1918.

1. At a date and time to be notified later the 13th Royal Scots will carry out a raid on enemy trenches in H.5.b.& d., H.6.a.& c., H.11.b. and H.12.a.

(a) Right Boundary, Hudson Alley to point of SNOUT, thence EAST. Left Boundary, Light Railway through H.5.b. for 400 yards to junction of NEWTON and new C.T. (H.5.b.97.30.) to NAVAL and along CIVIL.

(b) The furthest objective HOARY and HAGGARD between CHILI and CIVIL, blocks being made in CHILI, CALEDONIAN and CIVIL, 50 yards East of HOARY and HAGGARD.

2. The 15th Bn. M.G.C. will cooperate as follows:-

(a) "B" Coy.
2 guns at about H.9.b.13.45. (guns to be used 21 & 21a.)
Target. H.11.b.77.39. to H.11.b.80.03.
2 guns at about H.9.b.13.45. (guns to be used 22 & 22a.)
Target. H.11.b.96.40. to H.12.a.01.03.

(b) "C" Coy.
4 guns at about H.10.c.35.98.(guns to be used S9.10.11.12.)
Target. H.6.d. 44.75. to H.6.d.36.20.
4 guns about H.10.c.50.35. (guns to be used S5.6.7.8.)
Target. H.6.d.36.20. to H.12.b.56.68.

3. 51st Bn. M.G.C. will cooperate as follows:-
4 guns. Target. H.6.b.29.38. to H.6.d.39.78.
2 guns. Target. H.6.a.12.9?. to H.6.a.21.66.
2 guns. Target. H.6.a.56.93. to H.6.a.50.64.

4. Rate of fire:-
Z to Z plus 10 5 belts.
Z plus 10 to Z plus 40 8 belts.
Z plus 40 to Z plus65 10 belts.

5. All guns will return to their battle positions immediately after firing barrage.

6. "B" and "C" Coys. will use the extra belts which have been sent up.

7. Machine Guns will not open fire until the artillery barrage commences.

8. An Officer from each of "B" and "C" Coys, 15th Bn.M.G.C., and an Officer from 51st Bn.M.G.C. will synchronize watches at 45th Inf. Bde. Hqrs. (G.12.b.85.50.) at 10 p.m. on the night of the raid.

9. ACKNOWLEDGE.

V. Ketchin 2/Lieut. & A/Adjt.
15th Bn. Machine Gun Corps.

Distribution:- Copy No.1. "B" Coy.
2. "C" Coy.
3. 51st Bn. M.G.C.
4. 45th Inf. Bde.
5. 15th Div. "G".
6. War Diary.
7. File.

SECRET. COPY NO. 10

15th Bn. Machine Gun Corps.

OPERATION ORDER NO.30.

22nd June 1918.

Ref. Map 51 b
1/10,000

1. A raid will take place on the night of the 23/24th by the 46th Inf. Bde.

2. Objectives. SUNKEN ROAD in rear of ICELAND TRENCH (H.28.a.35.20. to H.28.a.35.30.) and Cave at H.28.a.60.40. To capture prisoners, secure identification and to capture or destroy enemy M.G's. and material.

3. At Z plus 3, barrage lifts from the objective and raiders and blocking parties rush in.
Two Lewis gun teams will remain on either flank 50 yards from the objective.

4. At Z plus 15 parties withdraw.
Signal for withdrawal.
(i) A red light fired low over the objective by the Commander of either of the two raiding parties
(ii) Bugle to sound "Come to the cookhouse door".
(iii) Officers to sound long blast on whistle.

5. Guide for return. A white flare lighted at H.27.a.5.9.

6. 15th Bn. M.G.C. will cooperate as follows:-

"C" Coy.
(a) Guns 9 & 10. Gun location H.26.a.85.80.
Target location H.28.a.40.80.
South gun traverses 25 yards North.
North gun traverses 50 yards North.

(b) Guns 11 & 12, and two reserve guns from Coy. Hqrs.
Battery location H.15.d.15.25.
Target location H.22.d.15.05 to H.23.c.10.50.

"D" Coy.
Guns S9. 10. 11 & 12.
Battery position EFFIE TRENCH H.16.a.50.48.
Target INDIAN TRENCH from railway embankment to 500 yards South of it.

"A" Coy.
Guns 21. 21a. 22. 22a.
Battery position Gun pits in H.10.c.
Target ITALIAN TRENCH from railway to 500 yards South of it.

Rate of fire:-
1 belt per 2 minutes.
Z plus 0 to Z plus 20.

7. 56th Bn. M.G.C. will cooperate with 4 guns from H.28.b. approx. on Target H.28.c.47.69. to H.28.c.55.30.

Rate of fire 1 belt per 2 minutes for 20 minutes.

8. Ammunition supply for "A" and "D" Coys.
10 belts per gun will be drawn from reserve of 80 belts held by O.C. "A" Coy. and placed by "A" Coy. in two battery positions. O.C. "A" Coy. will also send 3 boxes S.A.A. to battery position H.16.a.
40 belts will be collected by O.C. "C" Coy. from O.C. "A" Coy. These will be taken from the further reserve of 160 belts now held by him.

9. Opening of fire.
   Fire will not be opened until the artillery barrage commences.

10. On completion of firing all reserve guns will return to their normal positions.

11. Watches will be synchronized by O.C. Coys. concerned at the Hqrs. 46th Inf. Bde. at a time to be notified later.

12. Time of Zero hour will be notified later.

13. ACKNOWLEDGE.

J. Ketchen 2/Lieut. & A/Adjt.
15th Bn. Machine Gun Corps.

Distribution. Copy. No.1. "A" Coy.
2. "B" "
3. "C" "
4. "D" "
5. 45th Inf. Bde.
6. 46th Inf. Bde.
7. 15th Div. "G".
8. 56th Bn. M.G.C.
9. File.
10. War Diary.

SECRET. 15th Bn. Machine Gun Corps. M.G./T.47 1.

AMENDMENT NO.1. to 15th Bn. M.G.C. OPERATION ORDER NO.30. d/22.6.18.

Para. 1. for "23/24th" read "24/25th".

Para. 11. delete "a time to be notified later"
and read "7 p.m. 24th inst."

ACKNOWLEDGE.

[signature] 2/Lieut. & A/Adjt.
15th Bn. Machine Gun Corps.

23.6.18.

Copies to all recipients of O.O.30.

SECRET. COPY NO. 5

15th Bn. Machine Gun Corps.

OPERATION ORDER NO.31.

28th June 1918.

1. On the night 29/30th June "C" Coy. will relieve the gun of "D" Coy. at S2 position with one of their guns in Coy. reserve.
This position (approx. H.19.c.70.70.) will, after relief, be known as No.13 position.

2. "D" Coy. will place the two guns, at present at S1 and S2 positions, in TRIANGLE SWITCH at approx. H.19.c.20.00. as soon after S2 has been relieved as possible. The new positions will be known as S1 and S2 respectively from South to North.

3. The completion of relief ordered in para. 1 will be notified by the code word "CAT".
The completion of move mentioned in para. 2 will be notified by the code word "DOG".

4. ACKNOWLEDGE.

2/Lieut. & A/Adjt.
15th Bn. Machine Gun Corps.

Distribution:- Copy No.1. "C" Coy.
2. "D" Coy.
3. "A" Coy. For information.
4. "B" Coy. For information.
5. War Diary
6. File

SECRET. 15th Bn. Machine Gun Corps. M.G./T.530.

AMENDMENT NO.1 TO OPERATION ORDER NO.32 of 15th Bn. M.G.C. d/29.6.18.

The order of relieving front Coys. will be reversed. "A" Coy. Left Front will be relieved by "D" Coy. on the night 2/3rd instead of 3/4th, and "C" Coy. Right Front will be relieved by "B" Coy. on the night 3/4th instead of 2/3rd.

Acknowledge.

2/Lieut. & A/Adjt.
15th Bn. Machine Gun Corps.

30.6.18.

Copies to all recipients of O.O. No.32.

SECRET. COPY NO. 16.

15th Bn. MACHINE GUN CORPS.

OPERATION ORDER NO. 32.

Hqrs.
15th Bn. M.G.C.
June 29th 1918.

1. The following reliefs will take place on the nights 2/3rd and 3/4th proximo.

2.(a) Night 2/3rd Prox.

"B" Coy. will relieve "C" Coy. in the Right Front.
Details of relief to be arranged between Coy. Commanders concerned.
On completion of relief "C" Coy. will withdraw into reserve billets in ST. NICHOLAS vacated by "B" Coy.
Transport requirements to be notified direct to Transport Officer.
Completion of relief to be reported by wire by code word "WIRE".

(b) Night 3/4th prox.

"D" Coy. will relieve "A" Coy. in the Left Front.
Details of relief to be arranged between Coy. Commanders concerned.
On completion of relief "A" Coy. will move into support positions vacated by "D" Coy.
Transport requirements to be notified direct to Transport Officer.
Completion of relief to be reported by wire by code word "CLIPS".

3.(a) Harassing fire maps, Trench Stores (including water bottles of anti-gas solution), Programmes of work in hand, will be handed over.

(b) Transport Officer will arrange to relieve "B" Coy. transport (at present at ST. NICHOLAS) by "C" Coy. transport on night 4/5th prox.

4. ACKNOWLEDGE.

J Ketchin 2/Lieut. & A/Adjt.
15th Bn. Machine Gun Corps.

Distribution:- No.1. C.O.
2. "A" Coy.
3. "B" Coy.
4. "C" Coy.
5. "D" Coy.
6. Quartermaster.
7. Transport Officer.
8. Signal Officer.
9. 15th Div. "G".
10. 44th Inf. Bde.
11. 45th Inf. Bde.
12. 46th Inf. Bde.
13. 51st Bn. M.G.C.
14. 56th Bn. M.G.C.
15. War Diary.
16. File.

Instructions regarding War Diaries and Intelligence Summaries are contained in F. S. Regs., Part II. and the Staff Manual respectively. Title pages will be prepared in manuscript.

WAR DIARY
or
INTELLIGENCE SUMMARY.
(Erase heading not required.)

Army Form C. 2118.

WR 5

Place	Date	Hour	Summary of Events and Information	Remarks and references to Appendices
			CONFIDENTIAL VOLUME V FROM 1st JULY 1918 TO 31st JULY 1918	
			31st JULY 1918 R. [illegible] Lieut: Col. Commanding 15th Battn Machine Gun Corps	

D. D. & L., London, E.C.
(A8004) Wt. W1771/M2 31 750,000 5/17 Sch. 52 Forms/C2118/14

Instructions regarding War Diaries and Intelligence Summaries are contained in F. S. Regs., Part II. and the Staff Manual respectively. Title pages will be prepared in manuscript.

WAR DIARY
or
INTELLIGENCE SUMMARY.
(*Erase heading not required.*)

Army Form C. 2118.

Place	Date	Hour	Summary of Events and Information	Remarks and references to Appendices
	1/7/18		Normal Day HMS	
	2/7/18		Our guns fired 2,500 rounds on selected targets. During the day the enemy Artillery was extremely quiet. HMS	
	3/7/18		Our guns fired 3,000 rounds during the night HMS	
	4/7/18		Normal Day O.O. 33 issued HMS	O.O. 33 attd.
	5/7/18		Our guns fired 12,000 rounds during the night HMS	
	6/7/18		Our guns fired 3,000 rounds during the day, there was a slight increase in Enemy Artillery Activity in the back areas. Re-adjustment of positions ordered in O.O. 33 carried out successfully HMS	
	7/7/18		Normal day, there was an increase in the number of men returning to duty with the Battalion after "three days fever" HMS	
	8/7/18		Normal day.	
	9/7/18		Normal day O.O. 34 issued. HMS	O.O. 34 attd.
	10/7/18		Normal day Coy Commander of a Coy of 4th Bn. Can. MGC visited Battalion Hqrs, and arranged details of relief, proceeding later to D Coy Hqrs. HMS	
	11/7/18		Normal day. Commanding Officer and Adjutant of 1st Can Bn MGC visited Bn Hqrs HMS	O.O. 35 attd.
	12/7/18		Normal Day, our guns fired 12,000 4th Can Bn MGC relieved 8 guns of D Coy HMS	
	13/7/18		Enemy Artillery active on Railway Cutting. Remaining guns relieved as per O.O. 35 O.O. 36 issued. After Relief Coys moved to ARRAS HMS	O.O. 36 attd.

D. D. & L., London, E.C.
(A5004) Wt. W1 71/M2031 750,000 5/17 Sch. 52 Forms/C2118/14

Instructions regarding War Diaries and Intelligence Summaries are contained in F. S. Regs., Part II. and the Staff Manual respectively. Title pages will be prepared in manuscript.

WAR DIARY
or
INTELLIGENCE SUMMARY.
(Erase heading not required.)

Army Form C. 2118.

Place	Date	Hour	Summary of Events and Information	Remarks and references to Appendices
14/7/18			Relief Completed	
15/7/18			Battalion moved to billets in AUBIGNY. Transport lines moving to SAVVY. Warning order received that Battalion would entrain for a move to unknown destination at short notice, the Division to probably commence entraining at 2 on following day. Limbers were repacked, and arrangements made for move.	OO 37 attd
16/7/18			On receipt of orders from Division OO 37 issued.	
17/7/18			Battalion moved to new area Coys being attached to Infantry Brigade Groups. While on the move destination of the Battalion was altered, and after a 16 hr journey. Battalion detrained in the LIANCOURT area. Bn Hqrs B and D Coys being billeted in LIANCOURT. Remaining Coys remained with Infantry Brigade Groups in Brigade Areas.	
18/7/18			C Coy were moved to RATIGNY. Permission was obtained to concentrate the Battalion in one village at NOINTEL. OO 38 issued, but this was cancelled later on receipt of Divl Order stating the Division was moving to forward area by bus the following morning.	
19/7/18			Hqrs and D Coy embussed with Divl Hqrs Group, remaining Coys moving with their Infantry Bde Groups. Battalion debussed at HAUTE FONTAINE at 3 pm, where it was billeted in a wood (less A Coy who remained with [illegible] Bde Group) near TORSLY	

(A5001) Wt. W1-71/M2031 750,000 5/17 Sch. 52 Forms/C2118/14
D. D. & L., London, E.C.

Army Form C. 2118.

Instructions regarding War Diaries and Intelligence Summaries are contained in F. S. Regs., Part II. and the Staff Manual respectively. Title pages will be prepared in manuscript.

WAR DIARY
or
INTELLIGENCE SUMMARY.

(Erase heading not required.)

Place	Date	Hour	Summary of Events and Information	Remarks and references to Appendices
	20/7/18		~~Transport arrived remained billeted in the [illegible]~~ Transport arrived at a late hour in the evening	
	21/7/18	2.30 am	A Coy Transport left to move the Coy to HAUTE FONTAINE	
		6.30am	A Coy moved to wood near CHELLES. Orders were received later for the Battalion to again move forward and relieve the Machine Guns of 1st American Division. Battalion moved by road at night to wood W. of MONTGOBERT. During the march Enemy Aeroplanes were very active in bombing. 2/Lieut LINDSAY who had been sent forward to find accomodation for D Coy was slightly wounded.	
	22/7/18	3.30am	Battalion arrived in new area. C.O. went forward to carry out a reconnaissance. Coys also sent forward one officer each Coy. C.O. returned about 5pm and held a conference of Coy Commanders. Coys moved off from Bivouacs between 6 and 7pm and proceeded to the line. As the American Division were not able to definitely locate many of their Guns, the Battalion took up selected positions in the line, while the American Guns were withdrawn.	
	23/7/18		Orders received that the Division was to attack at 3am. Zero hour was later altered to 5am. LT LUNN was given a special task of firing on NOYANT and the high ground North of this place from the vicinity of BERZY-LE-SEC. While leading his teams into position LT. LUNN was wounded, and his Section Sergt took over command. Two Sections were detailed to move with the forward Infantry to	

Instructions regarding War Diaries and Intelligence Summaries are contained in F. S. Regs., Part II. and the Staff Manual respectively. Title pages will be prepared in manuscript.

WAR DIARY
or
INTELLIGENCE SUMMARY.

(*Erase heading not required.*)

Army Form C. 2118.

Place	Date	Hour	Summary of Events and Information	Remarks and references to Appendices
	23/7/18 cont		[illegible] consolidate position taken. At 5am our barrage opened and owing to the fact that the front line as marked over by the Americans on the map was about 1,000 yards behind its actual position on the map, the barrage came down 1,000 yards in advance of our troops. The Infantry were held up early in the attack by enemy Machine Gun fire, but at 9.30am a little ground had been gained and two guns were sent forward to consolidate a line just East of the SOISSONS Road. At 3.30pm another attempt was made, but with no greater success. Orders were then received to hold and consolidate ground gained, and accordingly our guns were disposed as follows: 2 in front of ACONIN FM and 2 in the cutting S of it, the latter facing SE down the valley and covering the right flank, the two in front of ACONIN FM facing N.E. These guns were moved later from a battery on the Sunken Road S of ACONIN FM. The enemy either observed movement here, or observed the position as he shelled the position very heavily killing two NCOs and 1 man. He also destroyed by direct hits one gun and tripod and the whole gun kit of one section. The remaining guns took up position on a line running parallel to the main SOISSONS Road about 1,000 to 1,500 yards west of it. Guns were placed on the forward slope of the ridge thus enabling them to cover the valley N of BUZANCY and the high ground N and S of the village. NOYANT was covered from positions behind BERZY-LE-SEC. SOS lines were laid out for all guns, which were disposed in 4 gun batteries.	

D. D. & L., London, E.C.
(A8001) Wt. W1-71/M2031 750,000 5/17 Sch. 52 Forms/C2118/14.

Instructions regarding War Diaries and Intelligence Summaries are contained in F. S. Regs., Part II. and the Staff Manual respectively. Title pages will be prepared in manuscript.

WAR DIARY
or
INTELLIGENCE SUMMARY.
(*Erase heading not required.*)

Army Form C. 2118.

Place	Date	Hour	Summary of Events and Information	Remarks and references to Appendices
	24/7/18		The day was spent in adjusting and making alterations where necessary. During the afternoon enemy heavily shelled MISSY-au-BOIS with H.E. and Gas, this shelling was continued during the night. The Battalion had 7 O.R. wounded and 16 sent down gassed during this period. All roads and approaches were heavily shelled during the night, and the Transport experienced great difficulties although sustaining no casualties. Orders received from Division that an attack would be carried out at 8.30 p.m., but this order was cancelled shortly after. [initials]	
	25/7/18		Disposition of the Battalion remained the same. Work was continued on position and S.A.A. dumps established. Enemy was very active on forward area during the day. Our casualties being 2 O.R. killed and 13 wounded. The 46th Inf Bde was relieved by the 44th Inf Bde during the night. O.O. 39 issued. [initials]	O.O. 39 attd.
	26/7/18		Enemy activity increased towards the evening. A Coy relieved C Coy during the night. A Coy reconnoitred barrage position for an impending attack, the following morning. [initials]	
	27/7/18		Preparations made for an attack by us which was imminent. Barrage positions were constructed as follows. A Coy on BOIS GERARD HILL. C Coy west of	

D. D. & L., London, E.C.
(A8001) Wt. W1771/M2031 750,000 5/17 Sch. 52 Forms/C2118/14

Instructions regarding War Diaries and Intelligence Summaries are contained in F. S. Regs., Part II. and the Staff Manual respectively. Title pages will be prepared in manuscript.

WAR DIARY
or
INTELLIGENCE SUMMARY.
(*Erase heading not required.*)

Army Form C. 2118.

Place	Date	Hour	Summary of Events and Information	Remarks and references to Appendices
	27/7/18 cont		ACONIN FM D Coy S.W. of ACONIN FM and the high ground S.W. of BERZY-LE-SEC	
			During the afternoon our Artillery commenced a bombardment of villages in Enemy lines on our front, and also on Enemy lines in front of Divn on our ~~left~~ Right with the object of deluding the Enemy as to the direction and frontage of our projected attack. OO 40 issued	OO. 40 attd.
	28/7/18		2/LT. HARBOTTLE and one Section were detailed to assist the 8th. Seaforths in **HMS** Consolidation. 2/LT. HARBOTTLE found OC A Coy of the SEAFORTHS and made all necessary arrangements with him. The two orderlies as detailed in OO 40 were left at HQrs of 8th SEAFORTHS for the purpose of bringing information to 2/Lieut HARBOTTLE. At Zero hour 12.30am the Barrage opened, and our guns opened fire accordingly. The attack was a complete surprise and our troops had little difficulty in reaching their objectives. The French on our right however were held up at the start by Machine Gun fire. This left our right flank exposed to heavy Machine Gun fire of the Enemy.	
		3.30pm	2/Lt. HARBOTTLE who was still at HQrs A Coy Seaforths up till this time had received no information as to the progress of the attack. Hearing that the objective had been reached (from a runner) he acted on his own initiative by leaving two guns under Sergt SMITH at A Coy HQrs of the Seaforths, and advancing with the two remaining gun teams he reached the corner of BOZANCY Chateau grounds. Here he left two guns under cover and reported to the Coy Commander of the	

D. D. & L., London, E.C.
(A8001) Wt. W1:71/M2031 750,000 5/17 Sch. 52 Forms/C2118/14

Army Form C. 2118.

WAR DIARY
or
INTELLIGENCE SUMMARY.
(Erase heading not required.)

Instructions regarding War Diaries and Intelligence Summaries are contained in F. S. Regs., Part II. and the Staff Manual respectively. Title pages will be prepared in manuscript.

Place	Date	Hour	Summary of Events and Information	Remarks and references to Appendices
	28/7/18 cont.		Seaforths. The situation was explained to him. The enemy had counter attacked on the left and right, and our right had been forced back. 2/Lt HARBOTTLE undertook to cover the left flank with his guns, and by bringing his guns into action succeeded in delaying the enemy's advance.	
		4pm	Meanwhile Sergt SMITH acting on his own initiative brought his guns into action and covered the right flank.	
		5pm	2/LT HARBOTTLE managed to withdraw his guns back to our original line as the Infantry had fallen back. He assisted in the defence of this line by placing his guns in consultation with the Seaforths.	
			Orders were received later that the Division was to side-step to the Divisional Front on our Right, our own front to be occupied by the Division relieved. This difficult move was carried out by withdrawing as many guns as possible during the early morning in readiness to move. [illegible]	
	29/7/18	2.30pm	2/LT. HARBOTTLE reported at his Coy Hqrs with his Section.	
			OO. 41 issued from Battalion Hqrs with details of move.	OO. 41 attd.
			The new Sector was reconnoitred during the day and positions sited.	
			The move was commenced during the night. The enemy shelled all main roads very heavily, especially the road through CHAUDUN. Infantry sustained several casualties but with the exception of 2 OR. missing and 6 wounded, also one limber and two mules lost, our move passed with few casualties.	
	30/7/18		The Battalion was disposed on this morning as follows. B and D Coys occupied front	

WAR DIARY
or
INTELLIGENCE SUMMARY.
(Erase heading not required.)

Army Form C. 2118.

Instructions regarding War Diaries and Intelligence Summaries are contained in F. S. Regs., Part II. and the Staff Manual respectively. Title pages will be prepared in manuscript.

Place	Date	Hour	Summary of Events and Information	Remarks and references to Appendices
	30/7/18		position. A Coy were in Support and C Coy were in reserve at VIERZY. The day passed without incident, but again in the evening the Enemy shelled roads and approaches very heavily. HMS	
	31/7/18		A bombardment of selected tanks took place at 2.30pm. One Section of D Coy was told off to watch for targets but with the exception of one [illegible] no targets of any size presented itself. During the night S.A.A. dumps were enlarged. OO 42 issued by Bn HQrs. HMS	OO 42 attd

R. Nasmith
LIEUT.-COL.
COMMANDING 15TH BATT. MACHINE GUN CORPS.

D. D. & L., London, E.C.
(A7001) Wt. W1 71/M2031 750,000 5/17 Sch. 52 Forms/C2118/14

SECRET. COPY NO. 8

Ref. Mw. [handwritten]

15th Bn. MACHINE GUN CORPS.

OPERATION ORDER NO. 33.

Ref. 51 B.N.W. 1/20,000.

Hqrs.
15th Bn. M.G.C.
July 5th 1918.

1. On night 6/7th inst. "C" Coy. will relieve a section (four guns) of "A" Coy. at positions S9. 10. 11. 12.

2. O.C., "A" Coy. will arrange to occupy, with section relieved by "C" Coy., as soon as possible after relief:-

Position R14.	approx.	G.23.d.90.~~50~~ 40.
R15.	"	G.23.d.90.~~25~~ 40.
R16.	"	G.29.b.~~30.70~~ 75.55.
R17.	"	G.29.b.~~80.60~~ 75.55.

3. Completion of relief and subsequent move to be reported by "A" Coy. to Battn. Hqrs. using code word 'DALYS'.

4. ACKNOWLEDGE.

[signature]
Capt. & Adjt.
15th Bn. Machine Gun Corps.

Distribution. Copy 1. "A" Coy.
2. "C" "
3. "B" "
4. "D" "
5. 15th Div. "G".
6. 44th Inf. Bde.
7. 45th Inf. Bde.
8. 46th Inf. Bde.
9. War Diary.
10. File.

SECRET. COPY NO. 15

15th Bn. MACHINE GUN CORPS.

OPERATION ORDER NO. 34.

Hqrs.
15th Bn. M.G.C.,
July 9th 1918.

1. The 15th Division will be relieved by the 4th Canadian Division and 1st Canadian Division.

2. The 15th Bn. Machine Gun Corps will be relieved by the 4th Bn. and 1st Bn. Canadian Machine Gun Corps as follows:-

(a) Night 12/13th July.
Guns 31. 32. 29. 30. 21. 21a. 22. 22a. of "D" Coy. S.13. and S.14. of "A" Coy. will be relieved by No.2.Coy of 4th Bn. Canadian Machine Gun Corps.
For the purposes of relief S13. & S14. will come under orders of "D" Coy. but will report at their own Coy. H.Q. on completion of relief.

13/14th (b) Night ~~14~~/15th July.
Guns 23. 24. 25. 26. 27. 28. 33. 34. of "D" Coy. will be relieved by a battery of No.1.Coy. 1st Bn. Canadian M.G.C.
Guns 7. 8. 11. 12. 15. 17. 18. 19. 20. of "B" Coy. will be relieved by a battery of No.1.Coy. 1st Bn. Canadian M.G.C.
Guns S5. S6. S7. S8. of "A" Coy. and S9. S10. S11. S12. of "C" Coy. will be relieved by a battery of No.1.Coy. 1st Bn. Canadian M.G.C. For purposes of relief guns S9. S10. S11. S12. will come under orders of "A" Coy. but will report at their own Coy. H.Q. on completion of relief.

(c) Night 14/15th July.
Guns 5. 6. 9. 10. 13. of "B" Coy. will be relieved by a battery of No.2.Coy. 1st Bn. Canadian M.G.C.
Guns S1. S2. S3. S4. R14. R15. R16. R17. of "A" Coy. will be relieved by a battery of No.2.Coy. 1st Bn. Canadian M.G.C.

3. On completion of reliefs Coys. will move back to ARRAS, further details regarding this and location of billets will be notified later.

4. On the morning of 15th July the Battalion will proceed to the SAVY area.

5. Coy. Commanders of 1st Canadian M.G.Bns. will visit "A" "B" & "D" Coys. H.Q. tomorrow, when all details of relief, guides etc. will be arranged between Coy. Cmdrs. concerned.

6. 14 belt boxes per gun, 2 petrol tins of water, ½ a pint of oil will be handed over at each occupied gun position.
All S.A.A. bombs, range cards, orders boards, maps, defence schemes, reserve rations, gas clothing, anti-gas solution and programmes of work, etc. will also be handed over and receipts taken. Copies of receipts to be retained until called for by Bn. H.Qrs.

7. 4th Bn. Canadian M.G.C. will hand over at Transport Lines DUISANS 140 filled belts and boxes and 20 petrol tins.
1st Bn. Canadian M.G.C. will hand over at same place 532 filled belts and boxes and 76 petrol tins.
The Quartermaster will give receipts for these on arrival.

8. Relief of Signalling personnel will be arranged between Signal Officer and Signal Officer of 1st Canadian M.G.Bn.

9. Every effort will be made to keep the relief concealed from the enemy.

10.(a) Completion of Relief in para. 2a to be notified to Bn. Hqrs., using code word "GAIETY", by Coys. concerned.

(b) Completion of relief in para. 2b to be notified to Bn. Hqrs., using code word "GARRICK", by Coys. concerned.

(c) Completion of relief in para. 2c to be notified to Bn. Hqrs., using code word "SAVOY", by Coys. concerned.

11. ACKNOWLEDGE.

Issued at 8 p.m.
through Signals.

Capt. & Adjt.
15th Bn. Machine Gun Corps.

Distribution:- Copy 1. "A" Coy.
2. "B" "
3. "C" "
4. "D" "
5. 44th Inf. Bde.
6. 45th Inf. Bde.
7. 46th Inf. Bde.
8. 15th Div. "G"
9. 15th Div. "Q"
10. 1st Bn. Canadian M.G.C.
11. 4th Bn. Canadian M.G.C.
12. Transport Officer.
13. Quartermaster.
14. Signal Officer.
15. War Diary.
16. File.

SECRET.

15th Bn. Machine Gun Corps. M.G./T.597.

Ref. OPERATION ORDER NO.34. d/9.7.18.

Para. 2 (b) :-

For Night 14/15th,

Read Night 13/14th

ACKNOWLEDGE.

Capt. & Adjt.
15th Bn. Machine Gun Corps.

10.7.18.

Copies to all recipients of O.O.34.

SECRET. COPY NO. 14

15th Bn. MACHINE GUN CORPS.

OPERATION ORDER NO.35.

Hqrs.
15th Bn. M.G.C.,
July 11th 1918.

1. "C" Coy. 15th Bn. M.G.C. (Res. Coy.) will be relieved by a battery of No. 1 Coy. 1st Bn. Canadian Machine Gun Corps, on night 13/14th July.

2. Battery Commander of 1st Bn. Canadian M.G.C. will arrange all details of relief with O.C., "C" Coy.

3. On completion of relief "C" Coy. will withdraw to billets in ARRAS.

4. Completion of relief to be notified to Bn. Hqrs. using code word "GLOBE".

5. ACKNOWLEDGE.

H M Sarson [signature]

Capt. & Adjt.
15th Bn. Machine Gun Corps.

Distribution:- Copy No.1. "C" Coy.
2. "A" "
3. "B" "
4. "D" "
5. 44th Inf. Bde.
6. 45th Inf. Bde.
7. 46th Inf. Bde.
8. 15th Div. "G".
9. 1st Canadian Bn. M.G.C.
10. Transport Officer.
11. Quartermaster.
12. Signal Officer.
13. War Diary.
14. File.

SECRET. COPY NO._____

15th Bn. MACHINE GUN CORPS.

OPERATION ORDER NO.36.

Ref. Map
51B N.W. 1/20,000.
51C N.E. 1/20,000.

Hqrs.
15th Bn. M.G.C.,
July 13th 1918.

1. The Battalion will move to Billets in AUBIGNY on the 15th inst.

2. Coys. will march from billets in ARRAS to B12 Loop (Light Railway) at G.20.d.2.8. Route RUE GAMBETTA - RUE D'AMIENS - Road Junction G.26.b.70.80. - Cross Roads G.20.d.02.48. Order of march "C" "A" "B" "D" Coys.

"C" Coy. will leave the GRANDE PLACE at 11:15 a.m. arriving at place of entrainment at 11:45 a.m. The remaining Coys. following at two minute intervals.

Care will be taken to see that billets in ARRAS are left thoroughly clean.

3. 5 Trains are being provided for the Battalion, each of 6 trucks.

Coys. will entrain as follows:-

No 1 Train. "C" Coy.
2 Train. 3 Sections "A" Coy. and Coy. H.Q.
3 Train. 1 Section "A" Coy. 2 Sections "B" Coy.
4 Train. 2 Sections "B" Coy. 1 Section "D" Coy. & "B" Coys. H.Q.
5.Train. 3 Sections "D" Coy. & "D" Coys. H.Q.

Capt. Stocker will act as entraining officer and will be at point of entrainment at 11:30 a.m.

The Senior Officer with each train will be in command of same during the journey.

4. Billeting arrangements have been issued separately to all concerned.

5. The train journey will take about 1 hour, and the Quartermaster will arrange that the dinners are ready for consumption on arrival of Coys.

Only breakfast rations will be sent to Coys. in ARRAS on the night of 14/15th inst.

6. Billeting Officers will arrange to meet their Coys. at AUBIGNY Light Railway Station, and guide them to billets.

7. The Transport will arrange to move to AUBIGNY by road under the Bn. Transport Officer. Starting point, Road Junction L.8.c. 42.40. Time to pass starting point 10:30 a.m. ROUTE. DUISANS - Cross Roads L.2.c.20.40. - ARRAS-St.Pol Main Road - Cross Roads E.13.a.05.55. - AUBIGNY.

A distance of 100 yards will be maintained between Coy. Transport.

The strictest march discipline will be maintained, and the C.O. expects an excellent turnout of men, animals and vehicles.

Drivers are to be carefully instructed in paying compliments etc. Brakesmen will carry their rifles and march in rear of their vehicles.

8. ACKNOWLEDGE.

Capt. & Adjt.
15th Bn. Machine Gun Corps.

Distribution:- Copies 1-4 A.B.C.& D. Coys. 8-11 4 Coy Billeting Officers
5 Quartermaster. 12. 15th Div. "G".
7 Signalling Officer. 6 Transport Officer. 13. 15th Div. "Q".
14 Town Major Aubigny.
15 " " Arras.
16 War Diary.
17 File.

SECRET.

COPY NO 18

15th Bn. MACHINE GUN CORPS.

OPERATION ORDER NO. 37.

Hqrs.
15th Bn. M.G.C.
15th July 1918.

1. The 15th Division will move by train from First Army to XXII Corps.

2. The 15th Bn. M.G.C. will move as under:-

a. "A" Coy. 16th inst.
Departure of train 8 a.m. from TINCQUES.
Coy. Transport to move off 3:30 a.m. to report to R.T.O. at Station at 5 a.m.
Coy. to march off at 5 a.m. to report to Staff Officer of 44th Inf. Bde. at 7 a.m.

b. "C" Coy. 16th inst.
Departure of train 9 a.m. from SAVY.
Coy. Transport to move off at 5:30 a.m. to report to R.T.O at station at 7 a.m.
Coy. to march off at 7:25 a.m. to report to Staff Officer 46th Inf. Bde. at 8 a.m.

c. "B" Coy. 16th inst.
Departure of train 10 a.m. AUBIGNY.
Coy. Transport to move off at 6:40 a.m. to report to R.T.O. at station at 7 a.m.
Coy. to march off at 8:50 a.m. to report to Staff Officer 45th Inf. Bde. at 9 a.m.

d. H.Q. and "D" Coy. 17th inst.
Departure of Train 1 a.m. AUBIGNY.
Transport to move off at 9:40 p.m. 16th inst. to report to R.T.O. at 10 p.m.
H.Q. and "D" Coy. to move off at 11:40 p.m. to report to Staff Officer 45th Inf. Bde. at 12 midnight.

3. Dress will be Marching Order, steel helmets to be worn. Water bottles to be filled before marching off. Rations for 16th inst. will be carried on the man. Meat and Bread ration for 17th will also be carried. Remainder of rations for 17th and rations for 18th will be carried on the train.

4. Signalling Officer will attach M.G. Signallers to Coys. 5th Section R.E. to move with Bn. Hqrs.

5. Transport Officer will arrange to attach 1 Water Cart to "A" Coy. and 1 to "D" Coy. He will also arrange that a "D" Coy. 1 limber accompanies "A" & "C" Coys. to their respective entraining stations to carry cooking utensils used for breakfast.

6. Advance Parties of 1 Officer and N.C.O. per Coy. & Bn. Hqrs. will report as follows:-

a. "A" Coy. to Staff Officer 44th Inf. Bde. before departure of first train from entraining station at 2:38 a.m. 16th inst.

b. "C" Coy. to Staff Officer 46th Inf. Bde. before departure of first train from entraining station at 3:26 a.m. 16th inst.

c. "B" Coy. to Staff Officer 45th Inf. Bde. before departure of first train from entraining station at 4:20 a.m. 16th inst.

d. Hqrs. & "D" Coy. to Staff Officer 45th Inf. Bde. before departure of first train from entraining station 4:20 a.m. 16th inst.

7. O.C. Coys. will have an accurate Parade State to hand to Staff Officer of their Brigade Group, showing numbers of Officers, men, animals, vehicles and bicycles under their command.

8. ACKNOWLEDGE.

Capt. & Adjt.
15th Bn. Machine Gun Corps.

Distribution:-

Copy No 1. "A" Coy.
2. "B" "
3. "C" "
4. "D" "
5. Transport Officer "A" Coy.
6. " " "B" "
7. " " "C" "
8. " " "D" "
9. 15th Division "G".
10. 15th Division "Q".
11. Town Major, Aubigny.
12. Quartermaster.
13. Signal Officer.
14. 44th Inf. Bde.
15. 45th Inf. Bde.
16. 46th Inf. Bde.
17. War Diary.
18. File.

War Diary

SECRET. COPY NO. 17

15th Bn. MACHINE GUN CORPS.

OPERATION ORDER NO 38.

Ref.
Map BEAUVAIS,
Sheet 32.

Hqrs.
15th Bn. M.G.C.,
July 18th 1918.

1\. (a) The Battalion (less "A" Coy.) will move to billets in NOINTEL tomorrow the 19th inst.

(b) Route LIANCOURT - SENECOURT - BREUIL-LE-SEC - NOINTEL.

2\. (a) Order of March. Hqrs. "C" Coy. "D" Coy. "B" Coy. Battn. Transport.

(b) Starting Point (with exception of "B" Coy.) will be gate of drive to Battn. Hqrs.

(c) Battn. Hqrs. will march off at 3 p.m. Head of "C" Coy. will pass starting point in rear of Bn. Hqrs. allowing an interval of 100 yards. "D" Coy. will follow in rear of "C" Coy. allowing an interval of 100 yards.
"B" Coy. will form up outside their billets, and will follow 100 yards in rear of "D" Coy.

3\. "A" Coy. will move independently from billets in RIEUX to NOINTEL, marching off at 3 p.m.
Route ANGICOURT - LIANCOURT - SENECOURT - BRUIL-LE-SEC - NOINTEL.

4\. Dress will be full marching order, steel helmets to be carried under pack straps. Water bottles to be filled before marching off.

5\. "C" Coy. Transport will halt at starting point, and will follow with Bn. Transport (less "B" Coy.) at five minutes interval from time "D" Coy. pass the starting point. "B" Coy. Transport will follow in rear of Bn. Transport when rear of column passes their billets.

6\. Billoting Parties(from all Coys.) of 1 Officer and 1 N.C.O. per Coy. will report to 2/Lieut. KETCHIN at 8 a.m. at Bn. Orderly Room, and will proceed in advance. On arrival, billets will be allotted by 2/Lieut. KETCHIN.

7\. ACKNOWLEDGE.

H. M. Barns
Capt. & Adjt.
15th Bn. Machine Gun Corps.

Distribution:-

Copy No. 1-4 "A" "B" "C" "D" Coys.
5 Quartermaster.
6 Signal Officer.
7 2/Lt. Ketchin.
8 15th Div. "G".
9 15th Div. "Q".
10 44th Inf. Bde.
11 45th Inf. Bde.
12 46th Inf. Bde.
13 C.R.E. 15th Div.
14 15th Divl. Train.
15 A.P.M. 15th Div.
16 A.D.M.S. 15th Div.
17 War Diary.
18 File.

SECRET.

COPY NO 13.

15th Bn. MACHINE GUN CORPS.

OPERATION ORDER NO. 39.

Advd. Bn. Hqrs.
15th Bn. M.G.C.
25th July 1918.

1. "A" Coy. will relieve "C" Coy. in the Right Sector on night 26/27th inst.

2. Details of relief to be arranged between Coy. Commanders concerned.

3. Officers and N.C.Os of "A" Coy. will carry out a thorough reconnaisance of the front to be taken over before the relief.

4. Any extra transport required will be notified to Bn. Hqrs. before 12 a.m. 26th inst.

5. Completion of relief to be reported by wire to 44th and 46th Inf. Bdes. and Bn. Hqrs. by code word "ROSE".

6. ACKNOWLEDGE.

H M Barns
Capt. & Adjt.
15th Bn. Machine Gun Corps.

Distribution:-

Copy No. 1 "A" Coy.
2 "B" Coy.
3 "C" Coy.
4 "D" Coy.
5 15th Div. "G".
~~6 15th Divl. Arty.~~
7 44th Inf. Bde.
8 45th Inf. Bde.
9 46th Inf. Bde.
10 Signalling Officer.
11 Quartermaster.
12 Transport Officer.
13 War Diary.
14 File.

SECRET. COPY NO 12

15th BN. MACHINE GUN CORPS.

OPERATION ORDER NO. 40.

Ref. Map SOISSONS.

Advd. Bn. Hqrs.
15th Bn. M.G.C.
27th July 1918.

1. The 15th Division, in conjunction with the 87th Division on the Right, will attack BUZANCY and the high ground East of it.
The attack is under the orders of G.O.C., 15th Division.
Five Companies 91st Regiment, 87th Division, will co-operate with the 15th Division.

2. The 91st Regiment, 87th Division, are to co-operate generally in the following manner :-

(a) Two companies will debouch from main road East of VILLEMONTOIRE Village at zero hour and will capture that portion of the objective from the road as far North as the road running South-east from BUZANCY to the BOIS L'EVEQUE.

(b) At an hour to be decided by O.C., 91st Regiment, one company will attack in a Northerley direction and mop up the wood South-west of BUZANCY.

(c) One company will attack in an easterly direction advancing from present front line just South of the 15th Divisional boundary, capture the work on the high ground South-west of BUZANCY and mop up the Northern portion of the wood South-west of BUZANCY and join up with the company attacking the wood from the South.
One platoon detailed by Right Battalion of the 44th Inf. Bde., will move with this latter company and establish liaison and assist them with their task in the wood.

(d) One company will be in reserve just East of VILLEMONTOIRE.

3. 44th Inf. Bde. will carry out the attack within that Brigade boundary, [illegible]. The details of the attack will be arranged by G.O.C., 44th Inf. Bde., which will be generally as follows :-

(a) One party, strength about two companies, will attack the village of BUZANCY moving by the North of the CHATEAU. This party will mop up the village working in a South-westerly direction and join up with troops of the 91st Regiment which have been detailed to attack the wood South-east of the village.

(b) One party, strength about one company, will attack and mop up the CHATEAU, and ground within the CHATEAU walls.

(c) Three companies will attack and capture that portion of the objective from the road running South-east of BUZANCY to BOIS L'EVEQUE to the Southern edge of wood South-east of CHIVRY FARM.

4. 45th Inf. Bde. will co-operate in the attack, within 45th Inf. Bde. area, and establish posts on the Northern edge of the wood just South-west of CHIVRY FARM.

5______

5. Zero hour will be 12.30 p.m. 28th July, at which hour the Infantry will attack.

6. (a) Artillery will bombard BUZANCY from 11.30 a.m. until rolling barrage comes down.

(b) At Zero – 2 minutes artillery barrage will fall 150 yards in front of front line as far North as ROZIERES-ACONIN FARM road.

7. 15th Bn. Machine Gun Corps will co-operate as follows :-

(a) <u>A. Coy.</u>

16 guns on BOIS GERARD Hill.
Barrage A. Targets.

4 guns	BUZANCY SQUARE	a.25.49.	to	BUZ. SQUARE	a.25.25.
4 guns	ditto	a.50.49.	to	ditto	a.50.25.
4 guns	ditto	a.75.49.	to	ditto	a.75.10.
4 guns	ditto	a.99.49.	to	ditto	a.99.20.

(To read this the kilometre square containing BUZANCY has been divided as in British maps).

Times of firing :- Zero to Zero + 14 mins.
Rate of fire 1 belt per 2½ minutes.

Barrage B.
At Zero + 14 minutes all 16 guns will lift on to the following line and will maintain a standing barrage at a slow rate of fire till Zero + 90 minutes, Junction of grid lines and track 500 yards North-east of <u>B</u>. in <u>BUZANCY</u> to square North of BUZANCY square b.60.40. (English method).

This line will be the S.O.S. line for these guns after Zero + 90 mins.

(b) <u>C. Coy.</u> 4 guns West of <u>A</u> in <u>A</u>CONIN FARM.
Target. Eastern half of that portion of NOYANT South of grid line.
Times of firing Zero to Zero + 90 minutes.
Rate of fire 1 belt per 3 minutes.

(c) <u>D. Coy.</u> 4 guns near Railway Cutting South-west of <u>A</u> in <u>A</u>CONIN FARM.
Target, Western half of that portion of NOYANT South of grid line.
8 guns on high ground S.W. of BERZY-LE-SEC.
Target, that portion of NOYANT N. of grid line.
Times of firing for <u>D</u>. Coy. Z. to Z + 90 mins.
Rate of fire, 1 belt per 3 minutes.
In addition to firing these barrages, C. and D. Coys. will prepare to engage any targets which may present themselves.

(d) O.C. C. Coy will detail 1 section to move tonight to area occupied by 8th Seaforth Highrs. This section will leave two ~~orderlies~~ runners at Bn. Hqrs. 8th Seaforth Highrs. O.C. 8th Seaforth Highrs. will send word by these runners to the section commander when the objective has been captured. The section will then move and occupy the best positions obtainable in the vicinity of N.E. corner of BUZANCY CHATEAU grounds wall.

8. A. Coy. will ensure that there is no movement on BOIS GERARD Hill tomorrow after daylight. Men are to be warned that such movement may draw heavy shell fire.

9. <u>Synchronization of watches.</u>
A. and C. Coys. will synchronise watches at Hqrs. 44th Inf. Bde. at 7 a.m. tomorrow 28th inst.
D. Coy. will synchronise watches at Hqrs. 45th Inf. Bde. at 8 a.m. 28th inst.

10. ACKNOWLEDGE.

H. K. Barnes [signature]
Capt. & Adjt.
15th Bn. Machine Gun Corps.

Distribution :-
Copy No.1 A. Coy.
2 B. Coy.
3 C. Coy.
4 D. Coy.
5 Bn. Hqrs. (Tech).
6 15th Div. "G".
7 44th Inf. Bde.
8 45th Inf. Bde.
9 46th Inf. Bde.
10 War Diary.
11 File.
12 File.

Ack. Bde. 437 - 30

<u>SECRET</u>. COPY NO 9

<u>15th Bn. MACHINE GUN CORPS.</u>

<u>OPERATION ORDER NO.41.</u>

Advd. Bn. Hqrs.,
15th Bn. M.G.C.,
29th July 1918.

1. The Battalion will be withdrawn from the line tonight, and will occupy positions in new sector as per attached map (to Brigades only).

B. Coy. on Right Front.
D. Coy. on Left Front.
A. Coy. in support.
C. Coy. in reserve at ~~....~~ VIERZY.
B. D. & A. Coy. Hqrs. will be in the tunnel.

2. Transport arrangements will be as follows:-

(a) <u>D. Coy</u>. Five limbers and four half limbers will be at Res. Coy. Hqrs. at 8.30 p.m. Five limbers are for moving gun kit, Coy. Hqrs. etc. O.C. D. Coy. will arrange to load 16 boxes S.A.A. at Res. Coy. Hqrs. into each of the four half limbers. One half limber will accompany each section to new position.

(b) <u>B. Coy</u>. Five limbers and three half limbers will be at Res. Coy. Hqrs. at 9 p.m. These three half limbers will each contain 16 boxes of S.A.A. One other half limber will proceed to B. Coy's old Hqrs. at MISSY-AU-BOIS and there pick up 16 boxes of S.A.A. and join Coy. at Res. Coy. Hqrs. This half limber will be at MISSY-AU-BOIS at 8.30 p.m. where O.C. B.Coy. will arrange to have four men to load S.A.A. One half limber will accompany each section to new position.

(c) <u>A.COY</u>. Five limbers will be at A. Coy's Hqrs. at 9.30 p.m. to move Gun kit and Coy. Hqrs. Four half limbers each containing 16 boxes S.A.A. will be at junction of CHADUN and LECHELLE roads at 11 p.m. where O.C. A.Coy. will arrange to have one guide per section to take each half limber to it's section.

(d) <u>C.Coy</u>. Three limbers will be at C.Coy. Hqrs. at 10 p.m. to move two sections and Coy. Hqrs., and two limbers will be at Res. Coy. Hqrs. at 11 p.m. to move two remaining sections. Two limbers each with 25 boxes S.A.A. will also be at Res. Coy. Hqrs. at 11 p.m.

(e) Rations in each case will be sent up with limbers that are moving Coys.

3. Completion of moves to be reported by wire to Advd. Bn. Hqrs. by code word "PUN". Each Coy. on arrival at new positions will send back a runner (with bicycle) to take orders for an operation tomorrow, if necessary.

4. ACKNOWLEDGE.

[signature]
Capt. & Adjt.
15th Bn. Machine Gun Corps.

Distribution:- Copy 1 A. Coy.
2 B. Coy.
3 C. Coy.
4 D. Coy.
5 Bn. Hqrs. (Corr).
6 15th Div. "G".
7 44th Inf. Bde.
8 45th Inf. Bde.
9 46th Inf. Bde. ✓
10 War Diary.
11 File.

SECRET. COPY NO 10

15th Bn. MACHINE GUN CORPS.

OPERATION ORDER NO. 42.

Advd. Bn. Hqrs.
15th Bn. M.G.C.,
31st July 1918.

Ref. map attached. (To Coys. only).

1. (a) The 15th Division will attack tomorrow 1st August 1918 with two Brigades in front and one in support.
Leading Brigades will take the first objective, Reserve Brigade will pass through and take final objective.

(b) 46th Brigade will be on the Right.
45th Brigade will be on the Left.
44th Brigade will be in support.

(c) Objectives and boundaries are as shown on the attached map.

2. 15th Bn. M.G.C. will co-operate as follows:-

(a) The following guns will be used for barrage :-
2 Sections A. Coy.)
2 Sections D. Coy.) All under O.C., D. Coy.

2 Sections A. Coy.)
2 Sections B. Coy.) All under O.C., B. Coy.

(b) The following barrages will be fired by the 16 guns under O.C., D. Coy.
A. Barrage 10 guns.
B. Barrage 6 guns.
E. Barrage 6 guns.
A. and B. Barrage will be fired during the first phases of the attack. A. Barrage will be maintained throughout and ultimately become the S.O.S. line for these 10 guns.
The 6 guns firing B. Barrage will lift with, or just before the artillery, on to E. Barrage. Time of lift to be notified later, and duration of fire on A.and E. Barrages to be notified later.
This barrage will finally be used as an S.O.S. line for these guns.

(c) The 16 guns under O.C., B. Coy. will fire the following barrages :-
C. Barrage 6 guns.
D. Barrage 10 guns.
These two barrages will be fired during the first phase of the attack, and will then lift to F. and G. barrages respectively. Time of lift will be with, or just before, the artillery barrage, which will be notified later.
F. and G. barrages will be finally utilized as S.O.S. lines for the guns firing them.
For firing F. and G. barrages guns will move forward to vicinity of ROUTE NATIONALE.

Instructions regarding War Diaries and Intelligence Summaries are contained in F. S. Regs., Part II. and the Staff Manual respectively. Title pages will be prepared in manuscript.

WAR DIARY
or
INTELLIGENCE SUMMARY.
(Erase heading not required.)

Army Form C. 2118.

Place	Date	Hour	Summary of Events and Information	Remarks and references to Appendices
			VOL 6	
			CONFIDENTIAL.	
			WAR DIARY of 15th Battn: MACHINE GUN CORPS	
			1st to 31st August 1918	
			VOLUME VI	
		31-8-1918	R. Nasmith Lieut. Col. Comdg: 15th Bn Machine Gun Corps	

D. D. & L., London, E.C.
(A8001) Wt. W1 71/M2031 750,000 5/17 Sch. 52 Forms/C2118/14

Instructions regarding War Diaries and Intelligence Summaries are contained in F. S. Regs., Part II. and the Staff Manual respectively. Title pages will be prepared in manuscript.

WAR DIARY
or
~~INTELLIGENCE SUMMARY.~~
(Erase heading not required.)

Army Form C. 2118.

Place	Date	Hour	Summary of Events and Information	Remarks and references to Appendices
	1st		By dawn all arrangements for the attack were complete. Between 8 & 8.30 am three white lights were dropped from an aeroplane fixing Zero at 9 am.	
			The final objective of the attack was to capture the Bois de HARTENNES.	
			The 45th Brigade gained its objective after severe fighting but the 46th Brigade was held up from the outset by heavy M.G. fire from the wooded knolls in front of the Bois D'HARTENNES. After repeated attempts to carry these positions it was finally decided to stop the attack & make another attempt when a further bombardment of the knolls had been carried out.	
			The second attempt, at 3.30pm. had no better results and about 6 pm the attack had to be abandoned. Guns now took up their defensive positions	
			During the operation the guns fired very well and the barrage ~~was~~ gave entire satisfaction.	
			The casualties for the day were, 1 OR killed. 12 OR 2Lt De-Vere & 2Lt Stevens wounded J.K.	
	2nd		At 9 am the enemy ~~was~~ was reported to have retired on our right. About 10 am patrols reported the enemy had retired on our front and immediately strong infantry patrols were ordered to push forward and take up positions on the line of the CRISE. This they succeeded in doing.	
			The battn was notified of the advance of our patrols at 12 noon. The transport was immediately ordered to VIERZY where it arrived about 3 pm.	

D. D. & L., London, E.C.
(A5001) Wt. W1 71/M2031 750,000 5/17 Sch. 52 Forms/C2118/14

Instructions regarding War Diaries and Intelligence Summaries are contained in F. S. Regs., Part II. and the Staff Manual respectively. Title pages will be prepared in manuscript.

WAR DIARY
or
~~INTELLIGENCE SUMMARY.~~
(Erase heading not required.)

Army Form C. 2118.

Place	Date	Hour	Summary of Events and Information	Remarks and references to Appendices
			Thence the transport set out to collect the guns of the Coys who, after a reconnaissance had been ordered to take up defensive positions in support of the infantry. A & C Coys assisted 44 & 45 Bdes, respectively to consolidate the ground gained. D Coy was in support near the Bois de CONCROIS & 'B' Coy was in reserve at VILLEMONTOIRE. Battn HQ were established at VIERZY at 6 pm.	
			Orders were now received that the infantry were to be relieved that night by the French, but the M G Battn was to remain in position till the French passed through them on the following day. J.K.	
	3rd		In the morning the French passed through our outposts and advanced towards the line of the VESLE. In view of this Coys were ordered to concentrate in VIERZY during the afternoon. The last Coy arrived at 7 pm.	
			The battn was now ordered to join the remainder of the Division in bivouac at VIVIERS on the following day. All arrangements for the march were made. OO No 43 issued. J.K.	OO 43 attached.
	4th		At 3 am orders were received ordering the Battn to embus at VIVIERS for LIANCOURT at 2 pm on 4th. At 6 am a French officer reported to Orderly Room that he had been ordered to convey British troops from VIERZY to VIVIERS by bus. Battn embussed at 9 am ~~at VIERZY~~ and arrived at VIVIERS at 1.30 pm. At 2.30 pm we re-embussed and moved off to LIANCOURT at 3 pm.	

D. D. & L., London, E.C. (A5011) Wt. W1771/M2031 750,000 5/17 Sch. 52 Forms/C2118/14

Army Form C. 2118.

Instructions regarding War Diaries and Intelligence Summaries are contained in F. S. Regs., Part II. and the Staff Manual respectively. Title pages will be prepared in manuscript.

WAR DIARY
or
INTELLIGENCE SUMMARY.
(Erase heading not required.)

Place	Date	Hour	Summary of Events and Information	Remarks and references to Appendices
	5th		Battn. arrived at LIANCOURT at 2am. and moved to billets. The day was spent in re-organising and cleaning. Limbers were re-packed and all preparations made for an impending train journey. Instructions for the move by train received and OO 44 issued. JK.	OO 44 attached.
	6th		A & C Coys with transport march to LAIGNEVILLE and PONT ST MAXENCE respectively where they entrain as per Orders. JK.	
	7th		A Coy arrived at TINQUES at 10.30 am. where they detrained and marched to rest billets in AMBRINES arriving 5.30 pm. C Coy detrained at PT. HOUVIN at 3.30 pm and arrived at AMBRINES at 6.15 pm. The remainder of Battn entrain as per programme. 'B' Coy arrived at AMBRINES at 10.15 pm. JK.	
	7th		H.Q. & D Coy arrived at AMBRINES at 5.30 am. The remainder of the day spent in cleaning & re-organising. JK.	
	9th		The Divisional General presented French honours gained during recent operations. In all 11 Croix de Guerre were presented. Among the recipients were Lt Col Nasmith M.C., 2Lt Harbottle, 2Lt Wallington and 2 Lt Ward. Pte D. Roper, Sgt D. Budge, Sgt Smith, Sgt Sucher, Sgt Key. JK	
	10th 11th 12th 13th		Day spent in cleaning and resting in accordance with Divisional Orders. JK.	

D. D. & L., London, E.C.
(A8001) Wt. W1·71/M2031 750,000 5/17 Sch. 52 Forms/C2118/14

Instructions regarding War Diaries and Intelligence Summaries are contained in F. S. Regs., Part II. and the Staff Manual respectively. Title pages will be prepared in manuscript.

WAR DIARY
or
~~INTELLIGENCE~~ SUMMARY.
(Erase heading not required.)

Army Form C. 2118.

Place	Date	Hour	Summary of Events and Information	Remarks and references to Appendices
	14th		The adjutant visited 56th Battn to make preliminary arrangements for the relief of that Battn. J.K.	
	15th		O.O. No 45 issued. B & C Coys transport left Ambrines at 1.30 pm & marched to Berneville. B & C Coys left Ambrines at 4 pm and marched to HERMEVILLE where they entrained on light railway for WAILLY. From WAILLY B Coy. marched to the line & relieved the Centre Coy of the 56th Battn. Two sections of 'C' Coy. relieved 2 sections of the 56th Battn. near Beaurains. The remaining 2 sections of 'C' Coy & Coy. H.Q. marched to reserve billets in DAINVILLE. C.O. & adjutant proceeded to H.Q. 56th Battn. at WARLUS. J.K.	
	16th		D Coy. left Ambrines at ~~4.30 pm and~~ marched to embussing point. They proceeded by bus to DAINVILLE. J.K.	
	17th		D Coy. relieved the left Coy. of the 56th Bn. Battn. H.Q. and details moved by bus from Ambrines to billets in WARLUS. A Coy. moved by bus to DAINVILLE and marched into the line. They relieved the Right Coy. of the 56th Battn. J.K.	
	18th		Battn. relief completed. During the afternoon strong suspicions of an enemy retiral on this front were increased by a prisoner's statement. Battn was ordered to send 1 section forward with 45 Bde & 1 with 46 Bde. to assist in consolidation of ground won. In view of this the 2 reserve sections	

D. D. & L., London, E.C. (A8001) Wt. W1771/M2031 750,000 5/17 Sch. 52 Forms/C2118/14

Instructions regarding War Diaries and Intelligence Summaries are contained in F. S. Regs., Part II. and the Staff Manual respectively. Title pages will be prepared in manuscript.

WAR DIARY
or
~~INTELLIGENCE SUMMARY.~~

(Erase heading not required.)

Army Form C. 2118.

Place	Date	Hour	Summary of Events and Information	Remarks and references to Appendices
			of 'C' Coy. moved from DAINVILLE to ARRAS to keep in close touch with Bdes concerned. J.K.	
	19th		At 7am 46th Bde were reported to have established posts near ~~[illegible]~~ FEUCHY CHAPEL cross roads; in view of which 2Lt Harbottle's section was ordered to proceed via BATTERY VALLEY to assist in the consolidation of ground won. About mid-day it was reported that 46th Bde outposts had been forced to withdraw and the section withdrew to ARRAS. In the evening arrangements were ~~again~~ made for 46 Bde to send forward patrols and establish outposts if possible in INVERGORDON Trench. 2 Lt Harbottle's section was again ordered forward to take up positions by night to consolidate this ground and 2 guns of D Coy were placed in Bois de BOEUF to protect the right flank. J.K.	
	20th		The infantry patrols found INVERGORDON Trench occupied and were ordered to withdraw. The section of 'C' Coy, that had advanced to consolidate, was ordered to withdraw to ARRAS and the 2 guns of D Coy resumed their normal position. OO No 47 issued. J.K.	OO 47 attached
	21st		Day was normal in the line. ~~by~~ The strictest watch was kept on all enemy movement. In view of an impending relief OO No 47 was cancelled.	
	22nd		Warning order issued. 'C' Coy was withdrawn from the line and spent the night in billets at DAINVILLE. OO 48 issued. J.K.	Warning O & OO 48 attached

D. D. & L., London, E.C. (A8001) Wt. W1771/M2031 750,000 5/17 Sch. 52 Forms/C2118/14

Instructions regarding War Diaries and Intelligence Summaries are contained in F. S. Regs., Part II. and the Staff Manual respectively. Title pages will be prepared in manuscript.

WAR DIARY
or
INTELLIGENCE SUMMARY.
(Erase heading not required.)

Army Form C. 2118.

Place	Date	Hour	Summary of Events and Information	Remarks and references to Appendices
	23rd	5 am.	'C' Coy entrained & proceeded as per orders to Braquement.	
			The C.O. proceeded to HQ 11th Battn. ~~at~~	
		5.30 pm.	Battn H.Q. and details move to ARRAS. JK.	
	24th		Relief completed. Battn less 'C' Coy assembled in ARRAS	
		7 am.	Entrained at Artillery Siding and arrived at GOUY SERVINS at 10 am.	
		4.30 pm	A & D Coy left GOUY SERVINS and marched to billets for the night in BRAQUEMENT.	
		5 pm	'C' Coy relief completed. JK	
	25th	4.30 pm	B. Coy & Battn HQ marched from GOUY SERVINS to BRAQUEMENT and arrived at 8 pm. A & D Coys. carried out a daylight relief.	
		8 pm	Battn relief completed. JK.	
	26th		The day was normal. The sector was extremely quiet and trenches and dugouts were in good repair.	
	27th		GG 4 G issued	
		4.30 pm	Relief completed JK	Chngs attached
	28th		Normal day. JK	
	29th		Two sections of A Coy. were withdrawn to BRAQUEMENT. JK	
	30th		Normal day JK	
	31st		Normal day JK.	

31/8/18.

R. Nasmith Lt. Col.
Cmdg 15 Bn M.G.C.

D. D. & L., London, E.C. (A8001) Wt. W1771/M2031 750,000 5/17 Sch. 52 Forms/C2118/14

SECRET.

COPY NO______

15th Bn. MACHINE GUN CORPS.

OPERATION ORDER NO. 43.

Advd. Bn. Hqrs.,
15th Bn. M.G.C.,
3rd August 1918.

Ref. Map DE L'AISNE A L'OURCQ.

1.(a) The Battalion will move tomorrow August 4th by March Route to Wood N.W. LONGAVESNE.

(b) Starting Point 200 yards W. of Main Gate (Old Res. Coy. Hq. VIERZY) on VIERZY-VAUXCASTILLE Road.

(c) Order of March, HQ. A.B.C.D. Coys. Head of column will pass the starting point at 9 a.m.

2. Route VIERZY-VAUXCASTILLE-BEAU REPAIRE FM-VERTE FEUILLE FM Cross Roads at M of MON FRE de MONTGOBERT-Road junction at M in LA BEAUVE MON FRE-MONTGOBERT-SOUCY-L'EPINE FE-Cross Roads 400 yards E of last E in LONGAVESNE.

3. The 4 Coy. Cookers, G.S. Wagon and Mess cart will proceed with Bn. and will march in rear of D. Coy. Remainder of Transport will move under Bn. Transport Officer at 8 a.m. and will proceed to old Transport Lines. All Transport, Details and .M. Stores will move from there when ready to new billeting area.

4. Billeting party of 1 Officer per Coy. and Bn. Hq. (with bicycles) will parade at 7 a.m. outside the CHATEAU VIERZY and will proceed in advance.

5. Coys. will each detail 1 N.C.O. and 8 men to report to Coy. Transport Officers at 7.30 a.m. to act as brakesmen and to assist in loading limbers at old transport lines. These men are permitted to ride in limbers.

6. All Officers' Mess Kits will be stacked outside ~~the~~ Bn. Hq. at 8.30 a.m. sharp.

7. ACKNOWLEDGE.

H.Mc[illegible]
Capt. & Adjt.
15th Bn. Machine Gun Corps.

Distribution. O.C., A.B.C.D. Coys.
T.O.
Q.M.
M.O.
S.O.
War Diary.
File.

SECRET. COPY NO 18.

15th Bn. MACHINE GUN CORPS.

OPERATION ORDER NO.44.

Bn. Qrs.
15th Bn. M.G.C.,
5th August 1918.

Ref. Map BEAUVAIS.

1. The 15th Division will be transferred by rail from the French Zone to First Army Area.

2. The 15th Bn. Machine Gun Corps will entrain as follows:-

(a) "A" Coy. (with 44th Inf. Bde. Group).
Entraining station LAIGNEVILLE.
Time of Entraining 8 p.m. Aug. 6th.
Time of departure of train 11:55 p.m. Aug. 6th.
Coy. will march off at 6:15 p.m.
Route, Cross Roads 300 yards South of G in Station LAIGNEVILLE.

(b) "B" Coy. (with 45th Inf. Bde. Group).
Entraining Station LIANCOURT.
Time of entraining 12:30 a.m. Aug. 7th.
Time of departure of train 4:30 a.m. Aug. 7th.
Coy. will march off at 11:00 p.m. Aug. 6th

(c) Bn. Hqrs. & "D" Coy. (Divl. Troops Group).
Entraining Station LIANCOURT.
Time of Entraining 4:30 a.m. Aug. 7th.
Time of departure of train 8:30 a.m. Aug. 7th.
Hqrs. and "D" Coy. will march off at 4 a.m.

(d) "C" Coy. (with 46th Inf. Bde. Group).
Entraining Station PONT ST. MAXENCE.
Time of Entraining 9:30 p.m. Aug. 6th.
Time of departure of train 1:31 a.m. Aug. 7th.
Coy. will march off at 5 p.m. Aug. 6th.
Route - ANGICOURT-RIEUX-BRENOUILLE-PONT ST.MAXENCE.

3. Coy. Transport will arrive at Entraining Station 4 hours before train is due to depart.

4. A complete Marching out State showing numbers of Officers, Men, G.S.Limbered and G.S.Wagons and two Wheeled Vehicles and Cycles should be sent down with Transport so that the accomodation on the train can be checked by the R.T.O.

5. Breast Ropes for horses will be provided by Coys. Ropes for lashing vehicles on the Flat Trucks will be provided by the Railway.

6. All doors of covered trucks and carriages on the Right hand side of the train, on the main line, should be kept closed.

7. Instructions as to the issue of Train Rations (for consumption on the 7th inst.) will be detailed by the Quartermaster to the 4 Coy. Q.M. Sergts.

8. Billeting Parties of 1 Officer and 1 N.C.O. per Coy. and Bn. Hq. (with bicycles) will report to Staff Captain of 45th Inf. Bde. at 12 noon tomorrow (6th inst.) All Officers of this party will report to Adjutant at Bn. Orderly Room at 9:30 a.m. tomorrow for further instructions as regards billeting.

9. Dress will be Full Marching Order. Water bottles to be filled before marching off.

10. ACKNOWLEDGE.

Capt. & Adjt.
15th Bn. Machine Gun Corps.

Issued at 11·0 p.m. through Signals.

Distribution:-

Copy No. 1. "A" Coy.
2. "B" Coy.
3. "C" Coy.
4. "D" Coy.
5-8. Coy. Transport Officers.
9. Signal Officer.
10. Quartermaster.
11. Medical Officer.
12. 15th Div. "G".
13. 15th Div. "Q".
14. 44th Inf. Bde.
15. 45th Inf. Bde.
16. 46th Inf. Bde.
17. War Diary.
18. File.

File

S E C R E T.

15th Div. No. G.S. - 8.5.18.

15th Bn. M.G.C.

With reference to para. 5. - 15th Div. O.O.250, the relief of M.Gs. therein referred to will take place on night 9/10th May and not as stated.

C.G.S. Campbell Capt
for Lieut. Colonel,
General Staff, 15th Division.

Copy to :-

17th Corps.
51st Divn.
44th Inf. Bde.
45th Inf. Bde.
46th Inf. Bde.
"Q".
15th Signals.

SECRET.   COPY NO 13

15th Bn. MACHINE GUN CORPS.

OPERATION ORDER NO.45.

Hqrs.
15th Bn. M.G.C.,
15th August 1918.

Ref. Map LENS 11.

1. The 15th Division is being transferred to the XVII Corps and will relieve the 56th Division in the Line during the period 15th to 18th August.

2. The 15th Bn. M.G.C. will relieve the 56th Bn. M.G.C. as follows:-

Night 15/16th inst. B. and C. Coys. 15th Bn. M.G.C. will relieve C. and A. Coys. 56th Bn. M.G.C. in Centre Section and Reserve respectively.

Night 16/17th inst. D. Coy. 15th Bn. M.G.C. will relieve D. Coy. 56th Bn. M.G.C. in Left Section.

Night 17/18th inst. A. Coy. 15th Bn. M.G.C. will relieve B. Coy. 56th Bn. M.G.C. in Right Section.

Signal Officer will arrange to relieve Signalling personnel on night 16/17th inst.

3. Coys. will move under Brigade Groups as follows:-

(a)

B. and C. Coys.	44th Inf. Bde. Group.
D. Coy.	45th " " "
A. "	46th " " "

Coys. will move by Light Railway. (or bus)
B. and C. Coys. will move as follows:-
Entrain HERMAVILLE Road Spur (J.5.a.) at 6.30 p.m. Detrain WAILLY at 9 p.m.
Guides from 56th Bn. M.G.C. will meet Coys. at detraining station. Arrangements have been made for 10 Limbers of 56th Bn. M.G.C. to meet these Coys.
Coys. will reach entraining station at 6 p.m. leaving AMBRINES at 4 p.m. Rations for the 16th inst. will be carried on the man.
Arrangements for remaining Coys. will be notified later.

(b) Transport will proceed by road under Brigade Groups.
Transport of B. and C. Coys. will move as follows:-
Starting Point - Station ½ mile E. of IZEL-le-HAMEAU.
Time of passing starting point 2.30 p.m. Route HERMAVILLE - HABARCQ - MONTENESCOURT - WARLUS - BERNEVILLE.

4. 18 Belt Boxes per gun will be taken over in the line. Coys. will each leave 12 Belt Boxes per gun outside Bn. Hqrs. at 12 noon 15th inst. These will be taken over by Quartermaster and handed over to 56th Bn. M.G.C..

5. Dress will be fighting order. All packs (containing Service Caps) will be left in the limbers.

6. ACKNOWLEDGE.

H McSaran [signature]

Capt. & Adjt.
15th Bn. Machine Gun Corps.

Distribution:-
Copy Nos.1-4 Coys.
5 Transport Officer.
6 Signal Officer.
7 Quartermaster.
8 Medical Officer.
9 15th Div. "G".
10 44th Inf. Bde.
11 45th Inf. Bde.
12 46th Inf. Bde.
13 War Diary.
14 File.

SECRET. COPY NO. 6

15th Bn. MACHINE GUN CORPS.

OPERATION ORDER NO.40.

Ref. Map 1/20000
51.B. S.W. & N.W.

Hqrs.
15th Bn. M.G.C.,
18th August 1918.

1. A deserter reports that enemy have in anticipation of a British attack withdrawn covered by a Rear Guard disposed as follows:-

2 Companies in CALIFORNIA and ZOUAVE trenches and along Railway Embankment.

2 Companies in WELLFORD trench.

One Battalion is in support and one Battalion is in reserve.

4 Field Artillery Batteries are in the MONCHY - HAPPY VALLEY area.

2. The 15th Division co-operating with the 51st Division on the left are at once to gain touch with the enemy's Rear Guard and maintain contact.

The 170th Inf. Bde. 57th Division, are under orders of 51st Division and will co-operate on the left of the 15th Division.

3. The Division will push out strong fighting patrols along the whole Divisional front, drive back any outlying posts and make good the area up to and including the line Eastern outskirts of NEUVILLE VITASSE - HUMBER trench - RANGOON trench - HALIFAX trench - CALIFORNIA trench.

4. (a) When the objective is reached it will be consolidated and posts pushed forward to CHAPEL HILL (N.10.a. and N.4.d.) and ORANGE HILL.

(b) Special parties will be detailed to maintain touch with Flank Divisions as well as parties to establish liaison between Brigades.

(c) Nucleus garrisons will be maintained in the Main Line of Resistance and in the present front line. These garrisons will not be moved without orders from Divisional Headquarters.

5. C.R.E. will detail one section Field Coy. R.E. to accompany each Inf. Bde. with special duty to examine dug-outs etc., none of which are to be entered by troops until pronounced as safe by the R.E.

6. The 15th Bn. M.G.C. will co-operate as follows:-

"C" Coy. will move 8 guns to "D" Coy's Hqrs. in RUE GAMBETTA. On hearing the objectives have been taken "C" Coy. will move 4 guns to N.33. Central and 4 guns to AIRY CORNER approx. (to fire S.E.)

"C" Coy. will also at the same time take over 4 guns of "B" Coy. in the line between TILLOY and TELEGRAPH HILL, also 4 guns at present in position near BEAURAINS.

"B" Coy. will be prepared to withdraw 16 guns from the line (on hearing the objectives have been taken) and will move into Divisional Reserve at AGNY, establishing their Headqrs. with "A" Coy. They will retain their fighting transport unless heavily shelled, or ordered to withdraw it.

7. ACKNOWLEDGE by wire.

Capt. & Adjt.
15th Bn. Machine Gun Corps.

Distribution:-

Copy No. 1. "A" Coy.
2. "B" Coy.
3. "C" Coy.
4. "D" Coy.
5/6. War Diary. 15th Div. "G"
7/6. File.

SECRET. 15th Bn. Machine Gun Corps. M.G.158.

To O.C."A" "B" "C" "D" Coys.
Transport Officer.
T.O. "A" "B" "C" "D" Coys.
Quartermaster.
Signal Officer.
Medical Officer.

WARNING ORDER.

1. On night 22/23rd "C" Coy. will move to 44th Bde. area which will be notified later; and will entrain on morning of 23rd inst.
Guns, tripods and 12 Belt boxes per gun will be carried on the train.

2. On night 22/23rd "D" Coy. will be relieved in the line by a Coy. of 2nd Canadian M.G. Bn. Details will be notified later. On completio of relief "D" Coy. will move to billets in ARRAS, and will entrain with 45th Bde. Group on morning of 23rd inst. Guns, tripods and 12 Belt boxe per gun will be carried on the train.

3. "A" & "B" Coys. will be relieved by two Coys. 3rd Canadian M.G. Bn. on night 23/24th. On completion of relief "A" & "B" Coys. will move to billets in ARRAS under arrangements to be made by Coy. Commanders. Details of relief will be notified later.
Bn. Hqrs. will move to ARRAS on night 23/24th and will entrain with "A" and "B" Coys. and Bn. Details with 46th Bde. Group on morning of 24th.
Guns, tripods and 12 Belt boxes per gun of "A" and "B" Coys. will be carried on the train.

4. Transport Officer will arrange for 5 limbers to assist "C" Coy., and 5 limbers to assist "D" Coy. to entrain.
Transport of "C" & "D" Coys. will move with 44th Bde. Group by Road on 23rd inst. Transport of "A" and "B" Coys. and Hqrs. will move with 46th Bde. Group by road 24th inst.

5. 3rd Canadian Divn. will be requested to assist "A" and "B" Coys. with 5 limbers per Coy, to entrain.

6. Packs will be carried on the limbers. Packs of Bn. Hqrs. will be carried on a lorry. Transport Officer will arrange that Wheelers tools, Pump, Chaff Cutter, extra shoes and forge are sent to Bn. Q.M. Stores on morning of 23rd inst.

7. The above orders are subject to alterations as more definite orders are received from Division.

8. Acknowledge.

[signature]
Capt. & Adjt.
15th Bn. Machine Gun Corps.

22.8.18.

SECRET. COPY NO 17

15th Bn. MACHINE GUN CORPS.

OPERATION ORDER NO. 47.

Ref. Maps 51B 1/10000
51C 1/20000

Hqrs.,
15th Bn. M.G.C.,
20th August 1918.

1. "B" Coy. 15th Bn. M.G.C. will be relieved in the line tomorrow night 21st/22nd inst. by "A" Coy. of the 1st (Life Guards) Bn. Guards M.G. Regt. (Coy. Commander Major Chumleigh).

2. O.C. "B" Coy. will arrange for guides to meet "A" Coy. 1st L.G. Bn. at Cross Roads M.4.c.00.80. at 9.15 p.m. 21st inst. O.C. "B" Coy. will also supply 4 Limbers to be at this point on the ACHICOURT Road to take up guns of the Life Guards Bn. from their lorries which will dump there.

3. 14 Belts per gun will be handed over in the line, and the Life Guards Bn. are sending an equal number per gun to WAILLY. "B" Coy. Transport Officer will arrange for a guide to meet a L.G. Lorry at Cross Roads R.22.b.20.60. at 11 a.m. tomorrow 21st inst. to guide this lorry to "B" Coy. Transport Lines.

4. All Maps, S.O.S. Lines, Programmes of Work in hand will be handed over and receipts obtained. "B" Coy. will bring out 1 water tin per gun.

5. "A" Coy. of Life Guards Bn. are bringing in one day's rations with them to the line. Their Coy. Q.M. Sergt. and staff will report to the Quartermaster of 15th Bn. M.G.C. at No.1 Camp WARLUS tomorrow. The Quartermaster will arrahge all subsequent rationing of this Coy., transport being supplied by 15th Bn. M.G.C. Arrangements are being made by 1st Life Guards Bn. for rations for their "A" Coy. to be delivered to Quartermasters Store of 15th Bn. M.G.C.

6. Section Officers from "A" Coy. 1st Life Guards Bn. will be at "B" Coy. Hqrs. at 10 a.m. tomorrow to reconnoitre the line.

7. On completion of relief "B" Coy. will move to billets in WAILLY and become Divisional Reserve. O.C. "B" Coy. will make all necessary arrangements as regards billeting..

8. 1st Life Guards Bn. are taking over all Signal Stations in "B" Coy. area. Relief to be arranged between Signal Officers concerned.

9. Completion of relief to be notified to Bn. Hqrs. by wire by phrase "Your M.G. 21 received at-----".

10. ACKNOWLEDGE.

Issued at by S.D.R.

Capt. & Adjt.
15th Bn. Machine Gun Corps.

Distribution:-
Copy No. 1. C.O.
2. O.C. "A" Coy.
3. O.C. "B" Coy.
4. O.C. "C" Coy.
5. O.C. "D" Coy.
6. 15th Div. "G".
7. 15th Div. "Q".
8. 1st (Life Guards)Bn. Guards M.G. Regt.
9. 44th Inf. Bde.
10. 45th Inf. Bde.
11. 46th Inf. Bde.
12. QQuartermaster.
13. Bn. Transport Officer.
14. Transport Officer "B" Coy.
15. Signal Officer
16. War Diary. 17. File.
18. 25th Bn. MGC
19 51st "

SECRET. COPY No. 20

15th Bn. MACHINE GUN CORPS.

OPERATION ORDER NO. 48.

Ref. Maps Lens 11.
51c NE. 1/20000

Hqrs.,
15th Bn. M.G.C.
22nd August 1918.

1. The 15th Bn. Machine Gun Corps (less "C" Coy.) will be relieved by the 2nd and 3rd Bns. Canadian M.G.C. on night 23/24th inst. and will concentrate in ARRAS as arranged.

2. The Battalion will move North and relieve the 11th Bn. M.G.C. in the HULLUCH Sector. (H.Q. BRAQUEMONT) as follows:-

(a) "C" Coy. will entrain with the 44th Inf. Bde. Group at DAINVILLE WOOD, L.28.c.60.90. at 5 a.m. 23rd inst. Guns, tripods & 12belt boxes per gun will be taken on the train.

Detrainment station VERDREL, where Coy. will be met by limbers and guide of the 11th Bn. M.G.C. and will march to billots in BRAQUEMONT taking over from the reserve Coy. of the 11th Bn.M.G.C. there.

On the 24th inst. "C" Coy. will relieve "D" Coy. 11th Bn. M.G.C. "C" Coys. transport will move with the 44th Bde. transport at about 3 a.m. tomorrow to BRAQUEMONT. Detailed time and place of starting will be communicated direct to "C" Coy. Transport Officer.

(b) The Battalion (less "C" Coy.) will entrain on the 24th inst. at time and place to be notified later, and will detrain at LA HAIE Junction W.18.b.2.6. and will be billeted at CHATEAU DE LA HAIE for the night 24/25th.

Guns, tripods and 12 belt boxes per gun will be taken on the train.

All transport (less "C" Coy. transport) will move to CHATEAU DE LA HAIE on the 24th inst. Time to be notified later.

"D" and "A" Coys. and their transport will march from CHATEAU DE LA HAIE on the 25th inst. at 6 a.m. to BRAQUEMONT, Route Gd SERVINS - HERSIN - Cross Roads ½ mile N. of F in FOSSE DITE DUPONT - BRAQUEMONT and occupy billets vacated by "C" Coy. and other billets which are being arranged.

On the afternoon of the 25th inst. "D" and "A" Coys. will relieve the right front and support Coys. respectively of 11th Bn. M.G.C.

Bn. H.Q. and "B" Coy. will march from CHATEAU DE LA HAIE at 3 p.m. moving by same route to BRAQUEMONT. There will be a halt for tea on route. "B" Coy. will take over reserve billets at BRAQUEMONT.

At CHATEAU DE LA HAIE "D" "A" and "B" Coys. will pack their guns, tripods and belt boxes in limbers and will carry packs on march to BRAQUEMONT.

16 belt boxes per gun will be taken over in the line, and 16 per gun will be handed over under Bn. arrangements at BRAQUEMONT to 11th Bn. M.G.C.

3. All Trench Stores, Maps etc. will be handed over to 2nd and 3rd Canadian M.G.Bns. by Coys. concerned. Reserve Rations will also be handed over, care being taken to see that amount handed over agrees with amount taken over from 56th Bn. M.G.C.

Copy of receipts for all Trench Stores and Rations handed over will be sent to Bn. Hqrs. before entering new sector.

4. Completion of reliefs on night 23/24th will be reported by runner to Bn. H.Q. which will move to ARRAS, location will be notified later.

Completion of reliefs in new sector will be wired to Bn. H.Q. using phrase "Your M.G. 51 received at ----"

5. ACKNOWLEDGE.

H M Barnes
Capt. & Adjt.
15th Bn. Machine Gun Corps.

Distribution:-

Copies 1-4 A.B.C. & D. Coys.
5-8 A.B.C. & D. T.Os.
9 Bn. Transp. Officer.
10 Signal Officer.
11 Quartermaster.
12 15th Div. "G".
13 15th Div. "Q".
14 44th Inf. Bde.
15 45th Inf. Bde.
16 46th Inf. Bde.
17 2nd Canad. M.G.Bn.
18 3rd Canad. M.G.Bn.
19 11th Bn. M.G.C.
20.21. War Diary & File.

SECRET. COPY NO. 16

15th Bn. MACHINE GUN CORPS.

OPERATION ORDER NO. 49.

Ref. Maps 44a)
44b) 1/40000
44a N.W.3. 1/10000.

Hqrs.,
15th Bn. M.G.C.
27th August 1918.

1. 46th Inf. Bde. will relieve 73rd Inf. Bde. in the left section of the 24th Divn. front today 27th inst. and night 27/28th inst.

2. "B" Coy. will relieve the left front Coy. of the 24th Bn. M.G.C. today 27th inst.

3. 1 Guide per section will meet "B" Coy. at Hqrs. 24th Bn. M.G.C. (L.28.c.80.50.). From this point sections will move at intervals of half an hour to M.2.b.9.1. where gun team guides will be met, and at which point guns and tripods will be unloaded from limbers.
   Location of Coy. Hqrs. is G.34.d.75.40.

4. All Trench Stores, Maps, etc. will be handed over and receipts given. Copy of receipts will be sent to Bn. Hqrs. as soon as possible after relief. In addition "B" Coy. will very carefully take over all details of S.O.S. lines and defensive arrangements.

5. Signalling Officer will arrange relief of Signalling personnel.

6. Completion of relief will be notified to Bn. Hqrs. using code phrase "Your M.G. 400 received at -----".

7. ACKNOWLEDGE.

H McBarron
Capt. & Adjt.
15th Bn. Machine Gun Corps.

Distribution:-
Copy No. 1. "A" Coy.
2. "B" "
3. "C" "
4. "D" "
5. Signalling Officer.
6. Transport Officer.
7. " " "B" Coy.
8. Quartermaster.
9. 15th Division "G".
10. " " "Q".
11. 44th Inf. Bde.
12. 45th Inf. Bde.
13. 46th Inf. Bde.
14. 24th Bn. M.G.C.
15. 16th Bn. M.G.C.
16. War Diary.
17. File.

Instructions regarding War Diaries and Intelligence Summaries are contained in F. S. Regs., Part II. and the Staff Manual respectively. Title pages will be prepared in manuscript.

WAR DIARY
or
~~INTELLIGENCE SUMMARY~~.
(Erase heading not required.)

Army Form C. 2118.

Vol 7

Place	Date	Hour	Summary of Events and Information	Remarks and references to Appendices

CONFIDENTIAL

WAR DIARY

OF

15th BATTN: MACHINE GUN CORPS

FROM :- 1st to 30th September 1918

VOLUME VII

30th September 1918

R. Nasmith
Lieut: Col:
Comdg: 15th Bn Machine Gun Corps

D. D. & L., London, E.C.
(A10266) Wt W5300/P713 750,000 2/18 Sch. 52 Forms/C2118/16

Instructions regarding War Diaries and Intelligence Summaries are contained in F. S. Regs., Part II. and the Staff Manual respectively. Title pages will be prepared in manuscript.

WAR DIARY
or
~~INTELLIGENCE SUMMARY.~~
(Erase heading not required.)

Army Form C. 2118.

Place	Date	Hour	Summary of Events and Information	Remarks and references to Appendices
	1st		Day was normal. We fired 5750 rounds harassing fire and 600 anti-air-craft fire. O O 50 issued. JK.	O O 50 attached.
	2nd	10 am	Two guns of 'B' Coy relieved as per O O 50. O O 51 issued. The reason for withdrawing 'A' Coy into reserve was to have a force in hand so that should the enemy retire this was available for immediate pursuit. JK.	O O 51 attached.
		7 pm	A Coy relief completed.	
	3rd		During the period our guns fired 4,750 rounds harassing fire. Suspicions of an enemy retiral on this front were very strong and every effort was made to gain reliable information as to his movements and intentions. The infantry were ordered to send out strong fighting patrols and to establish posts ~~wherever~~ possible. The reserve Coy was ordered to be ready to move on ~~[illegible]~~ ~~[illegible]~~ short notice. S.A.A. dumps were established in forward areas. JK.	
	4th		Day was normal. Our guns fired 4,500 rounds. Infantry carried out active patrolling by night. O O 52 issued. JK.	O O 52 attached.
	5th		Zero hour for the raid was 4.45 am. We fired 64,000 rounds barrage fire and 2,000 rounds ordinary harassing fire. All guns fired extremely well. JK	

Instructions regarding War Diaries and Intelligence Summaries are contained in F. S. Regs., Part II. and the Staff Manual respectively. Title pages will be prepared in manuscript.

WAR DIARY
or
~~INTELLIGENCE SUMMARY.~~
(Erase heading not required.)

Army Form C. 2118.

Place	Date	Hour	Summary of Events and Information	Remarks and references to Appendices
	6th		During the day there was a slight increase in enemy's Artillery activity	
		11 pm.	Zero for the raid. Barrage was fired as per O.O. 53 22,500 rounds were fired. The aggressive tactics were still maintained. Posts were established on the left of the Divisional front. O.O. 54 issued. JK	O.O. 54 attached.
	7th		Work on barrage positions for impending raid. ~~Ofte~~ ~~opening~~ The enemy's plan seems to have been to hold his front lightly by posts which on the slightest sign of attack retired to their main line. JK	
	8th		Early this morning a small raid was carried out. Our guns fired 36,000 rounds in support of same. The remainder of day was normal. O.O. 55 issued JK.	
	9th		The day was normal. Our guns fired 2,000 rounds harassing fire. During the night the enemy carried out a gas bombardment. Ten men were gassed. For three or four days the enemy had employed a fair amount of gas on this front. JK.	
	10th		The day was normal Our guns fired 3000 rounds. JK.	
	11th		In the early morning our Infantry patrols were very active	
		5 am	They established posts in the Quarries meeting with very little resistance. The remainder of the day was normal. Our guns had an opportunity of engaging enemy air-craft. 2,000 rounds were fired. JK	

D. D. & L., London, E.C.
A5001) Wt. W1 71/M2031 750,000 5/17 Sch. 52 Forms/C2118/14

Instructions regarding War Diaries and Intelligence Summaries are contained in F. S. Regs., Part II. and the Staff Manual respectively. Title pages will be prepared in manuscript.

WAR DIARY
or
INTELLIGENCE SUMMARY.
(Erase heading not required.)

Army Form C. 2118.

Place	Date	Hour	Summary of Events and Information	Remarks and references to Appendices
	12th		The day was normal. Our guns had an opportunity of engaging hostile air-craft. 750 rounds were fired. JK.	
	13th	5 am.	Infantry again pushed forward their posts. There was the normal amount of artillery activity for the remainder of the day. 1000 rounds harassing fire were fired. JK.	
	14th	5.30 am	Enemy bombarded old front line positions.	
		6 am	Under cover of a heavy barrage our outposts were attacked in the Quarries. Our posts were forced to withdraw slightly. 3000 rounds were fired on S.O.S. lines. JK.	
	15th		Activity in Quarry region still continued. At 1.40 pm our posts were again attacked and forced to withdraw slightly. These attacks took the form of parties working up C.Ts. & bombing or rushing our posts. No targets for M.G. fire were presented. OO 57 issued. JK.	OO 57 attached.
	16th	5 am.	The infantry raided the enemys trenches and established posts. 38,000 rounds were fired in support of the raid. The remainder of the day was normal. OO 56 issued. JK.	OO 56 attached
	17th		The morning was quiet.	
		4 pm	The infantry carried out a raid on the enemys trenches. There was a special barrage and a gas projector attack. Our guns fired 72,000 rounds in support. By night our patrols were very active. OO 58 issued. JK.	OO 58 attached
	18th		The day was normal. The usual patrolling by night was carried out. JK	
	19th		At 5.15 am the enemy attacked our post on the left. By a successful counter-attack his attack was broken up. Remainder of the day was normal. JK.	

D. D. & L., London, E.C.
(A8001) Wt. W1-71/M2031 750,000 5/17 Sch. 52 Forms/C2.118/14

Instructions regarding War Diaries and Intelligence Summaries are contained in F. S. Regs., Part II. and the Staff Manual respectively. Title pages will be prepared in manuscript.

WAR DIARY
or
INTELLIGENCE SUMMARY.
(Erase heading not required.)

Army Form C. 2118.

Place	Date	Hour	Summary of Events and Information	Remarks and references to Appendices
	20th	9.45am	The enemy after a barrage of our forward posts attempted strong bombing attacks. He again kept to trenches and made M.G. fire useless. 'D' Coy relieved 'B' Coy as per OO 58. The relief was completed by 3.30 pm. JK.	
	21st		The day was very quiet. Our guns fired 1250 rounds harassing fire. The usual patrolling was carried out by night. JK.	
	22nd		The day was normal. Our guns had an opportunity of engaging enemy air-craft. 1130 rounds A.A. fire were fired. To day one of our infantry Bdes took over from one Bde of the 16th Divn on our left. The M.G's covering this Bde front were attached to the 15th Bn. OO 59 issued. JK.	OO 59 Attached
	23rd	3.30pm	During the gas projector attack our guns fired 69,000 rounds. The barrage and projectors were placed as they had been for the raid on the 17th inst. except that the M.G barrage was put on the trench that then was the final objective. Our fire drew a considerable amount of retaliation. One sergeant & 2 privates were killed by a shell which burst in the emplacement. The remainder of the period was fairly quiet. During the night the enemy carried out a gas bombardment. JK.	
	24th		The day was normal. Our guns fired 5,000 rounds harassing fire. JK.	
	25th		The day was very quiet. Small engagements took place between patrols. JK.	

D. D. & L., London, E.C. (A8001) Wt. W1.71/M2031 750,000 5/17 Sch. 52 Forms/C2118/14

Army Form C. 2118.

Instructions regarding War Diaries and Intelligence Summaries are contained in F. S. Regs., Part II. and the Staff Manual respectively. Title pages will be prepared in manuscript.

WAR DIARY
or
INTELLIGENCE SUMMARY.
(Erase heading not required.)

Place	Date	Hour	Summary of Events and Information	Remarks and references to Appendices
	26th		The day was normal. Our guns carried out the usual harassing fire programme. GK.	
	27th		The day was normal. The enemy bombed one of our forward posts and forced it to retire. 5000 rounds were fired in harassing fire. GK	
	28th		The infantry continued to push forward their posts. The day was normal. OO 60 issued. In accordance with OO 60 65,000 rounds were fired GK	OO 60 attached
	29th		An organised attack by three parties of the enemy against one of our post was successfully repulsed. 45,000 rounds were fired in harassing fire GK.	
	30th		OO 61 issued. The day was normal but the enemy was reported as being very alert. 31,000 rounds were fired in harassing fire. GK.	

30-9-18

R. Nasmith Lieut: Col:
Comdg: 15th Bn Machine Gun Corps

D. D. & L., London, E.C. (A8001) Wt. W1771/M2031 750,000 5/17 Sch. 52 Forms/C2118/14

SECRET. COPY NO. 12

15th Bn. MACHINE GUN CORPS.

OPERATION ORDER NO. 50.

Ref. map
LOOS 44A N.W.3.
1/10000.

Hqrs.,
15th Bn. M.G.C.
1st September 1918.

1. The Boundary between 15th Division and 24th Division is being amended to run as follows:-
Junction of HEAVEN TRENCH and front line - HEAVEN TRENCH - HURRAH ALLEY - SCOTS ALLEY (all exclusive) as far as G.36.d.95.55. - G.36.c.60.60. - G.35.d.85.20. - G.32.d.0.5. - thence straight to present boundary at G.25.b.0.3. thence present boundary.

2. Consequent upon the change of the Right Divisional Boundary, the Boundary between 46th and 44th Inf. Bdes. will be amended to run as follows :-
Junction of front line and road at H.19.c.7.3. - G.23.c.9.0. - thence along present boundary.

3. On the night 1/2nd September, the 17th Inf. Bde. 24th Division will extend to the left and adjust to the new Inter Divisional Boundary relieving troops of the 46th Inf. Bde.
Relief is being completed by midnight 1/2nd September.

4. (a) On the night 1/2nd September, the 24th Bn. M.G.C. will take over the two guns at WHITE MOUND (H.31.c.30.60.) from "B" Coy. 15th Bn. M.G.C. All arrangements to be made between Co. Commanders concerned. On completion of relief the two guns of "B" Coy. will be accomodated in the vicinity of "B" Coy. Hqrs.
(b) Completion of relief to be notified to Bn. Hqrs. by wire using code phrase "Your M.G.560 received at -----"

5. ACKNOWLEDGE.

H.M. Barrons

Capt. & Adjt.
15th Bn. Machine Gun Corps.

Issued at 1.30 p.m. through Siggals.

Distribution:- Copy No. 1. "A" Coy.
2. "B" "
3. "C" "
4. "D" "
5. 15th Div. "G".
6. 44th Inf. Bde.
7. 45th Inf. Bde.
8. 46th Inf. Bde.
9. C.M.G.O. I Corps.
10. 24th Bn. M.G.C.
11. 16th Bn. M.G.C.
12. War Diary.
13. File.

SECRET. COPY NO. 14.

15th Bn. MACHINE GUN CORPS.

OPERATION ORDER NO. 51.

Ref. map
LOOS 44A N.W.3.
1/10000

Hqrs.,
15th Bn. M.G.C.
2nd September 1918.

1. In order to bring the whole of "A" Coy. into Reserve, the following moves and reliefs will take place commencing 8 a.m. 2nd September 1918.

No. 1 Move.
The 4 guns of "B" Coy. at Coy. H.Q. will relieve DUMPTY BATTERY and CURZON BATTERY of "D" Coy. (each 2 guns).
On completion of relief guns now at DUMPTY BATTERY and CURZON BATTERY will relieve PHILOSOPHE BATTERY and VERLOOS BATTERY of "A" Coy.
On completion of relief guns of "A" Coy. at PHILOSOPHE BATTERY and VERLOOS BATTERY will move to BRACQUEMONT.

No. 2 Move.
PONT BATTERY and REDOUBT BATTERY will be abandoned by "D" Coy., and the guns from same will relieve AVENUE BATTERY and LIMBER BATTERY of "C" Coy.
On completion of relief, guns now at AVENUE BATTERY and LIMBER BATTERY will relieve TOWER BATTERY and KEEP BATTERY of "A" Coy.
On completion of relief guns of "A" Coy. at TOWER BATTERY and KEEP BATTERY will move to BRACQUEMONT.

2. Coy. Commanders will arrange all details of guides by telephone.

3. In the case of No.1 move, Belt Boxes will be handed and taken over, and O.C. "B" Coy. will arrange to have 64 belt boxes on MAROC - LOOS Road at furthest point Transport is allowed in daylight, where limbers will be to bring them back to BRACQUEMONT, where they will be handed over to "A" Coy.

In the case of No. 2 move, belt boxes will not be handed or taken over.

4. "D" Coy. will arrange that all Trench Stores, Iron Rations, etc. left at PONT and REDOUBT BATTERIES are moved as soon as possible to Coy. Hqrs.
"A" Coy. will arrange that all Trench Stores etc. at their old Coy. Hqrs. at NOYELLES are withdrawn to BRACQUEMONT.

5. Coys. will each report completion of their reliefs by the code word "FROG" to Bn. Hqrs. by wire.

acknowledge

H M Barns.
Capt. & Adjt.
15th Bn. Machine Gun Corps.

Issued at 1 a.m. through Signals.

Distribution:- Copy No1. "A" Coy.
2 "B" "
3 "C" "
4 "D" "
5 Transport Officer.
6 Signal Officer.
7 15th Divn. "G".
8 15th Divn. "Q".
9 44th Inf. Bde.
10 45th Inf. Bde.
11 46th Inf. Bde.
12 16th Bn. M.G.C.
13 24th Bn. M.G.C.
14 War Diary. 15 File.
16 11th D.A.

SECRET. COPY NO 11

15th Bn. MACHINE GUN CORPS.

OPERATION ORDER NO.52.

Ref. Map
Loos 44A NW 3
1/10000.

Hqrs.,
15th Bn. M.G.C.
4th September 1918.

1. 46th Inf. Bde. will raid enemy's trenches tomorrow morning in the following area:-
Northern Boundary H.25.b.43.92. to H.19.d.72.06. Southern Boundary H.25.b.70.03. to H.26.a.07.22. Furthest limit East enemy's Support Line.

2. The 15th Bn. Machine Gun Corps will co-operate as follows:-
(a) "B" Coy. 4 guns at about G.36.a.30.65.
Target. 2 guns on hostile machine guns at H.26.b.01.01.
1 gun on Trench from H.26.b.01.01-H.26.b.18.15.
1 gun on hostile machine gun at H.26.b.15.20.
4 guns at about G.29.d.62.70.
Target HIVE ALLEY from H.19.d.52.35. - H.20.c.28.75.

"D" Coy. 6 guns at about G.29.b.55.51.
Target H.26.a.77.71. - H.20.c.56.05. - H.20.c.52.48.

(b) Rate of fire :-

Z	to Z plus 5	2½ belts.
Z plus 5	to Z plus 20	5 "
Z plus 20	to Z plus 30	5 "
Z plus 30	to Z plus 40	2½ "

3. Machine gun barrage will not open until the artillery barrage commences.

4. "B" and "D" Coys. will each send an officer to synchronise watches at 46th Bde. Hqrs. (G.34.d.75.33.) at 10 p.m. tonight.

5. A "Chinese" ~~attack~~ barrage will be carried out at the same time between HEMLOCK ALLEY and H.13.c.77.18.

6. The 15th Bn. M.G.C. will co-operate as follows:-
"D" Coy. 2 guns of LIMBER BATTERY.
Target. H.13.d.38.08. - H.13.d.33.27.

"B" Coy. 2 guns of CURZON BATTERY.
Target. HICKS ALLEY from H.19.b.00.81.- H.13.d.38.06.

"C" Coy. 4 guns of DALY BATTERY.
Target. HALIFAX TRENCH H.13.a.74.56. - H.13.b.10.60.

Rate of fire for all guns firing in "Chinese" barrage:-

Z	to Z plus 10.	5 belts.
Z plus 10	" Z plus 15.	1 "

All guns firing in this barrage will use normal night firing positions.
Zero hour will be notified later.

ACKNOWLEDGE.

Issued at 8pm.

[signature]
Capt. & Adjt.
15th Bn. Machine Gun Corps.

Distribution:- Copies 1 - 4. A.B.C.& D. Coys.
5. 46th Inf. Bde.
6. 44th Inf. Bde.
7. 45th Inf. Bde.
8. 15th Division "G".
9. 11th Divl. Arty.
10. 24th Bn. M.G.C.
11. War Diary.
12. File.

SECRET. 15th Bn. Machine Gun Corps. M.G.281.

Ref. OPERATION ORDER NO. 54. d/6.9.18.

"C" and "D" Coys. will each send an officer to 45th Inf. Bde. Hqrs. at PHILOSOPHE to synchronise watches at 6 p.m. to-day, 7th inst.

ACKNOWLEDGE.

7.9.18.

Capt. & Adjt.
15th Bn. Machine Gun Corps.

Copies to "C" Coy.
"D" "
45th Inf. Bde.

SECRET. COPY NO 11

15th Bn. MACHINE GUN CORPS.

OPERATION ORDER NO. 54.

Ref. Map Loos 44A NW 3
1/10000.

Hqrs.
15th Bn. M.G.C.
6th September 1918.

1. The 45th Inf. Bde. will probably carry out a raid on enemy's trenches from H.7.c.02.30. - G.12.d.97.42. on night 7/8th inst.

2. The 15th Bn. Machine Gun Corps will co-operate as follows:-

"D" Coy.-
6 guns at about G.17.c.79.65.
Guns to be used LONE and LIMBER.
Target HAMLET TRENCH from H.7.d.37.26. - H.7.c.90.63.

The 2 guns of CURZON POST firing from PONT BATTY.
Target Hostile Machine Gun H.7.c.66.52.

"C" Coy.
4 guns at about G.17.a.81.38.
DALY BATTY. to be used.
Target H.7.c.90.63. - H.7.c.67.92.

2 guns at CHAPEL BATTY. firing from night firing positions.
Target Hostile Machine Gun at G.12.b.43.82.

3. Rate of fire for all guns except DALY BATTY:-
Z to Z plus 8 4 belts.

DALY BATTY. will open fire at Z plus 4.
Rate of fire Z plus 4 to Z plus 8 2 belts.

From Z plus 8 to Z plus 38 all guns will fire bursts as follows:-

Z plus 13	1 belt.
Z " 18	½ "
Z " 25	80 rounds.
Z " 30	50 "
Z " 38	50 "

4. Machine gun barrage will not open until artillery barrage commences.

5. Zero hour and details regarding synchronisation of watches will be notified later.

6. ACKNOWLEDGE.

H M Barns.
Capt. & Adjt.
15th Bn. Machine Gun Corps.

Issued at 9 p.m.
through Signals.

Distribution:- Copies 1 - 4. A.B.C. & D. Coys.
5. 15th Division "G".
6. 44th Inf. Bde.
7. 45th Inf. Bde.
8. 46th Inf. Bde.
9. 11th Div. Arty.
10. 16th Bn. M.G.C.
11. War Diary.
12. File.

SECRET. 15th Bn. Machine Gun Corps. M.G. 375.

Reference 15th Bn. M.G.C. OPERATION ORDER No.56.

d/ 16th September 1918.

Ref. para 4. Zero hour will be 4 p.m. (four o'clock p.m.(September 17th.

"C" Special Coy. R.E. will co-operate in the raid, wind permitting, and will discharge 500 Gas Projectors into the HULLUCH Sector at Zero hour.

O.C. "C" Special Coy. will be responsible that the discharge does not take place if wind is unfavourable. The attached map (x) shows the Danger and Precautionary Zones and Targets.

Within Danger Zone all troops will be withdrawn and tunnel entrances closed from Zero - 5 until an Officer of "C" Special Coy. R.E. reports that the area is clear.

Within the Precautionary Zone all troops will be kept under cover and will wear their respirators from Zero - 5 till the area is reported "all clear".

Watches will be synchronised at the following times and places:-
"A" Coy. HQ. 44th Inf. Bde. 12 noon 17th Sept.
"B" Coy. HQ. 46th Inf. Bde. 11 a.m. 17th Sept.

ACKNOWLEDGE by wire.

H Mason
Capt. & Adjt.
15th Bn. Machine Gun Corps.

16.9.18.

(x) To Coys. only. Copies to all recipients of OO.56

SECRET.

COPY NO 4

15th Bn. MACHINE GUN CORPS.

OPERATION ORDER NO.56.

Ref. LOOS 44A
1/10000

Hqrs.
15th Bn. M.G.C.
16th September 1918.

1. The 46th Inf. Bde. will raid the enemy trenches in the area H.25.b. - 26.a. - 20.c. and 19.d. by daylight on Sept. 17th 1918.

2. Objectives :-
(1.) Enemy front line from it's junction with HONEY ALLEY to it's junction with HIVE ALLEY.
(2.) Enemy support line from it's junction with HONEY ALLEY to it's junction with HIVE ALLEY.
(3.) HULLUCH TRENCH from H.26.a.9.5. to H.20.c.25.75.

The Boundaries of the raid will be HONEY ALLEY (inclusive) on the South, and HIVE ALLEY (inclusive) on the North.

3. 15th Bn. Machine Gun Corps will co-operate as follows:-

(a) "B" Coy.

4 guns from BANKER and CRAP at about G.36.a.25.65. Target H.26.d.00.95. to H.26.b.30.20.

4 guns from CYCLONE and STUD at about G.30.a.75.50. Target H.26.d.05.90. to H.26.c.80.70.

4 guns from DUMPTY and CURZON BATTY. at about G.23.d.50.30. Target H.20.A.05.18. to H.19.b.96.55.

(b) "A" Coy.

4 guns from CURZON POST and LONE at about G.23.b.70.15. Target. Trench H.19.b.96.55. to H.19.b.80.90.

Rates of fire for all guns, Zero to Z plus 58 mins. a steady rate of fire averaging 1 belt in 3 minutes. Fire will cease at Z plus 58.

4. Zero hour will be notified later.

5. ACKNOWLEDGE by wire.

[signature]
Capt. & Adjt.
15th Bn. Machine Gun Corps.

Issued through Signals at 8 am.

Distribution:- Copy No. 1. "A" Coy.
2. "B" "
3. "C" "
4. 46th Inf. Bde.
5. 15th Division "G".
6. 24th Bn. M.G.C.
7. War Diary.
8. File.

SECRET. COPY NO 6

15th Bn. MACHINE GUN CORPS.

OPERATION ORDER NO.57.

Hqrs.
15th Bn. M.G.C.
15th September 1918.

1. Reference the operation to have taken place this afternoon by 44th and 45th Inf. Bdes. this operation will take place tomorrow morn morning.

2. 15th Bn. M.G.C. will co-operate as follows:-

"C" Coy.
2 guns firing on GANDER TRENCH from G.6.a.5.9.- A.30.c.80.30.
3 guns firing on GOAT TRENCH G.6.a.5.7. to it's junction with the ST.LAURENT-HULLUCH line.
2 guns firing on GANDER TRENCH G.6.a.5.9. - G.6.b.50.40.

Guns will remain on these barrage lines till 8 p.m. and will open on same if S.O.S. goes up.

"A" Coy.
2 guns will enfilade the ST.LAURENT-HULLUCH line from G.6.b. 50.40. - A.30.central.
A.Coy. will also place enfilade barrages on HOMER ALLEY, HAWK ALLEY and HABORN ALLEY for purposes of deceiving the enemy.
On c ompletion of tasks "A" Coy. guns will return to normal battle positions.

3. In the event of Bde. Commanders requiring M.Gs. to fire longer than 5.30 am. they are requested to advise O.C. "C" Coy. and O.C. "A" Coy. direct.

4. Rates of fire for all guns - 1 belt per 3 minutes.
Time of firing - Z to Z plus 30.

5. Zero hour will be 5 am 16th September.

6. Acknowledge.

[signature]
Capt. & Adjt.
15.9.18. 15th Bn. Machine Gun Corps.

Distribution:- Copy No.1. "A" Coy.
2. "C" "
3. 44th Inf. Bde.
4. 45th Inf. Bde.
5. 15th Division "G".
6. War Diary.
7. File.

SECRET. COPY NO 14

15th Bn. MACHINE GUN CORPS.

OPERATION ORDER NO. 58.

Hqrs.
15th Bn. M.G.C.
17th September 1918.

1. "D" Coy. will relieve "B" Coy. in the Right Sector of Divl. front on Sept. 20th. Relief to be completed by 7 p.m.

2. All necessary arrangements will be made between Os.C. Coys. concerned.

3. All Maps, Trench Stores etc. will be handed over. Copies of receipts to be forwarded to Bn. Hqrs. within 24 hours after completion of relief.

4. O.C. "D" Coy. will carefully hand over all instructions as regards the action of reserve coy. in case of omergency, and O.C. "B" Coy. will arrange for the necessary reconnaisance regarding action of reserve coy. as laid down in Provisional Defence Scheme and Warning Order M.G.249 of 3rd inst., to be carried out before leaving the line.

5. On completion of relief "B" Coy. will become Reserve Coy. and move to billets in BRACQUEMONT.

6. Completion of relief to be wired to Bn. Hqrs. using code word "COAL". This to be repeated to 45th Inf. Bde.

7. ACKNOWLEDGE. (Coys. only).

Capt. & Adjt.
15th Bn. Machine Gun Corps.

Issued at 2 p.m. through Signals.

Distribution:- Copy No.1. "A" Coy.
2. "B" "
3. "C" "
4. "D" "
5. Transport Officer.
6. Quartermaster.
7. Signal Officer.
8. 44th Inf. Bde.
9. 45th Inf. Bde.
10. 46th Inf. Bde.
11. 15th Division "G".
12. 16th Bn. M.G.C.
13. 24th Bn. M.G.C.
14 & 15. War Diary.
16. File.

SECRET. COPY NO _____

15th Bn. MACHINE GUN CORPS.

OPERATION ORDER NO. 59.

Ref. Map 44A NW3. 1/10,000.

Hqrs.
15th Bn. M.G.C.
22nd September 1918.

1. "C" Special Co. R.E. have installed 720 Gas Projectors at G.24.a.4.7. and G.18.a.9.1.
If weather conditions are favourable, these projectors will be fired on 23rd September, with artillery co-operation.
Wind limits are from S.W. through W. to W.N.W.

2. The attached map (to Coys. only) shows the targets, Danger and Precautionary Zones.
Within the Danger Zones, all troops will be withdrawn and tunnel entrances closed from Zero until an Officer of "C" Special Co. R.E. reports that the areas are clear.
Within the Precautionary Zones, all troops will keep under cover and will wear their respirators from Zero until the areas are reported clear.

3. In order to induce the enemy to expect a raid and man his trenches when the gas discharge takes place, artillery will co-operate in the following manner :-
(a). Fire Smoke S. of CITE St. ELIE and into HULLUCH from Zero till Zero plus 10 minutes.
(b). At Zero. Form a box barrage on HENDON and HABORN ALLEYS and enemy's support line between these two trenches.
(c). At Zero plus 2 minutes. Barrage lifts to HULL TRENCH.
(d). At Zero plus 4 minutes. Barrage lifts to HOCKEY TRENCH where it will stand till Zero plus 12.
All trenches leading out of gassed area to be barraged.
(e). At Zero plus 15 minutes. Any 18-pounders available fire two bursts of gun fire on HULLUCH TRENCH between HONEY and HIVE ALLEYS.

4. 15th Bn. Machine Gun Corps will co-operate as follows :-

(a). "A" Coy.
Guns to be used. LIMBER BATTY. AVENUE BATTY. LONE BATTY. CURZON POST. SCOTTISH BATTY.
Targets :-
LIMBER BATTY. - HULLUCH TRENCH from it's junction with HICKS ALLEY to H.19.b.95.80.
Remaining guns - HULLUCH TRENCH from H.20.a.00.40. to H.20.c.60.55.

(b). "C" Coy.
4 guns near DALY BATTY. (2 guns to be drawn from CHAPEL BATTY.).
Target :- HULLUCH TRENCH H.19.b.95.80. - H.20.a.00.40.

(c). "D" Coy.
All 16 guns of the Coy. from positions near their permanent battle positions, with the exception of NEW MACKAY and V.20. which will be moved forward for this operation.
Target:- HULLUCH TRENCH from H.20.c.60.55. to H.26.b.20.20.

Rate of fire for all guns will be 1 belt per 3 minutes. Fire will commence at Zero plus 15 mins. and continue till Zero plus 45 minutes.

5. Gas Projectors are being fired at Zero plus 7 mins.

6. Zero hour will be 3.30 p.m. 23rd September.

7. Watches will be synchronised as follows:-
"D" Coy. at Hqrs. 45th Inf. Bde. 9 a.m. Sept. 23rd.
"C" Coy.)
"A" Coy.) at Hqrs. 44th Inf. Bde. 10 a.m. Sept. 23rd.

O.O. No.59. contd:-

8. ACKNOWLEDGE by wire.

Capt. & Adjt.
15th Bn. Machine Gun Corps.

Distribution :- Copies 1 - 4. A. B. C. & D. Coys.
5. 44th Inf. Bde.
6. 45th Inf. Bde.
7. 46th Inf. Bde.
8. 15th Division "G".
9. 16th Bn. M.G.C.
10. 15th D.A.
11 & 12 War Diary.
13 File.

War Diary (2)

SECRET. COPY NO 14

15th Bn. MACHINE GUN CORPS.

OPERATION ORDER NO. 60.

Hqrs.
15th Bn. M.G.C.
28th September 1918.

1. Recent information tends to indicate that the enemy in front of the FIFTH ARMY has made all arrangements to effect a withdrawal, if it becomes necessary, by reason of action here or elsewhere.

2. For a period of 24 hours beginning at 8 a.m. 28th September, full use is to be made of all available Artillery to harass and inflict loss on the enemy.

3. It is important that we should obtain early information of any indication that the enemy intends to withdraw or is in process of withdrawing.
From this date patrols are being specially active and the enemy's front constantly tested in order that prompt action may be taken in the event of a withdrawal taking place.
45th Infantry Brigade are maintaining close touch and co-operating with the left of the 24th Division in any forward move and keeping Div. H.Q. informed of events on this flank.

4. On the early morning of the 30th September the I Corps are preparing to push forward posts along the line running G.5.b.9.3. - A.30.c.2.4. - A.30.a.2.8. - A.24.c.1.7. - A.18.c.3.4.

5. In consequence, on the morning of the 30th September, 46th Infantry Brigade are preparing to capture GIBBON TRENCH if this has not already been done.

6. At the same time, 45th Infantry Brigade will carry out a raid on HILDA TRENCH between HINDOO and HICKS ALLEYS.

7. 15th Bn. Machine Gun Corps will co-operate as follows :-

(a) By special Harassing Fire programme which will be issued to all concerned. (M.G. 494 of 28th inst.)

(b) For Operation mentioned in para.5 as follows :-

"C" Coy.

2 guns of STANSFIELD BATTY.
2 guns of TUNNEL BATTY.
4 guns of CHAPEL BATTY.

Target. Area bounded by the following co-ordinates :-
H.30.c.80.40. - H.30.d.30.40. - H.30.c.90.25.- H.30.b.50.20.

"A" Coy.

2 guns of LIMBER BATTY.

Target. Enfilade ST.LAURENT-HULLUCH line from H.30.c.80.30. to H.30.c.85.80.

Rate of fire for all guns - 1 belt per 3 minutes.

Period of fire Zero to Z. plus 30 minutes.

Zero hour will be 6.15 a.m. (six fifteen a.m.) 30th inst.

(c)..................

O.O. No. 60. contd:-

(c) For operation mentioned in para. 6 as follows :-

"D" Coy.

DUMPTY BATTY. Target. H.13.d.40.45. to H.13.d.25.72.

VENDIN BATTY. Target. H.13.d.40.09. to H.13.d.35.52.

Each gun will search 30' up.

Rate of fire:- Z to Z plus 5 2 belts.
Z plus 5 " Z plus 15 3 "
Z plus 15 " Z plus 25 5 "

Zero hour of this operation will be ~~notified later~~. 6.15 am 30th in

8. Watches will be synchronised as follows :-

"A" & "C" Coys. Hqrs. 46th Inf. Bde. 8 p.m. 29th inst.
"D" Coy. " 45th " " 7 p.m. 29th "

9. ACKNOWLEDGE by wire.

[signature]
Capt. & Adjt.
15th Bn. Machine Gun Corps.

Issued through Signals at 8 p.m.

Distribution :- Copy No.1. "A" Coy.
2. "B" "
3. "C" "
4. "D" "
5. O.C. Rt. Sub. Group, 16th Bn. M.G.C.
6. 15th Division "G".
7. 44th Inf. Bde.
8. 45th Inf. Bde.
9. 46th Inf. Bde.
10. 16th Bn. M.G.C.
11. 24th Bn. M.G.C.
12. COrps M.G.O. I Corps.
13. 15th D.A.
14/15. War Diary.
16. File.

SECRET. 15th Bn. Machine Gun Corps M.G. 501.

AMENDMENT NO.1 to OPERATION ORDER NO.60 d/28.9.18.

PARA.7. (b) line 7 :-

For H.30.c.80.40. - H.30.d.30.40. - H.30.c.90.25. - H.30.b.50.20.

Road A.30.c.80.40. - A.30.d.30.40. - A.30.a.90.25. - A.30.b.50.20.

Para 7. (b) "A" Coy.

For Target. Enfilade ST.LAURENT-HULLUCH line from H.30.c.80.30. to H.30.c.85.80.

Read Target. Enfilade ST.LAURENT-HULLUCH line from A.30.c.80.30. to A.30.c.85.80.

ACKNOWLEDGE.

H.M. Sar...

Capt. & Adjt.

29.9.18. 15th Bn. Machine Gun Corps.

Copies to all recipients of O.O.60.

Instructions regarding War Diaries and Intelligence Summaries are contained in F. S. Regs., Part II. and the Staff Manual respectively. Title pages will be prepared in manuscript.

WAR DIARY
or
INTELLIGENCE SUMMARY.
(Erase heading not required.)

Army Form C. 2118.

Vol 8

Place	Date	Hour	Summary of Events and Information	Remarks and references to Appendices

CONFIDENTIAL

WAR DIARY

OF

15th. BN. MACHINE GUN CORPS.

FROM 1st. to 31st. OCTOBER 1918.

VOL. VIII

31st. OCT. 1918.

R. Chasmith Lieut. [illegible]
Comdg 15th Bn. Machine Gun Corps

D. D. & L., London, E.C. (A8094) Wt. W1771/M2031 750,000 5/17 Sch. 52 Forms/C2118/14

Instructions regarding War Diaries and Intelligence Summaries are contained in F. S. Regs., Part II. and the Staff Manual respectively. Title pages will be prepared in manuscript.

WAR DIARY

~~or~~

~~INTELLIGENCE SUMMARY.~~

(Erase heading not required.)

Army Form C. 2118.

Place	Date	Hour	Summary of Events and Information	Remarks and references to Appendices
	1st		During the period the enemy artillery and M.G. activity was normal, his posts and patrols as usual. The line now held by us was roughly the HULLUCH–LA BASSEE line. The Bn. was disposed as follows:– D. Co. and A. Co. right and left front Cos respectively, B Co. in support and C. Co in reserve. The front Cos. took up positions in Old GERMAN SUPPORT Line. HB.	
	2nd		The infantry continued the advance meeting very little resistance.	
		11.20	Sections of opportunity of two front Cos. moved forward in rear of infantry.	
		12.00	The infantry were reported as having taken the VENDIN–DOUVRIN–LA BASSEE line and to have pushed patrols out beyond this. The enemy continued to offer very little resistance.	
		19.00	The sections of opportunity were reported as having taken up a position in the VENDIN–DOUVRIN–LA BASSEE line which was now being consolidated as per orders.	
		20.00	Forward Cos. reported that their front sections had moved forward and taken up positions to cover the main line	

D. D. & L., London, E.C. (A8004) Wt W1771/M2031 750,000 5/17 Sch. 52 Forms/C2118/14

Instructions regarding War Diaries and Intelligence Summaries are contained in F. S. Regs., Part II. and the Staff Manual respectively. Title pages will be prepared in manuscript.

WAR DIARY

~~or~~

~~INTELLIGENCE SUMMARY.~~

(Erase heading not required.)

Army Form C. 2118.

Place	Date	Hour	Summary of Events and Information	Remarks and references to Appendices
	2nd	2000	of resistance. These positions were taken up in the vicinity of BOIS DES DAMES and in front of BOIS DE QUATORZE on the right and S of HULLUCH and BENIFONTAINE and at PUITS 13bis on the left. The night was normal. Our patrols were reported as having reached a line through PONT A VENDIN and WINGLES. NB	
	3rd		During the day posts were established on the line of patrols. The reserve sections of D and A Cos. moved forward and occupied positions vacated by the sections that moved forward to positions on the main line of resistance. B Co. Support Co. occupied the positions vacated by the front Cos when they moved forward yesterday. Each Co. now had its own fighting limbers attached to it while No 3 limbers remained with Bn. transport. So far as possible sections retained their own transport. NB	
	4th		We had now advanced to a line through the centre of VENDIN LE VIEIL to E of WINGLES the METALLURGIQUE WORKS exclusive.	

Instructions regarding War Diaries and Intelligence Summaries are contained in F. S. Regs., Part II. and the Staff Manual respectively. Title pages will be prepared in manuscript.

WAR DIARY
or
~~INTELLIGENCE SUMMARY.~~
(Erase heading not required.)

Army Form C. 2118.

Place	Date	Hour	Summary of Events and Information	Remarks and references to Appendices
	4th		To cover this line a section took up position [illegible] W of VENDIN LE VIEL two sections were placed in the vicinity of CITIE-DES-DEUX-CENTS-QUATRE-VINGT-DIX and one section near slag heap N of WINGLES. The resistance now offered by the enemy was more determined. In spite of this our patrols made a slight advance. The enemy was very active with M.G's E of Canal. O.O. 62 issued and acted on. HB	O.O. 62 attached
	5th		The day was uneventful. The enemy continued to offer determined resistance. His M.G's on the E bank of the canal were especially active. This delayed our advance. HB	
	6th		Our patrols met with opposition everywhere. The enemy seemed determined to hold the line of the canal and a small Bridgehead west of it. HB	

D. D. & L., London, E.C. (A8004) Wt W1771/M2031 750,000 5/17 Sch. 52 Forms/C2118/14

Army Form C. 2118.

Instructions regarding War Diaries and Intelligence Summaries are contained in F. S. Regs., Part II. and the Staff Manual respectively. Title pages will be prepared in manuscript.

WAR DIARY

~~or~~

~~INTELLIGENCE SUMMARY.~~

(Erase heading not required.)

Place	Date	Hour	Summary of Events and Information	Remarks and references to Appendices
	6th	11.00	Our posts in the CENTRE of VENDIN were attacked and driven in, but during the afternoon all posts were successfully re-established. Our guns remained in the same positions which were improved as far as possible. The disposition of Bn. now was as follows:– Two Cos in front, with two forward sections out in support and one in reserve one Co in support in front one in our old front line system and one in reserve with two sections at PHILOSOPHE and two at MAZINGARBE. BN. HQ were at MAZINGARBE. NB.	
	7th		O.O. 63 issued. The day was normal. Enemy still maintained his resistance. NB	O.O. 63 attached
	8th		The enemy continued his harassing fire from the E bank of the canal. To overcome this a programme of harassing	

Army Form C. 2118.

Instructions regarding War Diaries and Intelligence Summaries are contained in F. S. Regs., Part II. and the Staff Manual respectively. Title pages will be prepared in manuscript.

WAR DIARY
or
~~INTELLIGENCE SUMMARY.~~

(Erase heading not required.)

Place	Date	Hour	Summary of Events and Information	Remarks and references to Appendices
	8th		fire was made out as per O.O. 64. This proved to be most satisfactory. HB	O.O. 64 attached
	9th	19.00	The relief of A Co. by C. Co. was carried out as per O.O. 63. Harassing fire as per O.O. 64 carried out. HB.	
	10th		The day was normal. The enemy continued to offer strong resistance but our patrols succeeded in establishing posts a little nearer the canal. O.O. 65 issued. HB.	O.O. 65 attached
	11th		The enemy still retained his footing W. of the canal. Aerial observation showed that all bridges over the canal had been destroyed. The division on our right succeeded making a small advance towards ANNAY. During the night front guns took up positions to	

D. D. & L., London, E.C. (A8004) Wt. W1771/M2 31 750,000 5/17 Sch. 52 Forms/C2118/14

Instructions regarding War Diaries and Intelligence Summaries are contained in F. S. Regs., Part II. and the Staff Manual respectively. Title pages will be prepared in manuscript.

WAR DIARY
or
~~INTELLIGENCE~~ SUMMARY.
(*Erase heading not required.*)

Army Form C. 2118.

Place	Date	Hour	Summary of Events and Information	Remarks and references to Appendices
	11th		Co operate with the infantry as per O.O. 65 Operation Instructions No 1 issued HB	O.I. No 1 attached
	12th		Our guns co operated with the infantry in their attack on the enemy W. of the Canal. This operation was entirely successful and a number of prisoners were taken. The right Bde. took over the front of the left Bde. of the 58 Div. on our left, this necessitated the moving of one Section into this area. This section took up position on the edge of ANNAY so as to cover the infantry about PONT MAUDIT. HB	
	13th		Enemy reported clear of W. of Canal. The day was normal. The section in front of ANNAY took up position during night HB	

D. D. & L., London, E.C. (A8604) Wt W1771/M2031 750,000 5/17 Sch. 52 Forms/C2118/14

Instructions regarding War Diaries and Intelligence Summaries are contained in F. S. Regs., Part II. and the Staff Manual respectively. Title pages will be prepared in manuscript.

WAR DIARY

~~or~~

~~INTELLIGENCE SUMMARY.~~

(*Erase heading not required.*)

Army Form C. 2118.

Place	Date	Hour	Summary of Events and Information	Remarks and references to Appendices
	14th		O.O. 66 issued. The right Co in preparation for the crossing moved its guns as follows:– Two sections just east of the COKE OVENS in VENDIN LE VIEIL, one E of ANNAY and one by Co H.Q. The day was normal. The enemy still held the E bank of canal. We still actively continued harassing fire on the enemy. NB	
	15th		The operation detailed in O.O. 66 was carried out: Our troops met with no opposition and no retaliation was reported. Enemy M.G.s still continued to fire from E bank of Canal. We carried out our usual harassing fire. Our patrols succeeded in crossing the canal and establishing bridge heads. BN H.Q. moved to LOOS. NB	
	16th		The enemy offered only slight opposition to our advance	

D. D. & L., London, E.C. (A8504) Wt W1771/M2031 750,000 5/17 Sch. 52 Forms/C2118/14

Instructions regarding War Diaries and Intelligence Summaries are contained in F. S. Regs., Part II. and the Staff Manual respectively. Title pages will be prepared in manuscript.

WAR DIARY

~~or~~

~~INTELLIGENCE SUMMARY.~~

(*Erase heading not required.*)

Army Form C. 2118.

Place	Date	Hour	Summary of Events and Information	Remarks and references to Appendices
	16th		A & C Co's passed through B & D. Cos as per Operation instructions No 1	
		13.00	Our advance patrols had passed through CARVIN and were reported on a line 1000x east of CARVIN. The two leading Cos were billetted close to the main line of resistance in PONT À VENDIN and MEURCHIN. BnHQ were at MEURCHIN. 2/Lt MASON. R.B. was killed.	
			NB.	
	17th	06.00	45 BDE passed through the out-post line of the Div and continued the advance as advance guard. C Co was attached to 45th BDE. After the advance guard had passed through the out-post line A & B Co's concentrated in CARVIN and EPINOY. D Co and Bn. HQ moved to MINES D'OSTRICOURT. The advance guard formed its out-post line for the night on a line E of LE BOSQUET and LIBECOURT.	
			NB	

D. D. & L., London, E.C. (A8001) Wt. W1771/M2031 750,000 5/17 Sch. 52 Forms/C2118/14

Instructions regarding War Diaries and Intelligence Summaries are contained in F. S. Regs., Part II. and the Staff Manual respectively. Title pages will be prepared in manuscript.

WAR DIARY
or
~~INTELLIGENCE SUMMARY.~~
(Erase heading not required.)

Army Form C. 2118.

Place	Date	Hour	Summary of Events and Information	Remarks and references to Appendices
	18th		The advance continued.	
		12.00 to 14.00	No opposition was met with until the main PONT A MARCQ – BERSEE road was reached. Here the enemy fought a small rear guard action but were unable to prevent this and advance to a line 1000x W of CAPELLE. During the action C Co was not called on. The remainder of the BN was disposed as follows for the night: BN H.Q and D Co in THUMERIES, B Co in LANEUVILLE, A Co in WAHAGNIES. WB	
	19th	09.00	The general advance continued. Progress was slow owing to a very thick mist. The opposition offered by the enemy was not serious. His MGs fired from successive positions but were not difficult to dislodge.	
		15.00	The out-post line for the night was 1000x E of FOURNES	

A7092). Wt. W12839/M1293 750,000. 1/17. D. D & L., Ltd. Forms/C2118/14.

Instructions regarding War Diaries and Intelligence Summaries are contained in F. S. Regs., Part II. and the Staff Manual respectively. Title pages will be prepared in manuscript.

WAR DIARY

or

~~INTELLIGENCE SUMMARY.~~

(*Erase heading not required.*)

Army Form C. 2118.

Place	Date	Hour	Summary of Events and Information	Remarks and references to Appendices
	19th		[illegible] to MINES DE COBRIEUX. BN. H.Q. and B. & D. Cos. were billeted in CAPELLE. A Co. in MOLPAS. The enemy did not bring any artillery into action during the day. [initials]	
	20th	08.00	The general advance continued and D. Co. replaced C. Co. as advanced Co. The enemy resistance was of a similar nature to that of previous days. The outpost line for the night was 1000x E of RUMES and LA GLANERIE. A. Co. concentrated during the morning on BLONDE RUE FOURNES. BN. H.Q. and B. Co. moved to same area and A. Co. to LA GLANERIE. [initials]	
	21st	0730	The advance continued. Very little opposition was met with in the early part of the day and the W. bank of the ESCAUT was easily gained on the right of the Div. front. On the left the enemy offered a little resistance but by night we had forced him back slightly.	

A7092). Wt. W12839/M1293 750,000. 1/17. D. D & L., Ltd. Forms/C2118/14.

Army Form C. 2118.

Instructions regarding War Diaries and Intelligence Summaries are contained in F. S. Regs., Part II. and the Staff Manual respectively. Title pages will be prepared in manuscript.

WAR DIARY
or
~~INTELLIGENCE SUMMARY.~~

(Erase heading not required.)

Place	Date	Hour	Summary of Events and Information	Remarks and references to Appendices
	21st		and established posts in BRUYELLE. The line in our left was continued to ST MAUR inclusive. His intention appeared to be to hold a bridgehead in front of TOURNAI.	
			Bn. H.Q. A Co and B Co. were billeted near PETIT RUMES, C Co in BERCU. D Co guns took up positions in the vicinity of MERLIN and JOLLAIN MERLIN forming a defensive left flank. HB	
	22nd		The enemy resistance showed no signs of slackening. He appeared to appeared to have arranged to hold this line. The front Cos improved their positions and established telephone communication with Bn H.Q. During the night the enemy did a considerable amount of shelling in forward areas. B Co and A Co maintained positions to cover the main line of resistance EBAIL – DE RODERIE road. HB	
	23rd		The enemy continued to resist on the same line. The front Cos was reported to be as being difficulty in positions and dug in at MERLIN & JOLLAIN MERLIN. During	

A7092). Wt. W12839/M1293 750,000. 1/17. D. D & L., Ltd. Forms/C2118/14.

Instructions regarding War Diaries and Intelligence Summaries are contained in F. S. Regs., Part II, and the Staff Manual respectively. Title pages will be prepared in manuscript.

WAR DIARY

or

~~INTELLIGENCE SUMMARY.~~

(Erase heading not required.)

Army Form C. 2118.

Place	Date	Hour	Summary of Events and Information	Remarks and references to Appendices
	23rd		The day the enemy continued to shell with gas and HE. One man was killed and one wounded. O.O. 67 issued. H.B.	O.O. 67 attached
	24th		The day was normal. The enemy continued to harass all roads and villages in forward area. Mustard gas was used. B. Co relieved D. Co as per O.O. 67. A. Co moved to support positions in GUINIES and C. Co moved from BERCU to billets vacated by A Co. O.O. 68 issued. H.B.	O.O. 68 attached
	25th		The day was normal. The enemy carried out his usual harassing fire. Several observed sniping shoots were carried out with most successful results an O.P. in BRUYELLE being used to observe from. A. Co. located ~~to~~ support positions and prepared the same for occupation. All companies retained their fighting limbers. H.B.	

A7092). Wt. W12839/M1293 750,000. 1/17. D. D. & L., Ltd. Forms/C2118/14.

Army Form C. 2118.

Instructions regarding War Diaries and Intelligence Summaries are contained in F. S. Regs., Part II. and the Staff Manual respectively. Title pages will be prepared in manuscript.

WAR DIARY

~~or~~

~~INTELLIGENCE~~ ~~SUMMARY.~~

(Erase heading not required.)

Place	Date	Hour	Summary of Events and Information	Remarks and references to Appendices
	26th		The period was normal. The enemy continued to shell all roads and villages in forward areas. The surface guns continued to engage successfully all targets that presented themselves. H.B.	
	27th		The day was normal. The approaches to MERLIN and JULLAIN MERLIN were continually shelled during the night. The reserve companies continued to train and re organise generally. H.B.	
	28th		The day was normal with usual harassing fire by enemy artillery. H.B.	
	29th		The day was normal. The enemy showed no signs of withdrawing, but continued to harass more actively. H.B.	

A7092). Wt. W12839/M1293 750,000. 1/17. D. D & L., Ltd. Forms/C2118/14.

Instructions regarding War Diaries and Intelligence Summaries are contained in F. S. Regs., Part II. and the Staff Manual respectively. Title pages will be prepared in manuscript.

WAR DIARY

~~or~~

~~INTELLIGENCE SUMMARY.~~

(Erase heading not required.)

Army Form C. 2118.

Place	Date	Hour	Summary of Events and Information	Remarks and references to Appendices
	30th		The day was normal.	
			M.G. 699 issued giving location of guns. HB	M.G. 699 attached
	31st		The day was normal.	
			O.O. 69 issued HB	O.O. 69 attached
			R. Nasmith Lieut. Col.	
			31-11-18 Comdg 15th Bn Machine Gun Corps	

A7092). Wt. W12839/M1293 750,000. 1/17. D. D & L., Ltd. Forms/C2118/14.

SECRET. COPY NO 14

15th Bn. MACHINE GUN CORPS.

OPERATION ORDER NO. 62.

Hqrs.
15th Bn. M.G.C.
4th October 1918.

1. The following reliefs and moves will take place as soon as possible :-

(a) The 4 guns of "B" Coy. at approx. H.8.d.42.60. will be relieved by 2 guns at AVENUE and 2 guns at G.17.b.7.9. of "A" Coy.

On completion of relief the 4 guns of "B" Coy. will occupy SCOTTISH BATTY. G.24.d.15.90.

(b) The 4 guns of "B" Coy. at approx. H.1.d.90.30. will be relieved by 4 guns of 16th Bn. M.G.C. at present at CENTRAL KEEP and SAVILLE POST.

Major T. FORESTER will continue to arrange for rationing of these teams.

4 guns of "B" Coy. on relief will occupy AVENUE BATTY. (G.18.d.10.50.)

(c) "B" Coy. will move the 2 guns TUNNEL POST to position vacated by "A" Coy. at G.17.b.7.9. and the 2 guns at G.11.b.15.90. to LIMBER BATTY. G.17.a.75.80.

(d) 2 guns of "B" Coy. which are now proceeding to take up position at approx. H.4.Central will come under command of O.C. "A" Coy.

(e) 16th Bn. M.G.C. guns :- 2 at H.1.a.80.40.
4 at G.5.d.10.80.
2 at G.4.b.40.20.
will be withdrawn, accomodation to be found near the HULLUCH Road.

Major T. FORESTER will notify Bn. Hqrs. of the location of this accomodation.

(f) "D" Coy. will move 4 guns at present at BANKER and STUD to a position covering the CITE ST.LAURENT - HULLUCH - LA BASSEE line from BOIS DE QUATORZE to HIVE ALLEY.

2. All arrangements for relief to be made between Coy. Commanders concerned.

3. Location of all guns will be reported by Coys, concerned as soon as possible after taking up new positions. Coys. will also notify Bn. Hqrs. of completion of all reliefs.

4. ACKNOWLEDGE by wire.

Capt. & Adjt.
15th Bn. Machine Gun Corps.

Issued by S.D.R. at 1330.

Distribution :-
Copies 1 - 4. A. B. C. & D. Coys.
5. Major T. FORESTER.
6. 15th Division "G".
7. 44th Inf. Bde.
8. 45th Inf. Bde.
9. 46th Inf. Bde.
10. 16th Bn. M.G.C.
11. 58th Bn. M.G.C.
12. C.M.G.O. I Corps.
13/14. War Diary.
15. File.

SECRET.   COPY NO 14

15th Bn. MACHINE GUN CORPS.

OPERATION ORDER NO. 63.

Hqrs.
15th Bn. M.G.C.
7th October 1918.

1. "C" Coy. will relieve "A" Coy. on the night 9/10th inst.

2. All necessary arrangements will be made between Coy. Commanders concerned.

3. Officers of "C" Coy. and as many N.C.Os. as possible will commence the necessary reconnaisance forthwith.

4. On completion of relief "A" Coy will become reserve Coy., and will be disposed as follows :-

Coy. Hqrs. MAZINGARBE.
2 Sections PHILOSOPHE.
2 Sections MAZINGARBE.

5. Completion of relief to be notified to Bn. Hqrs. by wire using code phrase "Your Ak 20 received at ---"

6. ACKNOWLEDGE.

Capt. & Adjt.
15th Bn. Machine Gun Corps.

Issued through Signals at 1200.

Distribution :- Copy Nos. 1 - 4. A. B. C, & D. Coys.
5. Transport Officer.
6. Quartermaster.
7. Signals.
8. 15th Division "G".
9. 44th Inf. Bde.
10. 45th Inf. Bde.
11. 46th Inf. Bde.
12. C.M.G.O. I Corps.
13. 16th Bn. M.G.C.
14. 58th Bn. M.G.C.
15. Major T. FORESTER, 15th Bn. M.G.C.
16--17. War Diary.
18. File.

SECRET. COPY NO 13

15th Bn. MACHINE GUN CORPS.

OPERATION ORDER NO.64.

Hqrs.
15th Bn. M.G.C.
8th October 1918.

1. Active harassing fire will be carried out commencing 1300 9th inst.

2. Guns to be used :-
Right Front Coy.

4 guns in H.29.a. to be known as "SASSE BATTERY."
4 guns in H.22.b. to be known as "ANNAN BATTERY."
4 guns in H.27.d. and H.33.b. to be known as "PETERKIN BATTERY."
4 guns in H.27.a. to be known as "TENTON BATTERY."

Left Front Coy.

4 guns in H.16.d. and H.16.a. to be known as "BURLEIGH BATTERY."

3. Positions will be prepared from which these guns can engage Targets as shown in Appendix I. These positions must be accessable by day without being observed by the enemy, and the actual gun positions made so that they can be used by day.
Locations of positions made will be notified to Bn. Hqrs.
In no case will the guns be fired within 200 yards of Battle Positions.

4. The following are the Targets to be engaged as laid down in Appendix I. In each case the Target is an area and will be searched.

"A" Area.	H.18.c.70.50.	H.18.a.78.00.	H.18.b.70.00.	H.18.d.72.50.
"B" Area.	H.18.c.70.00.	H.18.c.70.50.	H.18.d.72.50.	H.18.d.72.00.
"C" Area.	H.24.a.82.48.	H.18.c.70.00.	I.13.c.00.00.	I.19.a.00.50.
"D" Area.	H.24.b.00.00.	H.24.a.82.48.	I.19.a.00.50.	I.19.a.00.00.
"E" Area.	H.24.d.00.50.	H.24.b.00.00.	I.19.a.00.00.	I.19.c.00.50.
"F" Area.	H.24.d.00.00.	H.24.d.00.50.	I.19.c.00.50.	I.19.c.00.00.
"H" Area.	Square I.19.c.			

5. Rate of Fire will be 8 belts per gun in 2 hours, to be fired in 40 round bursts at irregular intervals.

6. "D" Coy. will send 2, and "A" Coy. 1 Fighting Limber to report to the Bn. Transport Officer for S.A.A. at 1100 tomorrow at Bn. Transport lines.

7. The closest liaison must be maintained with the Infantry with regard to patrols going out, and firing may at any time be suspended if necessary on account of this.

8. ACKNOWLEDGE by wire.

Capt. & Adjt.
15th Bn. Machine Gun Corps.

Issued by S.D.R. at 1000.
Distribution :- Copies 1 - 5. A. B. C. D. Coys.
5. Transport Officer.
6. 44th Inf. Bde.
7. 45th Inf. Bde.
8. 46th Inf. Bde.
9. 15th Division "G".
10. 15th D.A.
11. 58th Bn. M.G.C.
~~G.M.G.O.~~
12. C.M.G.O. I Corp
13.14. War Diary.
15. File.

SECRET. COPY NO ____

APPENDIX I to 15th Bn. MACHINE GUN CORPS

OPERATION ORDER NO. 64.

8th October 1918.

9th October 1918.

Battery.	Target.	Time.
"PETERKIN"	E & F	1300 to 1500
"ANNAN"	D & H	1500 to 1700
"BURLEIGH"	A & B	1700 to 1900
"SASSE"	H & F	1900 to 2100
"PETERKIN"	E & F	2100 to 2300
"ANNAN"	D & H	2300 to 2359.

10th October 1918.

Battery.	Target.	Time.
"ANNAN"	D & H	0001 to 0100
"BURLEIGH"	A & B	0100 to 0300
"TANTON"	C & D	0300 to 0500
"PETERKIN"	E & F	0700 to 0900
"ANNAN"	D & H	0900 to 1100
"BURLEIGH"	A & B	1100 to 1300
"TANTON"	C & D	1300 to 1500
"SASSE"	H & F	1500 to 1700
"ANNAN"	D & H	1900 to 2100
"BURLEIGH"	A & B	2100 to 2300
"TANTON"	C & D	2300 to 2359

11th October 1918.

Battery.	Target.	Time.
"TANTON"	C & D	0001 to 0100
"SASSE"	H & F	0100 to 0300
"PETERKIN"	E & F	0300 to 0500

If this harassing fire is to be continued a further programme will be issued.

Capt. & Adjt.
15th Bn. Machine Gun Corps.

Copies to all recipients of O.O. 64.

SECRET. 15th Bn. Machine Gun Corps. M.G.598.

O.C. "D" Coy.

Ref. 15th Bn. M.G.C. OPERATION ORDER No.64. d/8.10.18.

"TANTON" and "SASSE" Batteries will fire on Targets D and F respectively from 0500 to 0510 tomorrow, 10th inst.

Rate of Fire :- 4 belts per gun in 10 minutes.

ACKNOWLEDGE by wire.

Capt. & Adjt.
15th Bn. Machine Gun Corps.

9.10.18.

Copies to all recipients of O.O. No. 64.

SECRET. 15th Bn. Machine Gun Corps M.G.606.

Ref. APPENDIX I to 15th Bn. MACHINE GUN CORPS
OPERATION ORDER NO. 64.

10th October 1918.

The following additional harassing fire will be carried out on :-

11th October 1918.

Battery.	Target.	Time.
"ANNAN"	D & H	0700 to 0900
"BURLEIGH"	A & B	0900 to 1100
"TANTON"	C & D	1100 to 1300
"PETERKIN"	E & F	1300 to 1500
"SASSE"	H & F	1500 to 1700

ACKNOWLEDGE by wire.

H M Barn....
Capt & Adjt.
15th Bn. Machine Gun Corps.

Copies to all recipients of O.O.64.

SECRET.   COPY NO 16

15th Bn. MACHINE GUN CORPS.

OPERATION ORDER NO. ~~64~~.65

Ref. Map PONT à VENDIN
44A NW4 1/10000.

Hqrs.
15th Bn. M.G.C.
10th October 1918.

1. The 46th Inf. Bde. will carry out an operation to take the ground up to the West side of the HAUTE DEULE CANAL on the 12th October.
The 9th Royal Scots will attack on the Right, and the 10th Scottish Rifles on the left.
The Northern Boundary will be H.17.b.00.35. - H.18.a.00.55. - H.18.b.65.98.
Southern Boundary H.29.b.70.15. - H.30.a.35.50. - I.25.a.95.50.

2. The 15th Bn. Machine Gun Corps will co-operate as follows :-

(a) "D" Coy. (Right Front Coy).

"NOTTS" BATT. 4 guns at about H.28.d.50.50.
"KENT" BATT. 2 " " " H.29.a.72.10.
"HERTS" BATT. 4 " " " H.22.c.65.10.
"ESSEX" BATT. 4 " " " H.17.b.50.15.

"B" Coy. (Support Coy).

"FIFE" BATT. 4 guns at about H.22.b.20.00.
"DEVON" BATT. 4 " " " H.22.b.20.45.
"HANTS" BATT. 4 " " " H.22.b.80.88.
"BANFF" BATT. 4 " " " H.17.c.03.40.

"C" Coy. (Left Front Coy).

"DORSET" BATT. 4 guns at about H.17.a.00.78.

(b) Targets :-

"A" Barrage.

"NOTTS" BATT. H.24.d.50.43. to H.24.b.52.53.
"KENT" BATT. to take on any enemy Machine Guns seen firing from Northern outskirts of ANNAY, and not to fire unless enemy Machine Guns actually observed.
"HERTS" BATT. H.24.b.52.33. to H.24.b.55.73.
"FIFE" BATT. H.24.d.50.43. to H.24.d.51.90.
"DEVON" BATT. H.24.d.51.90. to H.24.b.52.33.
"HANTS" BATT. 2 guns Bridge at H.24.b.84.30.
2 guns Bridge at H.24.b.75.89.
"BANFF" BATT. 2 guns Bridge at H.18.d.74.36.
2 guns Bridge at H.18.d.75.95.
"DORSET" BATT. Area I.13.c.40.82. I.13.a.62.25. I.13.a.80.08. I.13.c.77.78. (This area contains 3 Pill Boxes).
"ESSEX" BATT. Sweep enemy Track from H.18.c.70.66. to H.18.c.80.01.

"B" Barrage.

"NOTTS" BATT. 2 guns I.19.c.60.29. to I.19.c.76.28.
2 guns I.19.c.60.65. to I.19.c.72.62.
"KENT" BATT. I.19.b.01.03. to I.19.b.30.20.
"FIFE" BATT. I.19.a.44.74. to I.13.c.43.16.
"DEVON" BATT. I.13.c.43.16. to I.13.c.43.55.
"HANTS" BATT. 2 guns Pill Box at I.13.a.68.56.
2 guns Pill Box at I.13.a.89.79.
"BANFF" BATT. 2 guns Pill Box at I.7.c.98.03.
2 guns Pill Box at I.7.d.09.41.

O.O.65 contd.

(c) LIFTS etc.

(i) The following Battery will lift on to it's "B" Barrage at Z plus 5:- "BANF" BATT.

(ii) The following Battery will cease fire at Z plus 8 :- "ESSEX" BATT.

(iii) The following Batteries will lift on to their "B" Barrages at Z plus 10 :-
"NOTTS" BATT.
"FIFE" BATT.
"DEVON" BATT.
"HANTS" BATT.

(iv) "HERTS" BATT. will cease fire at Z plus 10.

(v) If any enemy are seen in H.30.b. "NOTTS" BATT. will cease firing Barrage and will engage them.

(d) Rate of fire for all Batteries except "DORSET" BANFF" "HANTS" and "KENT" will be :-
Z to Z plus 10 4 belts. Z plus 10 to Z plus 56 9 belts.

Rate of fire for "DORSET", "BANFF" and "HANTS" Batteries :-
Z to Z plus 10 2 belts.
Z plus 10 to Z plus 20 4 belts.
Z plus 20 to Z plus 56 7 belts.
After Z plus 56 Barrage guns will stand by to fire as ordered until instructed to resume normal positions.

(e) Guns for Consolidation :-

(i) "ESSEX" BATT. will assist in the consolidation of the Left Battalion.
This Battery will send an Officer forward to reconnoitre the DUMP in H.18.b. c. and d. as soon as it is taken; this Officer should go forward just behind the Infantry.
The Battery will take up positions on or near the DUMP as quickly as possible after it is taken, and will 'stand by' to engage any hostile M.G. which may come into action on the East side of the Canal in either I.7.c. I.13.a. and c. or I. 19.a.
The 10th Scottish Rifles are establishing H.Q. at the present left front Coy. H.Q. and "D" Coy. will arrange to get in touch with them, and with the Coy. Commander carrying out the attack on the Left, to arrange details.

(ii) "D" Coy. will detail 2 guns under an Officer to be at 9th Royal Scots Advanced H.Q. at about H.23.c.19.52. during the action. If, when this battery has taken it's objective, it is much harassed by by enemy M.Gs. from the East side of the Canal, these two guns will go forward to engage same, the necessary information will be obtained from 9th Royal Scots H.Q.

(f) Signal Communication:-

Advanced Battn. H.Q. will be established at Section H.Q. at H.29.a.52.30. and O.C. No.5. Section R.E. will arrange for signal communication with all batteries except "ESSEX" and "KENT", and with 46th Inf. Bde. advanced H.Q. at H.28.b.80.50.

(g)..............

O.O.65 contd.

(g) Battle Maps will be prepared at Bn. H.Q. for "DORSET", "BANFF", "HANTS", "DEVON", "FIFE", "KENT" and "NOTTS" Batteries, so that if necessary, they can be switched as the situation demands.

3. Details regarding Zero hour and synchronisation of watches will be notified later.

4. ACKNOWLEDGE by wire.

Capt. & Adjt.
15th Bn. Machine Gun Corps.

Issued at____________

Distribution :-

Copy No.1. "A" Coy.
2. "B" Coy.
3. "C" Coy.
4. "D" Coy.
5. 44th Inf. Bde.
6. 45th Inf. Bde.
7. 8. 9. 46th Inf. Bde.
10. 15th Division "G".
11. 15th Divl. Arty.
12. O.C. No.5 Section R.E.
13. C.M.G.O. I Corps.
14. 58th Bn. M.G.C.
15. 16th Bn. M.G.C.
16.17. War Diary.
18.19.20. File.

SECRET. **15th Bn. Machine Gun Corps. M.G.623.**

Copy No 14

OPERATION INSTRUCTIONS NO. 1.

1. In the event of further withdrawal by the enemy, his pursuit will at once be taken up and touch maintained with his rearguards.

(a) The first objective on the East bank of the Canal will be; - ESTEVELLES - high ground in I.15.central - I.3.central.

Northern Divisional Boundary :- Road at C.25.c.1.8. - Cross Roads C.26.a.9.6. - Lime Kiln C.28.c.9.2. - ST.BARBE C.29.d.9.5. all inclusive.

Inter Brigade Boundary :- Approx grid line running East and West between I.8. and I.14.

Southern Divisional Boundary :- HAUTE DEULE CANAL.

2. The 15th Bn. M.G.C. will co-operate as follows :-

The Front two Coys. ("D" Coy. on the Right and "C" Coy. on the Left) will assist the Brigades in the crossing of the HAUTE DEULE CANAL, using two sections for direct covering fire and two sections for consolidating the Bridge Heads.

(a) "C" Coy. (Left Front Coy). will place the sections for covering fire about H.6.a.00.40. and H.11.b.95.25. respectively. The Sections to be used for consolidation of bridge heads will be located at DUMP in H.4. and about H.5.c.95.05. respectively.

All four sections will move to these locations as soon as possible, and "C" Coy. will report to Bn. Hqrs. when they are in position.

On information being received from the Infantry that they are starting to cross the canal, sections for covering fire will engage any enemy M.Gs, points of resistance, or any possible target asked for by the Infantry.

The sections for consolidation of Bridge Heads will at once move forward and cross the canal by the bridges put across by the Infantry; the Northern section by the bridges of the Left Battalion, and the Southern section by those of the Right Battalion, getting well forward with the Infantry to such positions as will prevent the enemy from harassing the bridges with rifle or machine gun fire.

(b) "D" Coy. (Right Front Coy). will as soon as possible move forward the two rear sections in H.27. and H.33. to positions in, or just rear of the VENDIN-DOUVRIN-LA BASSEE line.

On receiving information from the Infantry that they are advancing to cross the canal, one section will go to DUMP in H.18. and one will work forward in rear of the leading infantry to positions in houses just west of the canal in H.24.

These two sections will engage hostile machine guns etc. while the Infantry are crossing.

The remaining two sections will cross the bridges just in rear of the leading Infantry, one section in each Battalion area, and consolidate the Bridge Heads taking up positions sufficiently far forward to prevent the enemy harassing bridges with rifle and M.G. fire.

3. The actual locations of Infantry bridges across canal must be obtained from the Infantry, and the closest liaison must be maintained with them throughout by Section Officers.

4. On receipt of orders from Bn. Hqrs. "A" and "B" Coys. will move forward with fighting limbers as far as these can be taken, and will pass through "C" and "D" Coys. respectively, consolidating the first objective in co-operation with 44th and 46th Infantry Brigades

(a).........

M.G.623 contd.

(a) "A" Coy.

Suggested route :- HULLUCH - BENIFONTAINE - WINGLES - MEURCHIN Road - MEURCHIN.

One section to take up positions about I.3.a., one section about I.2.a., one section about I.9.central, the remaining section to be used as required.

(b) "B" Coy.

Suggested routs :- LOOS-VENDIN Road - PONT-A-VENDIN.

One section to take up positions about H.21.b., one section abput H.15.a., one section about H.14.c. or d., the remaining section to be used as required.

5. The R.E. are arranging to construct pontoon bridges for animals and transport at I.19.c.0.6. and H.6.d.7.3. If these are not completed by the time "A" and "B" Coys. reach the canal, sections will have to carry forward from there, and the transport will follow when pontoon bridges are completed.

6. If the enemy have not already withdrawn, "B" Coy. will move to billets in LOOS tomorrow the 12th inst. and "A" Coy. will move to area vacated by "B" Coy., moves to commence at 1300.

Completion to be reported to Bn. Hqrs. by wire.

7. S.A.A. dumps will be formed on west side of canal near pontoon bridgos, under battalion arrangements.

8. ACKNOWLEDGE by wiro.

H M Sams

Capt. & Adjt.
15th Bn. Machine Gun Corps.

11.10.18.

Distribution :-

Copies	
1 - 4.	A. B. C. D. Coys.
5.	Transport Officor.
6.	15th Division "G".
7.	44th Inf. Bde.
8.	45th Inf. Bde.
9.	46th Inf. Bde.
10.	C.M.G.O. I Corps.
11.	16th Bn. M.G.C.
12.	58th Bn. M.G.C.
13.14.	War Diary.
15.	Filo.

SECRET.

15th Bn. Machine Gun Corps. M.G.630.

ADDENDUM I to OPERATION INSTRUCTIONS NO.I. d/11.10.18.

On receipt of orders, "C" Coy. Fighting Transport will proceed to WINGLES, picking up on the way as much ammunition as it can carry from Dumps on HULLUCH Road. This ammunition will be dumped on W. side of the HAUTE DEULE Canal; approx. H.S.d.30.30.

"D" Coy. Fighting Transport will proceed to VENDIN-Lt-VIEIL, picking up on the way as much ammunition as it can carry from dumps on LOOS-VENDIN Road. This ammunition will be dumped on W. side of Canal at approx. H.24.d.97.05.

Battn. Hqrs. and remainder of Transport will probably move to HULLUCH. Exact location will be notified later.

Capt. & Adjt.
15th Bn. Machine Gun Corps.

12.10.18.

Copies to all recipients of O.I.No.1, plus "C" and "D" Coy. Transport Officers.

SECRET. 15th Bn. Machine Gun Corps. M.G.634.

ADDENDUM 2 to OPERATION INSTRUCTIONS NO1. d/11.10.18.

1. In view of today's operations, as soon as the enemy have been mopped up on ~~this-side~~ the West side of the Canal, "D" Coy. will get their Covering Fire Sections, as detailed in para 2 (b), into position, and will move forward to suitable places the sections for consolidation of Bridge Heads.

2. Ref. para 1. Southern Divisional Boundary to be amended and read as follows :- H.36.c.00.30. - I.31.c.00.00. - I.27.c.60.50. - I.22.d.60.00.

3. ACKNOWLEDGE.

Capt. & Adjt.
15th Bn. Machine Gun Corps.

12.10.18.

Copies to all recipients of O.I. No.1.

SECRET. 15th Bn. Machine Gun Corps. M.G.646.

ADDENDUM 3 to OPERATION INSTRUCTIONS No.1. d/11.10.18.

Reference para 2 (b). In view of additional front taken over by 15th Division, "D" Coy. will place one section about I.31.a. at once.

During the crossing of the canal, this section will fire at enemy machine guns or any other target seen in PONT-A-VENDIN.

The direct covering fire for crossing the canal will be carried out by one section with two guns on DUMP in H.18. and two guns in H.24.b. These guns to be placed in position at once.

The remaining two sections of the company will be used, as already arranged, for the consolidation of the bridge heads.

Please acknowledge.

[signature]

Capt. & Adjt.

15th Bn. Machine Gun Corps.

13.10.18.

Copies to all recipients of O.I. No.1.

SECRET. 15th. Bn. MACHINE GUN CORPS. COPY NO. 12

OPERATION ORDER NO. 67.

Ref. Maps 44 & 37
1/40,000

Hdqrs.
15th. Bn. M.G.C.
23rd. October 1918

1. "D" Coy. will be relieved by "B" Coy. to-morrow 24th. inst. commencing 1230.

Details of relief will be arranged between Coy. Commanders concerned.

Completion of relief to be notified to Bn. Hdqrs. by code word "BELL".

2. (a). In the event of 16th. Division securing the crossings over the River to-morrow morning prior to relief and the 45th. Inf. Bde. passing through them and making good the Bridgeheads on the line VEZONCHAUX-BOURGEON-FONTENOY-GUERONDE, "D" Coy. will be prepared to co-operate by moving two sections to houses on West bank of river ~~about V.15.~~ * to engage any suitable targets. Remaining two Sections to cross the canal immediately after the leading Infantry and to take up positions covering the Bridgehead Line. One Section about V.18.a. or c., one section about V.30.a.

* one section about V20 & V26 - one section # about V15

In the event of no covering fire being required or when the Infantry no longer require same one of the covering fire Sections will move to a position about V.24.a. and the other covering fire section to about V.22.b. or V.23.a.

Immediately on receipt of information from the Infantry that they are about to cross the River, "D" Coy. will act as above, therefore the closest liaison must be maintained between Section Officers and Infantry.

2. (b). On receipt of orders from Battn. Hdqrs. "A" Coy. will at once move forward by route already reconnoitred to area W. of River in V.15.a. and c. Provided that the Infantry are across the River two Sections of "A" Coy. will cross by the northernmost bridge which will probably be at V.15.b.00.60. and will form a defensive flank facing North and N.E. covering the ground from about V.11.c. to V.10.a.00.00. (GUERONDE inclusive). One Section to be about V.11.c. and one Section about V.10. central. Remaining two Sections will be kept in reserve on the W. bank of the River.

2. (c). It is probable that limbers can be used as far as the River, beyond the River guns will most probably have to be carried unless pontoons are in position. On no account must the non-arrival of pontoons delay the moving forward of Sections.

3. On completion of relief of "D" and "B" Coys. "B" Coy. will be prepared to carry out ~~the instructions detailed in Para 2.a.~~

4. Acknowledge by wire.

[signature]
Capt. & Adjt.
15th. Bn. Machine Gun Corps.

Issued at 2330.

Distribution :-

Copies 1 - 4. A.B.C.& D.Coys.
5. Signalling Officer
6 - 8. 44th, 45th, 46th, Inf. Bdes.
9. 15th. Division "G".
11-12 War Diary
13 File

SECRET. 15th. Bn. MACHINE GUN CORPS COPY NO. 15

OPERATION ORDER NO. 68.

Ref. Maps 44 & 37.
1/40,000.

Hdqrs.
15th. Bn.M.G.C.
24th.Oct.1918.

1. The 16th. Division are to secure small Bridgeheads at the River Crossings at ANTOING as soon as possible. They will establish Posts on the East bank of the River as far South as BRUYELLE to cover the road leading from BRUYELLE to ANTOING.

2. As soon as the above operation is complete 46th. Inf. Bde. will move under cover of these Posts, cross the river and secure a Bridgehead on the line VEZONCHAUX-BOURGEON-FONTENOY-GUERONDE.
The front battalion will establish Bridgeheads in front of VEZONCHAUX and BOURGEON, the battalion located at GUIGNIES will continue the bridgehead line round FONTENOY and GUERONDE. The 55th. Division should continue this line to the left but in case they are unable to a definsive flank, facing N. & N.E. will be formed coming back to the River about V.9.b.
Two foot bridges are being constructed for each Battalion of 46th. Inf. Bde. and the 16th. Division are responsible for the construction of one Transport Bridge.

3. The 15th. Bn. M.G.C. will co-operate as follows :-
(a). "B" Coy. (Front Coy.).
On receipt of information from the Infantry that they are about to move forward to cross the River "B" Coy. will move two Sections to houses on West bank of River, one Section about V.20. or V.26., one Section about V.15. to engage any suitable target. Remaining two Sections to cross the River immediately after the leading Infantry and to take up positions covering the bridgehead line. One Section about V.18.a. or c. one section about V.30.a.
In the event of no covering fire being required or when the Infantry no longer need same, one of the covering fire sections will move forward to about V.24.a. and the other to about V.22.b. or V.23.a.

(b). "A" Coy. (located at GUIGNIES).
On receipt of information from the Infantry that they are about to move forward to cross the River, "A" Coy. will at once move [illegible] to area West of River in V.15.a. and c. and will send two Sections, just in rear of the leading Infantry, across by the Northernmost Bridge (probably about V.15.B.00.50.) and will form a defensive flank facing North covering the ground from about V.11. to about V.9.b.80.70. One Section to be about V. 11.c. and one about V.10. central. The remaining two Sections will be kept in Reserve on the W. bank of the River. Should any part of the Line taken be threatened, these two Sections will be available to be used as the situation may demand.

4. "B" Coy. will establish H.Q. near the H.Q. of the Front Infantry Battalion at the CHATEAU in WEZ-VELVAIN and "A" Coy. will establish H.Q. near H.Q. of the Infantry Battalion located at GUIGNIES. The closest liaison will be maintained from now onwards and during the operations with these Infantry Battn. Commanders.
The Seconds in Command of "A" and "B" Coys. will remain near 46th. Inf. Bde. H.Q. for purposes of liaison.

5. It is practically certain that limbers can be used as far as the River; beyond the River guns will most probably have to be carried, as pontoons will not be in position in time.

O.O. 68. (cont.)

The C.R.E. is trying to arrange for bridges to take pack animals across on, and those could probably be used for getting forward ammunition to carry on with until the limbers can get across.

6. "A" & "B" Coys. will send guides for rations on the day the River is crossed to the Western end of the Transport Bridge.

7. This Order cancels para 2.(a), (b), (c) and 3 of O.O.67 dated 23.10.18.

8. Acknowledge by wire.

H M Sam

Capt. & Adjt.,
15th. Bn. Machine Gun Corps.

Distribution :-

Copies	1 to 4.	"A","B","C","D", Coys.
"	5 to 8.	46th. Inf. Bde.
"	9.	15th. Division "G".
"	10.	Signalling Officer.
"	11.	16th. Bn. M.G.C.
"	12.	44th. Inf. Bde.
"	13.	45th. Inf. Bde.
"	14.	C.M.G.O. I Corps.
"	15 to 16.	War Diary.
"	17 to 18.	File.

SECRET.

15th. Bn. MACHINE GUN CORPS.

COPY No. 15

OPERATION ORDER No. 67.

Hdqrs.
15th. Bn. M.G.C.
31st. Oct.1918.

1. The following reliefs will take place during daylight on November 2nd, 1918.

(a). "A" Coy. will relieve "B" Coy. in the Line.

(b). "C" Coy. will occupy billets vacated by "A" Coy.
All moves to commence at 1000 hours.

2. All arrangements will be made between Os.C. Coys. concerned. Details of actions of Coys. as laid down in 15th. Bn. M.G.C. O.O. 63. of 24.10.18. will be carefully handed and taken over, also all details regarding Battle Positions to be used in cases of emergency.

3. On completion of relief "B" Coy. will withdraw to billets vacated by "C" Coy.. Coy. Hdqrs. being located at B.12.a.9.9.

4. Completion of reliefs to be reported to Bn.H.Q. and H.Q.44th. Inf.Bde. by wire, using Code Phrase " YOUR A.K. 20. RECEIVED AT .... ".

5. ACKNOWLEDGE by wire.(Coys.only).

[signature] Capt. & Adjt.
15th. Bn. Machine Gun Corps.

Issued at 0700. 1.11.18.

Distribution :-.

Copy No.1. "A" Coy.
2. "B" "
3. "C" "
4. "D" "
5. Transport Officer.
6. Signalling Officer.
7. 15th. Division "G".
8. 44th. Inf. Bde.
9. 45th. Inf. Bde.
10. 46th. Inf. Bde.
11. C.M.G.O. 1 Corps.
12. 16th. Bn. M.G.C.
13. 58th. Bn. M.G.C.
14-15. War Diary.
16. File.

SECRET. 15th. Bn. Machine Gun Corps No. M.G.699.

15th. Division "G".
44th. Inf. Bde.
45th. " "
46th. " "
16th. Bn. M.G.C.
58th. Bn. M.G.C.
C.M.G.O. 1 Corps.

The 15th. Bn. M.G.C. is at present disposed as follows:-

(a). Bn. H.Q. :- B.12.a.4.2.

(b). FRONT COY.

H.Q. :- WEZ VELVAIN CHATEAU. C.5.c.9.8.

Positions of Guns :-

2 Guns about U.30.b.0.4.
2 " " U.30.b.8.3.
2 " " V.25.b.6.4.
2 " " V.25.c.9.3.
2 " " D.1.a.4.1.
2 " " C.6.a.7.1.
2 " " C.11.d.1.3.
2 " " C.17.b.6.1.

(c). SUPPORT Coy.

H.Q. & Coy. :- GUIGNIES.

Battle Positions for Guns :-

1 Section about U.28.c.1.6.
1 " " U.28.d.9.8.
1 " " C.9.b.2.5.
1 " In Reserve.

(d). 1 Coy.

H.Q. & Coy. :- B.12.a.9.9.

Battle Positions for Guns :-

2 Guns about U.26.c.8.5.
1 Section " C.2.d.1.7.
2 Guns " C.8.c.4.7.
2 " " C.7.c.6.1.
2 " " C.13.c.1.1.

1 Section in Reserve.

(e). 1 Coy.

H.Q. & Coy. :- B.12.a.1.9.

[signature]

30. 10. 18.

Capt. & Adjt.
15th. Bn. Machine Gun Corps.

15

Instructions regarding War Diaries and Intelligence Summaries are contained in F. S. Regs., Part II. and the Staff Manual respectively. Title pages will be prepared in manuscript.

WAR DIARY
or
~~INTELLIGENCE~~ SUMMARY.

(Erase heading not required.)

Army Form C. 2118.

9

Place	Date	Hour	Summary of Events and Information	Remarks and references to Appendices
			CONFIDENTIAL	
			WAR DIARY	
			OF	
			15th BATT: MACHINE GUN CORPS	
			FROM :- 1st NOVEMBER 1918	
			TO :- 30th NOVEMBER 1918	
			VOLUME IX	
			30-11-18	
			R. Nasmith Lieut Col Comdg 15th Bn Machine Gun Corps	

A5834 Wt. W4973/M687 750,000 8/16 D. D. & L. Ltd. Forms/C.2118/13.

Instructions regarding War Diaries and Intelligence Summaries are contained in F. S. Regs., Part II. and the Staff Manual respectively. Title pages will be prepared in manuscript.

WAR DIARY
~~or~~
~~INTELLIGENCE~~ SUMMARY.
(*Erase heading not required.*)

Army Form C. 2118.

Place	Date	Hour	Summary of Events and Information	Remarks and references to Appendices
	1/11/18		The Battalion was disposed as follows:- "A" Coy. & Coy. H.Q. at GUIGNIES "B" Coy. – H.Q. at WEZ VELVAIN CHATEAU Two Sections at CHATEAU LANNOY One Section near BRUYELLE One Section in JOLLAIN-MERLIN "C" Coy. and Coy. H.Q. in billets at PETIT RUMES, B.12.a.1.9 "D" Coy. and Coy. H.Q. in billets at LA LAITRE near PETIT RUMES Battalion Headquarters at PETIT RUMES. B.12.a.4.2	[illegible]
	2/11/18		During daylight "A" Coy. relieved "B" Coy. in the Line "C" Coy. moved to billets vacated by "A" Coy. at GUIGNIES "B" Coy. moved back to billets vacated by "C" Coy. at PETIT RUMES "D" Coy. remained at LA LAITRE near PETIT RUMES Battalion Headquarters at PETIT RUMES	[illegible]
	3/11/18		The day was normal No change.	[illegible]

A5834 Wt. W4973/M687 750,000 8/16 D. D. & L. Ltd. Forms/C.2118/13.

Army Form C. 2118.

WAR DIARY
~~or~~
~~INTELLIGENCE SUMMARY.~~
(*Erase heading not required.*)

Instructions regarding War Diaries and Intelligence Summaries are contained in F. S. Regs., Part II. and the Staff Manual respectively. Title pages will be prepared in manuscript.

Place	Date	Hour	Summary of Events and Information	Remarks and references to Appendices
	4/11/18		The day was normal. No change	HMS
	5/11/18		The day was normal No change	HMS
	6/11/18		The day was normal No change	HMS
	7/11/18		The day was normal No change	HMS
	8/11/18		The day was normal No change	HMS
	9/11/18		The Advance was resumed and the River SHELDT crossed. Bridgeheads were established on the Line VEZONCHAUX - BOURGEON - FONTENOY - GUERONDE	
			"C" Coy. moved to FONTENOY	
			"B" Coy. moved to GUIGNES	
			Battalion Headquarters and "D" Coy to ANTOING	HMS
	10/11/18		The Advance continued.	

A5834 Wt. W4973/M687 750,000 8/16 D. D. & L. Ltd. Forms/C.2118/13.

Instructions regarding War Diaries and Intelligence Summaries are contained in F. S. Regs., Part II. and the Staff Manual respectively. Title pages will be prepared in manuscript.

WAR DIARY

~~or~~

~~INTELLIGENCE SUMMARY.~~

(Erase heading not required.)

Army Form C. 2118.

Place	Date	Hour	Summary of Events and Information	Remarks and references to Appendices
	10/11/18		Battalion Headquarters moved to TOURPES "A" Coy. to WILLIAPUIS "D" Coy. to HUISSINIES.	[illegible]
	11/11/18		The advance continued until 1100 hrs when the Battalion was distributed as follows:- Battalion Headquarters at JARDIN C. Coy:- Coy. Hdqrs. at JARDIN with one section, 3 sections in TONGRE NOTRE DAME "B" Coy. at BOLIGNIES "D" Coy. at CHIEVRES "A" Coy. remained for the night at WILLIAPUIS	[illegible]
	12/11/18		"B" Coy. moved to FARM DE BEAUMONT, JARDIN "A" Coy. moved to BETISSART.	[illegible]
	13/11/18		The day was spent in generally cleaning up and making billets comfortable.	[illegible]

A5834 Wt. W4973/M687 750,000 8/16 D. D. & L. Ltd. Forms/C.2118/13.

Army Form C. 2118.

Instructions regarding War Diaries and Intelligence Summaries are contained in F. S. Regs., Part II. and the Staff Manual respectively. Title pages will be prepared in manuscript.

WAR DIARY
or
~~INTELLIGENCE SUMMARY.~~
(Erase heading not required.)

Place	Date	Hour	Summary of Events and Information	Remarks and references to Appendices
	14/11/18		Cleaning of equipment etc. during the day	HMS
	15/11/18		Cleaning of equipment etc continued	HMS
	16/11/18		B Coy with Transport inspected by The Commanding Officer in the morning. In the afternoon A Coy. with Transport inspected by the Commanding Officer. Capt: J. D. MACLEOD, LIEUT: E. ROGERS and LIEUT. J. P. RUNCIMAN joined the Battalion from Base	HMS
	17/11/18		C Coy. moved to JARDIN D Coy moved to BETISSART	HMS
	18/11/18		Normal Routine	HMS

A5834 Wt. W4973/M687 750,000 8/16 D. D. & L. Ltd. Forms/C.2118/13.

Instructions regarding War Diaries and Intelligence Summaries are contained in F. S. Regs., Part II. and the Staff Manual respectively. Title pages will be prepared in manuscript.

WAR DIARY
or
~~INTELLIGENCE SUMMARY.~~
(Erase heading not required.)

Army Form C. 2118.

Place	Date	Hour	Summary of Events and Information		Remarks and references to Appendices
	19/11/18		Normal day. Ordinary routine carried on	HMS	
	20/11/18		Normal day. Ordinary routine carried on	HMS	
	21/11/18		Cleaning up of billets and packing limbers etc. preparatory to moving to GAGES area	HMS	Order No 7 issued (copy attached).
	22/11/18		Battalion Headquarters and "B" and "D" Coy. moved to GAGES "A" Coy moved to CAMBRON-CASTEAN "C" Coy. moved to CAMBRON CASTEAU.	HMS	
	23/11/18		Re-allotting of billets and improving same	HMS	
	24/11/18		Normal day. Ordinary routine carried on.	HMS	
	25/11/18		Day spent in cleaning up generally preparatory to G.O.C's Inspection	HMS	
	26/11/18		Battalion, including Transport inspected by the G.O.C.	HMS	

A5834 Wt. W4973/M687 750,000 8/16 D. D. & L. Ltd. Forms/C.2118/13.

Army Form C. 2118.

WAR DIARY

~~or~~

~~INTELLIGENCE SUMMARY.~~

(Erase heading not required.)

Instructions regarding War Diaries and Intelligence Summaries are contained in F. S. Regs., Part II. and the Staff Manual respectively. Title pages will be prepared in manuscript.

Place	Date	Hour	Summary of Events and Information	Remarks and references to Appendices
		27/11/18	Normal day. Usual routine carried on. HMs	
		28/11/18	Normal day. Usual routine carried on. HMs	
		29/11/18	Normal day. Usual routine carried on. HMs	
		30/11/18	Normal day. Usual routine carried on. HMs	

30-11-18

R. Chasmitt [illegible] Lieut. Colonel
Commanding 15th Bn Machine Gun Corps

A5834 Wt. W4973/M687 750,000 8/16 D. D. & L. Ltd. Forms/C.2118/13.

SECRET.

Copy No. 16

15th Bn. MACHINE GUN CORPS.

ORDER NO. 71.

Ref. Map Sheet 38 1/40000.

Battalion Headquarters.
21st November 1918.

1. The Battalion will move tomorrow, 22nd instant, to GAGES and CAMBRON-CASTEAU. Moves will take place in accordance with the March Table attached.

2. One Billeting Officer per Coy., and one from Battalion Headqrs. will be at Maires Office at villages their coys. are to be billeted in, at 0900 tomorrow, 22nd instant, and will arrange for billets for their Coys.

3. Dress will be Full Marching Order; Service Caps will be worn.

4. Blankets at present in possession of Coys. will be carried on Fighting Limbers.

5. "A" Coy. mules will be sent back tomorrow afternoon to BETISSART under "A" Coy. Transport Officer, and will remain there until out of quarantine. The animals at present infected will not be used.

6. Battalion Headquarters will close at JARDIN at 1000 and will re-open at Farm P.26.b.5.2. on arrival. Coys. will report their arrival in new billeting area to this location.

7. ACKNOWLEDGE.

H M Baron ... Capt. & Adjt.
15th Bn. Machine Gun Corps.

Distribution :- Copy. 1. O.C., "A" Coy.
2. O.C., "B" "
3. O.C., "C" "
4. O.C., "D" "
5. Transport Officer.
6. Signal Officer.
7. Quartermaster.
8. 15th Division "G".
9. 15th Division "Q".
10. 44th Inf. Bde.
11. 45th Inf. Bde.
12. 46th Inf. Bde.
13. C.M.G.O. III Corps.
14. D.A.P.M.
15. 15th Divl. Train.
16,17. War Diary.
18. File.

MARCH TABLE issued in conjunction with 15th Bn. Machine Gun Corps Order No.71 d.21.11.18.

Ref. sheet 38. 1/40000. Starting Point - Road Junction O.19.b.2.6.

Coy.	From.	Destination.	Time of passing Starting Point.	Route.	Remarks.
Battn. Hqrs. Plus No.3 Limbers,	JARDIN.	GAGES.	10.24	- Cross Roads U.12.a.25.85. - BRUGELETTE. - GAGES.	
B.	JARDIN.	GAGES.	10.33	- Cross Roads U.12.a.25.85. - BRUGELETTE. - GAGES.	
D.	BETISSART.	GAGES.	10.42	- Cross Roads U.12.a.25.85. - BRUGELETTE. - GAGES.	Route to Starting Point Level Crossing N.28.d.60.70. - Cross Roads N.18.a.90.50.
C.	JARDIN.	CAMBRON -CASTEAU	11.00	- Road Junction V.7.c.20.25. - Level Crossing V.2.c.15.20. - CAMBRON-CASTEAU.	
A.	BETISSART.	CAMBRON -CASTEAU.	11.09	- Road Junction V.7.c.20.25. - Level Crossing V.2.c.15.20. - CAMBRON-CASTEAU.	Route to Starting Point -Level Crossing N.28.d.60.70. - Cross Roads N.18.a.90.50.

NOTE :_ Normal 10 mins. halts per hour will be observed.

Instructions regarding War Diaries and Intelligence Summaries are contained in F. S. Regs., Part II. and the Staff Manual respectively. Title pages will be prepared in manuscript.

11

WAR DIARY
or
~~INTELLIGENCE SUMMARY.~~
(Erase heading not required.)

Army Form C. 2118.

V8/10

Place	Date	Hour	Summary of Events and Information	Remarks and references to Appendices
			CONFIDENTIAL WAR DIARY OF 15th BATTN: MACHINE GUN CORPS FROM :- 1st December 1918 TO :- 31st December 1918 VOLUME X	

31st December 1918

R. Nasmith Lieut: Colonel
Comdg. 15th Bn Machine Gun Corps

D. D. & L., London, E.C.
(A8004) Wt. W1771/M2031 750,000 5/17 Sch. 52 Forms/C2118/14

Instructions regarding War Diaries and Intelligence Summaries are contained in F. S. Regs., Part II. and the Staff Manual respectively. Title pages will be prepared in manuscript.

WAR DIARY

or

~~INTELLIGENCE SUMMARY.~~

(Erase heading not required.)

Army Form C. 2118.

Place	Date	Hour	Summary of Events and Information	Remarks and references to Appendices
In the Field	1/12/18		Church Parades HMS	
	2/12/18		Battalion bathed at Baths at BRUGELETTE HMS	
	3/12/18		No. 66911 Private E. DAWES tried by F.G.C.M. for "absence without leave" Day spent on usual routine HMS	
	4/12/18		"A" Coy: moved from CAMBRON-CASTEAU to billets in BRUGELETTE HMS "C" Coy: moved from CAMBRON-CASTEAU to billets in GIBECQ "B" and "D" Coys Ordinary Routine	Order No. 72.
	5/12/18		Ordinary Routine i.e. Education, P.T. and Ceremonial Drill in morning Recreational Training in afternoon. HMS	
	6/12/18		Representatives of the Battalion i.e. C.O., Adjutant, 6 Subalterns and 100 Other Ranks proceeded to WILLAUPUIS for review by H.M. King GEORGE V on 7th inst. Remainder of Battalion Ordinary routine HMS	

D. D. & L., London, E.C.
(A8001) Wt. W1771/M2031 750,000 5/17 Sch. 52 Forms/C2118/14

Instructions regarding War Diaries and Intelligence Summaries are contained in F. S. Regs., Part II. and the Staff Manual respectively. Title pages will be prepared in manuscript.

Army Form C. 2118.

WAR DIARY
~~or~~
INTELLIGENCE SUMMARY.
(*Erase heading not required.*)

Place	Date	Hour	Summary of Events and Information	Remarks and references to Appendices
Field	7/12/18		No change. Ordinary Routine	Hms
	8/12/18		Church Parades	Hms
	9/12/18		Battalion bathed at baths at BRUGLETTE	Hms
	10/12/18		No change. Ordinary routine	Hms
	11/12/18		First man of the Battalion sent to U.K. for demobilization No change Ordinary routine	Hms
	12/12/18		6 other Ranks to U.K. for Demobilization. Ordinary routine carried on. Battalion association Football Team played 52nd Bn M.G.C. at CAMBRON-ST-VINCENT. Result 15th Bn M.G.C. 2. 52nd Bn M.G.C. 1.	Hms
	13/12/18		No change. Ordinary routine. Orders received stating the Division would be moving to BRAINE-LE-CHATEAU – WATERLOO – NIVELLES – BRAINE-LE-COMPTE Area on 16th and 17th inst.	Hms

A5834 Wt. W4973/M687 750,000 8/16 D. D. & L. Ltd. Forms/C.2118/13.

Army Form C. 2118.

Instructions regarding War Diaries and Intelligence Summaries are contained in F. S. Regs., Part II. and the Staff Manual respectively. Title pages will be prepared in manuscript.

WAR DIARY
or
~~INTELLIGENCE SUMMARY.~~

(Erase heading not required.)

Place	Date	Hour	Summary of Events and Information	Remarks and references to Appendices
In the Field	14/12/18		Preparation made for the move on 16th and 17th inst. HMS	Order No. 73.
	15/12/18		Billeting Party proceeded to LILLOIS-WITTERZEE to billet for the Battalion HMS	
			Final cleaning up and preparations completed for move	
	16/12/18		Battalion marched to BRAINE-LE-COMPTE, leaving GAGES at 0830 hrs and arriving at BRAINE-LE-COMPTE about 1630 hrs. HMS	
	17/12/18		March continued. Battalion left BRAINE-LE-COMPTE at 0900 hrs arriving at final billeting area, LILLOIS-WITTERZEE, at 1600 hrs. Heavy rain during latter part of the march. HMS	
	18/12/18		Day spent in cleaning up generally and making billets comfortable. HMS	
	19/12/18		Cleaning up continued under Coy. arrangements. HMS	

A5834 Wt. W4973/M687 750,000 8/16 D. D. & L. Ltd. Forms/C.2118/13.

Army Form C. 2118.

Instructions regarding War Diaries and Intelligence Summaries are contained in F. S. Regs., Part II. and the Staff Manual respectively. Title pages will be prepared in manuscript.

WAR DIARY
or
~~INTELLIGENCE SUMMARY.~~
(*Erase heading not required.*)

Place	Date	Hour	Summary of Events and Information	Remarks and references to Appendices
In the Field	20/12/18		Active Service Army School classes re-commenced in Communal Schools in LILLOIS. Ordinary Routine	HMS
	21/12/18		No change. Ordinary routine	HMS
	22/12/18		No change. Ordinary routine	HMS
	23/12/18		No change. Ordinary routine	HMS
	24/12/18		Day spent in decorating halls etc. and preparing Xmas Dinner and Entertainments for the troops. Battalion Concert Party gave a concert for Bn Hdqrs and "A" and "B" Coys.	HMS
	25/12/18		C. of E. Service in morning Remainder of day observed as a general holiday	HMS

A5834 Wt. W4973/M687 750,000 8/16 D. D. & L. Ltd. Forms/C.2118/13.

Army Form C. 2118.

Instructions regarding War Diaries and Intelligence Summaries are contained in F. S. Regs., Part II. and the Staff Manual respectively. Title pages will be prepared in manuscript.

WAR DIARY
or
~~INTELLIGENCE SUMMARY.~~

(*Erase heading not required.*)

Place	Date	Hour	Summary of Events and Information	Remarks and references to Appendices
Field	25/12/18		Battalion Headquarters and Each Coy: gave the troops a Special Xmas Dinner and Sing Song afterwards. All the troops spending a jolly and happy Xmas	HMS
	26/12/18		Beyond usual fatigues, day was observed as a holiday. CAPT: A. MURDOCH and 37 other Ranks proceeded to U.K. for demobilization. Batt: Concert Party gave a concert for "C" and "D" Coys. in the evening	HMS
	27/12/18		Battalion bathed at baths at BRAINE L'ALLEUD. 2nd Lieut P. MALBY, appointed Town Major of LILLOIS. 1 O.R. proceeded to U.K. for demobilization	HMS
	28/12/18		Ordinary routine. No change. 2 O.Rs. proceeded to U.K. for demobilization	HMS
	29/12/18		Church Parades. 9 O.Rs. proceeded to U.K. for demobilization	HMS

D. D. & L., London, E.C.
(A8004) Wt. W1771/M2031 750,000 5/17 Sch. 52 Forms/C2118/14

Instructions regarding War Diaries and Intelligence Summaries are contained in F. S. Regs., Part II. and the Staff Manual respectively. Title pages will be prepared in manuscript.

WAR DIARY
or
~~INTELLIGENCE~~ SUMMARY.
(*Erase heading not required.*)

Army Form C. 2118.

Place	Date	Hour	Summary of Events and Information	Remarks and references to Appendices
In the Field	30/12/18		Usual routine. No change 2 O.R^s proceeded to U.K. for demobilization	[initials]
	31/12/18		Usual routine. No change 5 O.R^s proceeded to U.K. for demobilization Battn. association Football Team played 7/8th K.O.S.B. at LILLOIS Result 15th Bn M.G.C. 3. 7/8th K.O.S.B. 1. In the evening the Battalion Concert Party assisted by the "LES AMIS DU PROGRESS" band gave a concert for the Battalion and civilian friends	[initials]

31st December 1918

R. Nasmith Lieut Colonel
Comdg 15th Bn Machine Gun Corps

D. D. & L., London, E.C.
(A8001) Wt. W1771/M2031 750,000 5/17 Sch. 52 Forms/C2118/14

SECRET.

COPY No. 19

15th. Bn. MACHINE GUN CORPS.

ORDER No. 73.

Battn. Hdqrs.
14th. Dec. 1918.

Ref. Maps :-
BRUSSELS 6. 1/100,000.
SHEET.38. 1/40,000.

---

1. The Battalion will move to BRAINE-LE-COMTE on the 16th. inst.

2. (a). ORDER OF MARCH:- Battalion Headquarters, "A", "D", "B", and "C" Coys. All Transport in rear in same order, No.3.limbers with Battalion Headquarters.Transp ort.
Intervals of 10 yards will be maintained between Coys.
" " 20 " " " " " Transport.

   (b). STARTING Point for Battalion Headquarters, "A", "D", and "B" Coys.:- Cross Roads P.27.a.20.80.
   TIME :- Head of column to pass starting point at ~~0900~~ 0830 hrs.

   (c). STARTING Point for "C" Coy.:- Road Junction P.5.b.75.40.
   TIME :- ~~0900~~ 0930 hrs.

   (d). The usual hourly halts will be observed by "A" & "C" Coys. on their way to Starting Point.

3. ROUTE :- Road Junction P.5.b.75.40 - SOIGNIES - BRAINE-LE-COMTE. There will be a halt for an hour about noon for dinners.

4. DRESS. Full Marching Order. S.D. Caps will be worn. Offic ers will carry haversacks, revolvers, field glasses, and box respirators.

5. BILLETTING PARTY. 1 Officer per Coy. mounted on horses or bicycles and one N.C.O. on bicycle from Battalion Headquarters will report to Cap t. J. D. MACLEOD, at Orderly Room at GAGES at 0700 hrs. on 16th. inst. This party will proceed to BRAINE-LE-COMTE to billet for the Battalion.

6. A party of one Officer (to be detailed later), the Provost Serjeant and 2 policemen will march in rear of the Battalion. This party will bring along any stragglers in a formed body moving at the pace of the slowest man.

7. Two lorries have been allotted to the Battalion and will be used as follows :-
One lorry will report to "A" Coy. and remain there for night 15/16th. "A" Coy. will arrange to have all their blankets loaded in this lorry and the lorry sent off to "C" Coy. at GIBECQ by ~~0600~~ hrs. 0630 hrs. 16th. inst. "C" Coy. will have all blankets ready for loading at 0700 hrs. and immediately on arrival of lorry will arrange for them to be loaded and the lorry despatched to BRAINE-LE-COMTE.

"B" & "D" Coys.

"B" & "D" Coys. will have their blankets stacked ready for loading outside their Coy. Hdqrs. at 0700 hrs. and Battn. Hdqrs. outside the Signal Office at the same time.
The remaining lorry will collect those ; Coys. and Battn. Hdqrs. each arranging their own loading party.
The Quartermaster will arrange that each lorry has a guide.
Each Coy. will send two men and Battn. Hdqrs. 1 man with their blankets to act as unloading party.
All blankets will be tightly rolled in bundles of 10 and properly labelled.

8. (a). On the 17th. inst. the Battalion will move from BRAINE-LE-COMTE to the final billeting area LILLOIS-WITTERZEE.

(b). Order of March . Battalion Headquarters, "C", "A", "B", "D" Coys. All Transport in rear in same order, No.3.Limbers with Battalion Headquarters Transport. The same intervals will be maintained as on the 16th. inst.

(c). ROUTE :- PONT-DU-JOUR - RONQUIERES - NIVELLES -

(d).Details re Starting Point, time, collection of blankets etc. will be notified later.

(e).A Billetting party consisting of Lieut. J. KETCHIN, one Oficer per Coy. and one N.C.O. from Battalion Headquarters with rations up to and including 17th. inst. mounted on bicycles will rendezvous at Orderly Room CAGES at 0800 hrs. to-morrow the 15th. inst.
This party will proceed to LILLOIS WITTERZEE area and there billet for the Battalion.

9: ACKNOWLEDGE.

Issued at 1830 hrs.

Capt. & Adjt.
15th. Bn. Machine Gun Corps.

Distribution :-

Copy No.1. "A" Coy.
2. "B" "
3. "C" "
4. "D" "
5. Bn. Education Officer.
6. Transport Officer.
7. Signalling Officer.
8. Medical Officer.
9. Quartermaster.
10. Lieut. J. KETCHIN.
11. 15th. Division "G".
12. " " "A".
13. 44th. Inf. Bde.
14. 45th. " "
15. 46th. " "
16. D.A.P.M. 15th. Div:
17. 15th. Divl. Train.
18. C.M.G.O. 111 Corps.
19,20. War Diary.
21. File.

SECRET. COPY NO. 16

15th. Bn. MACHINE GUN CORPS.

ORDER NO.72.

Battn. Hdqrs.
3rd. December 1918.

1. The following moves will take place to-morrow the 4th. inst. :-

(a). "A" Coy. will move to area already shown to Billetting Officer in BRUGELETTE U.5.d., U.6.c., U.12.a.

(b). "C" Coy. will move to GIBECQ. x

2. "A" Coy. will march off at 0940 hrs.
(a)Route :- Road Junction V.7.c.20.30. - BRUGELETTE.

(b). "C" Coy. will march off at 0930 hrs.
Route :- GAGES - Road Junction P.21.b.10.19 - GIBECQ.

3. Arrangements for transportation of blankets will be notified later.

4. Coy. Commanders will ensure that all billets are left in a thoroughly clean and sanitary condition.

5. Billetting returns will be completed and forwarded to Battalion Headquarters by evening D.R.L.S. 4th. inst.

6. Completion of moves and arrival in billets will be reported by runner to Battalion Headquarters.

7. ACKNOWLEDGE. ("A" and "C" Coys. only.)

H. Benningfield
Lieut. & Adjt.
15th. Bn. Machine Gun Corps.

~~x Destination of "C" Coy. is at present uncertain.~~ HB

Distribution :-

Copy No. 1. "A" Coy.
2. "B" "
3. "C" "
4. "D" "
5. Transport Officer.
6. Signalling Officer.
7. Quartermaster.
8. 15th. Division "G".
9. 15th. Division "A".
10. 44th. Inf. Bde.
11. 45th. Inf. Bde.
12. 46th. Inf. Bde.
13. C.M.G.O. 111 Corps.
14. 15th. Divl. Train.
15. D.A.P.M.
16.-17. War Diary.
18. Battn. Education Officer.
19. File.

C Coy will move as already arranged to GIBECQ

H. Benningfield
Lieut & Adjt

Instructions regarding War Diaries and Intelligence Summaries are contained in F. S. Regs., Part II. and the Staff Manual respectively. Title pages will be prepared in manuscript.

WAR DIARY
or
INTELLIGENCE SUMMARY.
(Erase heading not required.)

Army Form C. 2118.

15

Vol 11

Place	Date	Hour	Summary of Events and Information	Remarks and references to Appendices
			CONFIDENTIAL	
			WAR DIARY	
			OF	
			15th BATTN: MACHINE GUN CORPS	
			FROM:- 1st JANUARY 1919	
			TO :- 31st JANUARY 1919	
			VOLUME XI	
	31st January 1919		R. Naismith Lieut: Colonel Comdg 15th Bn Machine Gun Corps	

D. D. & L., London, E.C. (A5023) Wt. W1 71/M2031 750,000 5/17 Sch. 52 Forms/C2118/14

Instructions regarding War Diaries and Intelligence Summaries are contained in F. S. Regs., Part II. and the Staff Manual respectively. Title pages will be prepared in manuscript.

WAR DIARY
or
~~INTELLIGENCE SUMMARY.~~
(Erase heading not required.)

Army Form C. 2118.

Place	Date	Hour	Summary of Events and Information	Remarks and references to Appendices
Field	1/1/19		Day was observed as a General holiday 14 other Ranks to U.K. for Demobilization	[initials]
	2/1/19		Normal Day Ordinary Routine carried on. 3 other Ranks to U.K for Demobilization Battalion Association Football Team played R.A.M.C Result 15th Bn M.G.C. 1 R.A.M.C. 0.	[initials]
	3/1/19		Battalion bathed at Baths at BRAINE L ALLEUD Battalion Rugby Football Team played 7/8th K.O.S.Bs Result :- 7/8th K.O.S.Bs 8 points 15th Bn M.G.C. 6 points 1 other Rank to U.K. for demobilization	[initials]
	4/1/19		Normal day. Ordinary Routine carried on No.34937 Pte. H. TURNER and No 10747 Pte D. SCANNEL tried by F.G.C.M. for " absence without leave" Lieut D. BEVAN and 4 other Ranks to U.K. for Demobilization Battalion Association Football Team played 8th Seaforth Highrs Result :- 15th Bn M.G.C. 4. 8th Seaforth Highrs 2.	[initials]

D. D. & L., London, E.C.
(A8001) Wt. W1:71/M2031 750,000 5/17 Sch. 52 Forms/C2.118/14

Instructions regarding War Diaries and Intelligence Summaries are contained in F. S. Regs., Part II, and the Staff Manual respectively. Title pages will be prepared in manuscript.

WAR DIARY

or

~~INTELLIGENCE~~ SUMMARY.

(*Erase heading not required.*)

Army Form C. 2118.

Place	Date	Hour	Summary of Events and Information	Remarks and references to Appendices
Field	5/1/19		Church Parades HWS	
	6/1/19		Normal Day. Usual routine. No change HWS	
	7/1/19		3 other Ranks to U.K. for Demobilization Usual routine carried on. Battalion Association Football Team played 4/5th Black Watch. Result:- 15th Bn M.G.C. 1 4/5th Black Watch 0 HWS	
	8/1/19		Normal Day. No change HWS	
	9/1/19		1 other Rank to U.K. for Demobilization Normal Day. Usual routine. HWS	
	10/1/19		10 other Ranks to U.K. for Demobilization Usual Routine. No change HWS	

D. D. & L., London, E.C. (A8001) Wt. W1 71/M2031 750,000 5/17 Sch. 52 Forms/C2118/14

Instructions regarding War Diaries and Intelligence Summaries are contained in F. S. Regs., Part II. and the Staff Manual respectively. Title pages will be prepared in manuscript.

WAR DIARY
or
~~INTELLIGENCE~~ SUMMARY.

(*Erase heading not required.*)

Army Form C. 2118.

Place	Date	Hour	Summary of Events and Information	Remarks and references to Appendices
Field	11/1/19		21 other Ranks to U.K. for Demobilization Normal Day. No change	HMS
	12/1/19		Church Parades 7 other Ranks to U.K. for Demobilization	HMS
	13/1/19		Normal Day. Usual routine. No change 15 other Ranks to U.K. for Demobilization	HMS
	14/1/19		Usual routine, No change. Battalion Association ~~Football~~ Team played 15th M.T. Coy. Result :- 15th Bn M.G.C. 1 15th M.T. Coy. 1 25 other Ranks to U.K. for Demobilization	HMS HMS
	15/1/19		Normal Day. No change. Football match with 15th M.T. Coy. replayed Result :- 15th Bn M.G.C. 2. 15th M.T. Coy. 1	HMS

D. D. & L., London, E.C.
(A8001) Wt. W1-71/M2031 750,000 5/17 Sch. 52 Forms/C2118/14

Instructions regarding War Diaries and Intelligence Summaries are contained in F. S. Regs., Part II. and the Staff Manual respectively. Title pages will be prepared in manuscript.

WAR DIARY
or
~~INTELLIGENCE SUMMARY.~~

(*Erase heading not required.*)

Army Form C. 2118.

Place	Date	Hour	Summary of Events and Information	Remarks and references to Appendices
Field	16/1/19		Normal Day. Usual routine. No change	HWS
	17/1/19		Normal Day. Usual routine. No change	HWS
	18/1/19		22 Other Ranks to U.K. for Demobilization Battalion bathed at BRAINE L'ALLEUD.	HWS
	19/1/19		17 Other Ranks to U.K. for Demobilization Church Parades.	HWS
	20/1/19		11 Other Ranks to U.K. for Demobilization Normal Day. Usual routine. No change.	HWS
	21/1/19		All animals of the Battalion inspected by a board of Veterinary Officers for classification No change	HWS

D. D. & L., London, E.C.
(A5001) Wt. W1 71/M2031 750,000 5/17 Sch. 52 Forms/C2118/14

Instructions regarding War Diaries and Intelligence Summaries are contained in F. S. Regs., Part II. and the Staff Manual respectively. Title pages will be prepared in manuscript.

WAR DIARY
or
~~INTELLIGENCE SUMMARY.~~
(*Erase heading not required.*)

Army Form C. 2118.

Place	Date	Hour	Summary of Events and Information	Remarks and references to Appendices
Field	22/1/19		22 other Ranks to U.K for Demobilization Usual routine. Battalion Football Team (association) played 1/9th Royal Scots in Semi-final of Divisional Competition. Result:- 15th Bn M.G.C. 1 1/9th Royal Scots 0.	HMS
	23/1/19		The Composite Coy. detailed to take part in Ceremonial parade and "March Past" the King of Belgium, in BRUSSELS on January 26th paraded for inspection by the Commanding Officer No change	HMS
	24/1/19		Battalion bathed at baths at BRAINE L ALLEUD Blankets were also disinfected. No change.	HMS
	25/1/19		The Composite Coy proceeded by lorries to billets in BRUSSELS, to take part in the "March Past" the King of Belgium by	HMS

D. D. & L., London, E.C. (A8001) Wt. W1 71/M2031 750,000 5/17 Sch. 52 Forms/C2118/14

Army Form C. 2118.

WAR DIARY
or
~~INTELLIGENCE~~ SUMMARY.
(*Erase heading not required.*)

Instructions regarding War Diaries and Intelligence Summaries are contained in F. S. Regs., Part II. and the Staff Manual respectively. Title pages will be prepared in manuscript.

Place	Date	Hour	Summary of Events and Information	Remarks and references to Appendices
Field.	25/1/19		representative troops of the III Corps on the 26th January 1919 The Composite Company was composed as follows:- Coy: Commander:- Major F.E. DAVIES M.C Coy: 2nd in Command - Capt A.J. BARLOW C.S.M :- C.S.M. BUTCHER G C.Q.M.S :- C.Q.M.S BRIGNELL A. 2 Subalterns per Coy 1 Composite Section of 32 O.R.s per Coy	HWS
			5 other Ranks proceeded to U.K for demobilization	
	26/1/19		owing to the Ceremonial parade in BRUSSELS, no church parades were held.	HWS
	27/1/19		Lieut: DONALDSON and 22 other Ranks proceeded to U.K. for demobilization Normal Day, Usual routine. No change	HWS

D. D. & L., London, E.C.
(A8001) Wt. W1771/M2031 750,000 5/17 Sch. 52 Forms/C2118/14

Instructions regarding War Diaries and Intelligence Summaries are contained in F. S. Regs., Part II. and the Staff Manual respectively. Title pages will be prepared in manuscript.

WAR DIARY
or
~~INTELLIGENCE~~ SUMMARY.

(*Erase heading not required.*)

Army Form C. 2118.

Place	Date	Hour	Summary of Events and Information	Remarks and references to Appendices
Field	28/1/19		24 other Ranks proceeded to U.K. for Demobilization. The Composite Coy: returned from BRUSSELS No change. Visit to LILLOIS for 3 days of the Divisional Concert Party "THE JOCKS"	
	29/1/19		Lieut. F.R. KENDRICK and 6 other Ranks proceeded to U.K. for demobilization. All animals of the Battalion classified for Demobilization by the Remount Board	
	30/1/19		No change usual routine.	
	31/1/19		No change usual routine.	

31st January 1919

R. Nasmith Lieut Colonel
Comdg 15th Bn Machine Gun Corps

D. D. & L., London, E.C.
(A2001) Wt. W1771/M2031 750,000 5/17 Sch. 52 Forms/C2118/14

Instructions regarding War Diaries and Intelligence Summaries are contained in F. S. Regs., Part II. and the Staff Manual respectively. Title pages will be prepared in manuscript.

WAR DIARY
or
~~INTELLIGENCE~~ SUMMARY.

(*Erase heading not required.*)

Army Form C. 2118.

Vol 12

Place	Date	Hour	Summary of Events and Information	Remarks and references to Appendices
			CONFIDENTIAL WAR DIARY OF 15th BATTN: MACHINE GUN CORPS FROM:- 1st FEBRUARY 1919 TO:- 28th FEBRUARY 1919 VOLUME XII	

28th February 1919

R. Nasmith Lieut: Colonel
Comdg 15th Bn Machine Gun Corps

D. D. & L., London, E.C.
(A10266) Wt W5300/P713 750,000 2/18 Sch. 52 Forms/C2118/16

Instructions regarding War Diaries and Intelligence Summaries are contained in F. S. Regs., Part II. and the Staff Manual respectively. Title pages will be prepared in manuscript.

WAR DIARY
~~or~~
~~INTELLIGENCE~~ SUMMARY.
(*Erase heading not required.*)

Army Form C. 2118.

Place	Date	Hour	Summary of Events and Information	Remarks and references to Appendices
LILLOIS-WITTERZEE	1/2/19		No change Usual routine 5 other Ranks to U.K. for Demobilization	HMS
	2/2/19		Church Parades Capt J.D. MACLEOD and 21 other Ranks to U.K. for Demobilization	HMS
	3/2/19		No change Usual routine carried on. Lieut D. BEVAN and 6 other Ranks to U.K. for Demobilization	HMS
	4/2/19		No change Usual routine carried on	HMS
	5/2/19		No change Usual routine	HMS
	6/2/19		No change Usual routine 3 other Ranks to U.K. for Demobilization	HMS
	7/2/19		No change Usual routine	HMS

D. D. & L., London, E.C.
(A10266) Wt W5300/P713 750,000 2/18 Sch. 52 Forms/C2118/16

Instructions regarding War Diaries and Intelligence Summaries are contained in F. S. Regs., Part II. and the Staff Manual respectively. Title pages will be prepared in manuscript.

WAR DIARY
or
~~INTELLIGENCE SUMMARY.~~
(Erase heading not required.)

Army Form C. 2118.

Place	Date	Hour	Summary of Events and Information	Remarks and references to Appendices
LILLOIS WITTERZEE	8/2/19		No change. Usual routine 6 other Ranks to U.K. for Demobilization	
"	9/2/19		2nd Lieut. P. MALBY and 19 other Ranks to U.K for Demobilization Battalion Association Football Team played 6th Cameron Highrs in the final for the Divisional Cup at BRAINE-LE-COMPTE Result. 6th Cameron Highrs: 3 15th Bn Machine Gun Corps 1	
"	10/2/19		No change Usual routine 14 other Ranks to U.K. for Demobilization	
	11/2/19		No change Usual routine	
	12/2/19		No change Usual routine	

D. D. & L., London, E.C.
(A10266) Wt W5300/P713 750,000 2/18 Sch. 52 Forms/C2118/16

Instructions regarding War Diaries and Intelligence Summaries are contained in F. S. Regs., Part II. and the Staff Manual respectively. Title pages will be prepared in manuscript.

WAR DIARY
or
~~INTELLIGENCE~~ SUMMARY.
(*Erase heading not required.*)

Army Form C. 2118.

Place	Date	Hour	Summary of Events and Information	Remarks and references to Appendices
LILLOIS - WITTERZEE	13/2/19		No change. Ordinary routine	
			Lieut BRIDGE and 11 other Ranks to U.K. for Demobilization	JMS
	14/2/19		No change. Ordinary routine	
			2nd Lieut TURNER and 11 other Ranks to U.K. for Demobilization	
			Regimental concert in "M.G. PALACE" in the evening	JMS
	15/2/19		Lieut. H. H. J. WARD, 2nd Lieut. B.C. SIMMONDS and 17 other Ranks to U.K. for Demobilization	JMS
	16/2/19		No change. Ordinary routine	
			15 other Ranks to U.K. for Demobilization	JMS
	17/2/19		No change usual routine	
			MAJOR A HAMILTON M.C., 2nd Lieut. C.A. LINDSAY and 12 other Ranks to U.K. for Demobilization.	JMS

D. D. & L., London, E.C.
(A10266) Wt W5300/P713 750,000 2/18 Sch. 52 Forms/C2118/16

Instructions regarding War Diaries and Intelligence Summaries are contained in F. S. Regs., Part II. and the Staff Manual respectively. Title pages will be prepared in manuscript.

WAR DIARY

~~or~~

~~INTELLIGENCE SUMMARY.~~

(*Erase heading not required.*)

Army Form C. 2118.

Place	Date	Hour	Summary of Events and Information	Remarks and references to Appendices
LILLOIS-WITTERZEE	18/2/19		No change. Ordinary routine	[initials]
"	19/2/19		No change Ordinary routine	[initials]
"	20/2/19		Audit Board held to examine and report on the Mobilization Equipment of the Battalion Lieut. D.V. CHARLTON, Lieut. T. PEARCE, and 22 other Ranks to U.K. for Demobilization Return visit for 2 nights of the Divisional Concert Party "The Jocks"	[initials]
"	21/2/19		No change Lieut J.H.S PETERKIN and 14 other Ranks to U.K for Demobilization	
	22/2/19		10 "Y" Horses sent to Concentration Camp for Demobilization	[initials]

D. D. & L., London, E.C.
(A10266) Wt W5300/P713 750,000 2/18 Sch. 52 Forms/C2118/16

Instructions regarding War Diaries and Intelligence Summaries are contained in F. S. Regs., Part II. and the Staff Manual respectively. Title pages will be prepared in manuscript.

WAR DIARY

~~or~~

~~INTELLIGENCE SUMMARY.~~

(*Erase heading not required.*)

Army Form C. 2118.

Place	Date	Hour	Summary of Events and Information	Remarks and references to Appendices
LILLOIS-WITTERZEE	23/2/19		No change usual routine 15 other Ranks to U.K. for Demobilization	
	24/2/19		No change usual routine	
	25/2/19		No change usual routine	
	26/2/19		No change usual routine	
	27/2/19		No change usual routine	
	28/2/19		No change usual routine	

28th February 1919

Lieut. Colonel
Comdg 15th Bn Machine Gun Corps

D. D. & L., London, E.C.
(A10266) Wt W5300/P713 750,000 2/18 Sch. 52 Forms/C2118/16

D. A. G.
3rd Echelon
G. H. Q. France

H'QRS. 15th BATTALION
No. M.G.1/19
DATE. 9 - 4 - 19
MACHINE GUN CORPS

Herewith War Diary of this Unit up to and including date of Embarkation for U.K. i.e. 31st March 1919

[signature] Capt
for Lieut Colonel
Comdg 15th Cadre Bn M.G.C.

Dibgate Camp Stn
Shorncliffe.

Instructions regarding War Diaries and Intelligence Summaries are contained in F. S. Regs., Part II. and the Staff Manual respectively. Title pages will be prepared in manuscript.

11

WAR DIARY

~~or~~

~~INTELLIGENCE SUMMARY.~~

(Erase heading not required.)

Army Form C. 2118.

Vol 13

15

Place	Date	Hour	Summary of Events and Information	Remarks and references to Appendices
			CONFIDENTIAL	
			WAR DIARY	
			OF	
			15th BATTN: MACHINE GUN CORPS	
			FROM :- 1st MARCH 1919	
			TO:- 31st MARCH 1919	
			VOLUME XIII	

31-3-19

R. [illegible] Lieut Colonel
Comdg 15th Bn M.G.C

D. D. & L., London, E.C.
(A10266) Wt W5300/P713 750,000 2/18 Sch. 52 Forms/C2118/16

Instructions regarding War Diaries and Intelligence Summaries are contained in F. S. Regs., Part II. and the Staff Manual respectively. Title pages will be prepared in manuscript.

WAR DIARY

~~or~~

~~INTELLIGENCE~~ SUMMARY.

(*Erase heading not required.*)

Army Form C. 2118.

Place	Date	Hour	Summary of Events and Information	Remarks and references to Appendices
LILLOIS-WITTERZEE	1/3/19		All "Y" and "Z" Riders of the Battalion inspected by a Remount Officer. Ordinary Routine carried on.	
"	2/3/19		Ordinary Routine. No change	
		2300	Summer Time came into force. All clocks put forward one hour	
	3/3/19		No change. Ordinary Routine	
"	4/3/19		No change Ordinary Routine	
			MAJOR F.E.DAVIES M.C. (Second-in-Command of Battalion) proceeded to U.K. under authority A.G./7896/5 (O) dated 13/2/19	
			Orders issued for move from LILLOIS-WITTERZEE to WAUTHIER-BRAINE on 6th inst.	Order No. 74 attached
	5/3/19		Day spent in cleaning up billets and packing up preparatory to move on 6th inst.	
			Battalion Association Football Team played 10th Liverpool Scottish at BRUSSELS in 3rd round of Fifth Army Cup. Result:- 10th Liverpool Scottish 6, 15th Bn M.G.C. 1	
"	6/3/19	1000	Battalion marched off from LILLOIS-WITTERZEE	

D. D. & L., London, E.C.
(A10266) Wt W5300/P713 750,000 2/18 Sch. 52 Forms/C2118/16

Army Form C. 2118.

WAR DIARY
~~or~~
~~INTELLIGENCE SUMMARY~~.
(*Erase heading not required.*)

Instructions regarding War Diaries and Intelligence Summaries are contained in F. S. Regs., Part II. and the Staff Manual respectively. Title pages will be prepared in manuscript.

Place	Date	Hour	Summary of Events and Information	Remarks and references to Appendices
WAUTHIER-BRAINE	6/3/19	1130	Battalion arrived at WAUTHIER-BRAINE with Battalion Headquarters at Billet No. 14	
— — —	7/3/19		Unpacking and re-arranging billets etc.	
— — —	8/3/19		All "Z" animals of the Battalion inspected by the Remount Board No change	
— — —	9/3/19		No change MAJOR J. SEAFIELD-GRANT M.C. proceeded to U.K. under authority :- A.G./7896/5 (O) dated 13/2/19	
— — —	10/3/19		80 Mules, 13 Riders, and 4 L.D. Horses proceeded to Divisional Staging Camp for despatch to "CORCOL O". Ordinary Routine No change	

D. D. & L., London, E.C.
(A10266) Wt W5300/P713 750,000 2/18 Sch. 52 Forms/C2118/16

Instructions regarding War Diaries and Intelligence Summaries are contained in F. S. Regs., Part II. and the Staff Manual respectively. Title pages will be prepared in manuscript.

WAR DIARY

or

~~INTELLIGENCE~~ SUMMARY.

(*Erase heading not required.*)

Army Form C. 2118.

Place	Date	Hour	Summary of Events and Information	Remarks and references to Appendices
WAUTHIER-BRAINE	11/3/19		No change. Usual routine	
— " —	12/3/19		5 "Z" horses of the Battalion proceeded to Divnl. Staging Camp for despatch to 'CORCOL O'.	
			MAJOR H. COLE, CAPT: H.H. BENINGFIELD and 2 other Ranks proceeded to U.K. for demobilization	
— " —	13/3/19		Orders received that draft for 2nd Battn. M.G.C was cancelled, and instead a draft of 126 other Ranks, 2 Cooks and 1 Tailor were to be detailed and to "Stand By" to proceed to 9th Battn Machine Gun Corps (Army of Occupation)	
— " —	14/3/19		No change usual routine	
— " —	15/3/19		No change usual routine	
— " —	16/3/19		Lieut: G.D. CUMMING, Lieut J.P. RUNCIMAN and 18 other Ranks	

D. D. & L., London, E.C.
(A10266) Wt W5300/P713 750,000 2/18 Sch. 52 Forms/C2118/16

Army Form C. 2118.

WAR DIARY
or
INTELLIGENCE SUMMARY.
(Erase heading not required.)

Instructions regarding War Diaries and Intelligence Summaries are contained in F. S. Regs., Part II. and the Staff Manual respectively. Title pages will be prepared in manuscript.

Place	Date	Hour	Summary of Events and Information	Remarks and references to Appendices
WAUTHIER-BRAINE	16/3/19		proceeded to U.K. for Demobilization	
			29 Vehicles of the Battalion proceeded to LEMBECQ, ready for entrainment	
			2nd Lieut. W. LEECH M.M. and 23 other Ranks proceeded to LEMBECQ to take over duties as guards on Battalion Vehicle Park	
— " —	17/3/19		No. 128489 Pte ALNER P.G. "B" Coy. tried by F.G.C.M. at TUBIZE for "Absence without leave"	
			8 "Z" horses sent to Divisional Staging camp for despatch to 'CORCOL'	
— " —	18/3/19		Orders received that Cadre of Battalion would entrain for DUNKIRK on 24th inst	
— " —	19/3/19		All Bulk S.A.A. on charge of Battalion taken to Dump at GHISLENGHIEN.	
— " —	20/3/19		All Stores shifted to LEMBECQ, in readiness for entrainment	

D. D. & L., London, E.C.
(A10266) Wt W5300/P713 750,000 2/18 Sch. 52 Forms/C2118/16

Army Form C. 2118.

Instructions regarding War Diaries and Intelligence Summaries are contained in F. S. Regs., Part II. and the Staff Manual respectively. Title pages will be prepared in manuscript.

WAR DIARY

~~or~~

~~INTELLIGENCE SUMMARY.~~

(Erase heading not required.)

Place	Date	Hour	Summary of Events and Information	Remarks and references to Appendices
WANTHIER-BRAINE	21/3/19		Remainder of Limbers packed and moved to LEMBECQ	
"	22/3/19		Wire received from DW saying that all movement of troops to bases were cancelled owing to threatened Railway strike in England.	
LEMBECQ	23/3/19		Cadre of Battalion moved to billets in LEMBECQ, preparatory for entrainment for DUNKIRK	
–	"		All other officers and other Ranks not on the Cadre, moved to billets in TUBIZE and were attached for rations and discipline to 7/8th K.O.S.B. pending further instructions	
		1700hrs	Wire received from Division saying that Cadre would entrain for DUNKIRK on 24th inst	
	24/3/19	1145	All Limbers and wagons loaded on train.	

D. D. & L., London, E.C.
(A10266) Wt W5300/P713 750,000 2/18 Sch. 52 Forms/C2118/16

Instructions regarding War Diaries and Intelligence Summaries are contained in F. S. Regs., Part II. and the Staff Manual respectively. Title pages will be prepared in manuscript.

WAR DIARY

~~or~~

~~INTELLIGENCE SUMMARY~~.

(*Erase heading not required.*)

Army Form C. 2118.

Place	Date	Hour	Summary of Events and Information	Remarks and references to Appendices
LEMBECQ	24/3/19	1320	Train left LEMBECQ	
DUNKIRK	25/3/19	0700	Arrived at DUNKIRK.	
		1000	All Limbers and wagons unloaded from Train and were parked on wharf. Cadre marched to Camp 'B' for a hot meal, and afterwards proceeded to the Baths were deloused, Bathed and medically inspected, afterwards proceeding to No. 1 Embarkation Camp	
— " —	26/3/19		Ships rations for 1 day drawn	
— " —	27/3/19		Still at No. 1 Embarkation Camp	
— " —	28/3/19		Still at No. 1 Embarkation Camp	
— " —	29/3/19		Orders received to load Limbers and wagons on to ship on the morning of the 30th and that Cadre would	

D. D. & L., London, E.C.
(A10266) Wt W5300/P713 750,000 2/18 Sch. 52 Forms/C2118/16

Instructions regarding War Diaries and Intelligence Summaries are contained in F. S. Regs., Part II. and the Staff Manual respectively. Title pages will be prepared in manuscript.

Army Form C. 2118.

WAR DIARY

~~or~~

~~INTELLIGENCE~~ SUMMARY.

(*Erase heading not required.*)

Place	Date	Hour	Summary of Events and Information	Remarks and references to Appendices
DUNKIRK	29/3/19		Sail on the 31st March 1919	
" "	30/3/19	1200	All Limbers and wagons loaded on ship "KOURSK"	
" "	31/3/19	1030 hrs	Cadre of Battalion paraded and marched to Docks for Embarkation to England	
	"	1200	All personnel and stores aboard	
	"	1430	Boat sailed from DUNKIRK for SOUTHAMPTON.	

31st March 1919

R. [illegible] Lieut. Colonel
Comdg. 15th Battn Machine Gun Corps

D. D. & L., London, E.C.
(A10266) Wt W5300/P713 750,000 2/18 Sch. 52 Forms/C2118/16

15th. BN. MACHINE GUN CORPS. COPY NO.

ORDER NO. 74.

Battalion Headquarters,
LILLOIS-WITTERZEE.
March 4th. 1919.

Ref. sheet. BRUSSELS 1/100,000.

1. The Battalion will move to WAUTHIER-BRAINE on the 6th. inst.

2. ORDER OF MARCH.

Battalion Headquarters, "A", "B", "C", and "D" Coys. Bn. Transport

3. STARTING POINT.

Cross Roads at PT. 26. (1/2 kilo S.W. of C in COURS d' EAU).

4. TIME OF PASSING STARTING POINT.

Head of the Column to pass the Starting Point at 1000 hrs.

5. ROUTE.

Fork Road S.W. of B in BOIS-SEIGNEUR-ISAAC - NIVELLES-BRAINE-LE-CHATEAU-HAL Road - Fork Road 1/2 kilo N. of U in HAUT-ITTRE - WAUTHIER BRAINE.

6. BILLETING PARTY.

Billeting Party consisting of Lieut. G.McD.MIALL, 2nd.Lt.WAITE, 2nd.LT. WHEELHOUSE and two runners (one to be detailed by Signal Officer and one by O.C. "D" Coy.) will rendezvous outside "D" Coys' Officers Mess at 0800 hrs. and proceed in advance. Officers will be mounted and runners will proceed by bicycle.

7. TRANSPORT AND LOADING PARTIES.

(a). All Packs, Leather Jerkins, Blankets, Coy. Officers Mess Kit, Packsaddlery, and bulk ammunition and transport equipment will be carried on the limbers.

(b). Lieut. HESSEL "B" Coy., and 1 N.C.O. (not below rank of Serjeant) and 3 men per Coy. will be detailed as loading party. N.C.O.s and men detailed by Coys. to report to Lieut.HESSEL at 0930 hrs

(c). 3 Lorries have been allotted to the Battalion, and will report at an hour to be notified later. Lorries will make two journeys. The Quartermaster will move all stores at present at LILLOIS Station with these lorries by the first journey. The lorries will then report back to LILLOIS Station where they will be met by Lieut.HESSEL who will arrange to load all guns, tripods, and belt boxes at present in Coy. Stores. To facilitate loading of this equipment, Coys. will arrange to form a dump in a convenient place, and their N.C.O. detailed for loading party will act as guides to lorries. As soon as the Battalion moves off Lieut. HESSEL will arrange that one man per Coy. of the loading party is left in charge of each Coy. Gun Dump. The Loading party will travel by lorries with guns, and on arrival in new billeting area will report to the Quartermaster and hand all guns etc. over to him.

(d)........

(d). The loading of blankets etc. on Coy. Limbers will be done under Coy. Arrangements.

8. RATIONS.

Haversack rations will be carried. Dinner will be prepared on arrival in new billeting area.

9. DRESS.

Fighting Order. Service Caps will be worn.

10. HALTS.

The normal 10 minutes halts per hour will be maintained.

11. ACKNOWLEDGE. (Batt. Cy)

HRS[illegible]

Captain & Adjutant.
15th. Battn. Machine Gun Corps.

Distribution :-

Copy No. 1. "A" Coy.
2. "B" "
3 "C" & "D" Coys.
4. Transport Officer.
5. Signal Officer.
6. Quartermaster.
7. Medical Officer.
8. 15th. Division "G".
9. 15th. Division "Q".
10. 15th. Divl. Train.
11. Demobilization Officer.
12-13. War Diary.
14. File.

www.ingramcontent.com/pod-product-compliance
Lightning Source LLC
Chambersburg PA
CBHW082010220426
43670CB00014B/2595
* 9 7 8 1 4 7 4 5 0 9 5 0 3 *